"THE SIGNET AMERICAN WI... NEARLY EVER... NEEDS TO UNDERSTAND AND APPRECIATE AMERICAN WINES."

—*William Rice,*
Executive Food Editor
THE WASHINGTON POST

What can you expect when you sample a wine made from the Cabernet Sauvignon grape, or the Chardonnay, or the Pinot noir, or the Zinfandel? Is it true that all New York State wines have a "foxy" taste? How do American wines fare in blind tastings with the vintages of Europe, and how can you train your palate to appreciate the best and spot the worst in American wines? What is the intriguing story behind the American wine you ordinarily drink, and what awaits you in all the new and different bottles now crowding the shelves? How can you pick the most outstanding values in jug wine on the market?

These are just some of the questions answered in the first total guide to the wines of America. It is an absolutely essential book in every wine lover's library.

PETER QUIMME became a confirmed wine lover while living in France in the early 1960's. Since then he has developed a particular interest in American wines, and has traveled from coast to coast visiting wineries and vineyards, sampling wines, and gathering research on the material in this book. Mr. Quimme writes frequently on wine and other gourmet topics for leading magazines, including *New York* and *House Beautiful*, and is the author of the highly praised THE SIGNET BOOK OF COFFEE AND TEA and THE SIGNET BOOK OF CHEESE. An inveterate epicure, he lives in New York and travels as much as possible.

SIGNET Books of Special Interest

THE
SIGNET BOOK
OF
AMERICAN
WINE

Revised Edition

by
Peter Quimme

A SIGNET BOOK
NEW AMERICAN LIBRARY
TIMES MIRROR

to Marge, Mac, Bea, and Bob

COPYRIGHT © 1975, 1977 BY PETER QUIMME

All rights reserved.

Library of Congress Catalogue Card Number: 77-82575

SIGNET TRADEMARK REG. U.S. PAT. OFF. AND FOREIGN COUNTRIES
REGISTERED TRADEMARK—MARCA REGISTRADA
HECHO EN CHICAGO, U.S.A.

SIGNET, SIGNET CLASSICS, MENTOR, PLUME and MERIDIAN BOOKS
are published by The New American Library, Inc.,
1301 Avenue of the Americas, New York, New York 10019

FIRST PRINTING, MAY, 1975

4 5 6 7 8 9 10 11 12

Acknowledgments

A book of this sort cannot be written without the cooperation and help of scores of people involved, in one way or another, with American wine. While I cannot acknowledge here everyone who aided my research, I wish to thank those individuals and wineries who were especially generous with their time and help: David Bennion of Ridge Vineyards; David Bruce of David Bruce Winery; Donn Chappellet of Chappellet Vineyard; Jack Davies of Schramsberg Vineyards; the late Mary Schaw Day of Hanzell Vineyards; Dr. Konstantin Frank of Vinifera Wine Cellars; Guild Wineries and Distilleries; Gold Seal Vineyards; J. E. Heitz of Heitz Wine Cellars; Heublein, Inc.; Frederick McCrea of Stony Hill Vineyard; Penn-Shore Vineyards; Pleasant Valley Wine Co.; J. Leland Stewart of Souverain Cellars; Taylor Wine Co.; Robert Travers of Mayacamas Vineyards; Warner Vineyards; Dan Wheeler of Nicasio Vineyards; Widmer's Wine Cellars; and Hermann Wiemer of Bully Hill Vineyards.

Naturally I have consulted and drawn upon what has been written before on the subject of American wines, and some of the books I found particularly useful are mentioned in the appendix under "Further Reading." For much of the historical matter in this book I have drawn on the collection of material in the Napa Valley Wine Library in St. Helena. For their kind assistance in answering questions on technical matters, I wish to thank Professor Maynard A. Amerine and Dr. Curtis J. Alley of the Department of Viticulture and Enology at the University of California at Davis, Professor Nelson Shaulis and Professor G. S. Stoewsand of the Department of Pomology and Viticulture at the New York State Agricultural Experiment Station at Geneva, and the Wine Institute of California.

I wish to thank Susan Sachnoff for cheerfully typing from my scrawl, and I owe a special debt to William Peter Burns for his unstinting support of my efforts on this book.

Undoubtedly, errors and mistakes have found their way into this book, in spite of having done my best to eliminate them. I trust they are small, infrequent, and forgivable. But they are mine alone, as are the opinions and enthusiasms expressed herein.

October, 1974   PETER QUIMME

Acknowledgments to the Revised Edition

In addition to those thanked in the acknowledgments to the first edition—many of whom were kind enough to extend, once again, their time, help, and generosity—I would like to take this opportunity to thank some of the many individuals who not only made this revised edition possible, but also made it a very pleasant task: Richard Arrowood; David Akin; David Breitstein; Brother Timothy; Charles Carpy; David Clark; William Clifford; Jim Concannon; Joe Concannon; Mario Daniele; Ray Davidson; John De Luca; Michael Dixon; Paul Draper; Tom Ferrell; Ric Forman; Stanley Forster; Jim Friedman; Jerry Gleeson; Mary Ann Graf; John Graff; Mike Grgich; Allan Hemphill; Jan Haraszthy; William Jaeger; Dan Kingman; Joel Klein; Jim Lucas; Marjorie Lumm; Louis P. Martini; Klaus Mathes; Ernest Mittelberger; Marcia, Mike, and Tim Mondavi; Bruce Neyers; John Parducci; John Pedroncelli; Richard Peterson; Harvey Posert; Angela Rinaldi; Mike Robbins; Michaela Rodeno; Brian St. Pierre; Anthony Sarjeant; Walter Schug; Sam and Don Sebastiani; Tom Selfridge; David Stare; Peter Stern; Joseph Stillman; André Tchelistcheff; Gary Topper; Bernie Turgeon; Peter Watson-Graff; Brad Webb; Eric Wente; Warren Winiarski; Phil Woodward. In many ways, they should be credited for whatever improvements this edition makes on the former, although of course they are in no way responsible for any shortcomings. I only wish I had the space to include many more of those who have widened my understanding and deepened my appreciation of American wine.

PETER QUIMME

May, 1977

Contents

Maps

Illustrations

How to Use This Book

For the reader's convenience, this book is divided into two parts: Part I, a handbook of American wine; and Part II, a brief guide to the wineries and wines of the United States.

Part I discusses the history of American wine, American wine types, winemaking, grape varieties, and labeling laws, as well as buying, tasting, and storing American wines. The information given in Part I is intended not only to enhance the reader's appreciation of American wine, but also to help the reader make his or her own evaluations among the ever-growing number of American wines each new vintage brings.

Part II is a region-by-region guide to American wineries and their wines. Discussion of each region's climate, vinification practices, and historical trends is found at the beginning of the appropriate chapter, along with a list of suggested samplings from the wines of that region. The sections on the wineries themselves are brief, covering each winery's location, size, general reputation, and a bit of its history if particularly colorful. So that the reader will have some idea of what to expect from the wines of a given producer, I've attempted to characterize the typical style and general quality of the wines from most of the wineries mentioned here, giving examples where appropriate.

Although this book has been designed to be read straight through, the contents, index, and glossary allow it to be used as a reference guide to American wines, wineries, wine topics, and wine terms.

PART I

A Handbook
of American Wine

Chapter 1

Introduction

Not many years back, when I first began to share my enthusiasm over American wine with fellow wine lovers, I used to get a lot of raised eyebrows and patronizing replies such as, "Well, sounds very interesting, Zinfandel and all that, but now admit it, how does that American stuff stack up against Château What-Not?" The answer is that a lot of "that American stuff" stacks up very well against the best of Europe—as any number of well-publicized comparative tastings of the past few years (not to mention all the private transatlantic tasteoffs) have made abundantly clear.

Happily, a large and growing number of enophiles now rightly regard the best American wines as highly as they regard the best European wines, and talk as excitedly of wines like Heitz Cabernet Sauvignon, Freemark Abbey Chardonnay, Oregon White Riesling, or a new winery's Gamay as they do of Mouton-Rothschild, Bâtard-Montrachet, Piesporter, or the latest Beaujolais.

But even though it's no longer necessary to argue stridently that American wine is worthy of attention, because a good many people *are* paying attention, there is still a great need for accurate information on American wine. A distressingly large number of American enophiles outside California (where wine consciousness is the highest in the United States) are well-informed on the wines of every country but their own. Many have probably never heard of any but the largest producers discussed in this book, much less tasted their wines. If asked their opinion of American wine, they often display an appalling hodgepodge of misinformation: "All vintages are the same in California." "Aren't all jug wines pasteurized?" "All New York wines are foxy." "No American wine is worth aging." "You mean to say drinkable wine is made in Maryland? Washington? Pennsylvania?" Etcetera.

Such wine enthusiasts are surprised to discover that differences in California vintages are less extreme than those in Europe but hardly unimportant, that some of the best wines in the country come from New York State, that American

3

wines can be as long-lived as any fine wines and, at their
peak, a match for the world's best.

There are, of course, already a number of books out on
the subject, but precious few of them come right out and describe and evaluate the wines, which, after all, is something
everyone wants to know about. There are sound reasons for
not making snap judgments about American wine, and I go
into them in detail later. I must stress that in attempting to
evaluate American wines, I have ventured into what are
largely uncharted and treacherous waters. Unlike the wines
of Europe, there are few guideposts to quality among U.S.
wines, and wine reputations are in constant evolution. No one
would think a wine writer particularly original if he pro-
claimed Montrachet as the greatest French White Burgundy,
and few would challenge his opinion. I have not found it difficult to resist proclaiming who makes, say, the greatest
Chardonnay in the country, because I really am not sure myself. I've tasted at least a dozen superb ones, and in various vintages they seem to trade the top spot. The same could
be said of other wines, and I am not about to suggest other
winemakers couldn't join the list. Past a certain point of quality, it is a matter of preference for one or another equally
fine and equally valid style of winemaking.

Nor have I tasted every wine in production in the U.S.
(the list is far longer than most people suppose), and frankly,
I would be greatly disappointed to think that I had tasted every American wine worth tasting. Personally I am looking
forward to a good many more pleasant surprises, and I hope
not too many of my enthusiasms (especially over new
wineries) prove to be unwarranted in the long run.

Since I believe most rating scales are not very informative
and often misleading, I have tried to *characterize* wines
within four basic categories of quality: "ordinary," "good,"
"fine," and "great." By "ordinary" wine I mean nothing derogatory. I simply mean sound, well-made wine suitable for everyday consumption. It is not wine to be studied, but to be
used as a lubricant to food. At best it is pleasant, at worst a
little coarse. It is always very simple in flavor. A synonym I
tend to use for this category is "jug wine," in reference to its
handiest form. By "good" wine I mean wine a step above the
ordinary, typically the standard "premium" (or wine sealed
with a cork) wine of California. It is a little more complex in
flavor than "ordinary" and, in fact, may be quite delicious. It
may even be a vintage-dated varietal, as not all wines so la-

beled are automatically "fine." "Fine" is a term I reserve for wines of character and distinction, which can range from excellent to outstanding. Most often these are vintage-dated varietal wines from the best grape varieties. A near-great wine I usually call "superb," as I prefer to reserve the term "great" for wines that are literally unforgettable.

Finally, since this book is supposed to be a handy, useful guide rather than the sort of reference work that doubles as a flower-press, not every producing winery in the country is discussed here. For my purposes, what qualified a winery for discussion was whether or not it has national distribution (like Gallo), or has had an important impact (like Dr. Frank's Vinifera Cellars), or produces outstanding wines (like Stony Hill). Wineries whose products are not particularly remarkable and whose distribution is mostly local trade (of which there are many scattered all over the country) are not mentioned at all, since they would not concern anyone not living in the immediate locale. Readers should also be warned that not every wine discussed here is going to be found at the corner liquor store—especially the finer wines—any more than every important European wine can be found there. As everywhere in the world, the finest wines are produced in very small quantities.

A word about being up-to-date: Naturally I've made a great effort to be as up-to-date as possible, but the U.S. wine industry hardly seems to stand still long enough to be discussed in print. Few months go by without the birth of a new winery, a takeover or merger, or even (though rarely) a winery going out of business. This rapidly growing, increasingly competitive, anything-but-static industry produces some very interesting wine. In fact, there seems to be no end to the astonishing accomplishments of American winemakers. That is, of course, one of the reasons why the subject is so fascinating, and it is the simple purpose of this book to introduce the reader to some of the surprises and delights American wine offers.

Chapter 2
Americans and Wine

It is said often these days that Americans discovered wine in the mid- and late sixties. Actually, what happened was that Americans rediscovered wine; this country has always had a rather dramatic relationship with the grape, ranging from outright prohibition of wine (and other alcoholic beverages) to extraordinary and successful efforts to make some of the greatest wine in the world.

Early History

Histories of wine in America often begin by evoking a picture of Leif Ericson peering through the mists at the North American continent and, seeing nothing but a tangle of vines, dubbing the coast "Vineland." Whether there is anything to this story is debatable, but it does serve to point up the fact that America possesses its own native species of grapes. These grape varieties—*Vitis labrusca, rotundifolia, riparia,* etcetera—were found flourishing in North America when the first European settlers arrived. Such varieties yielded undistinguished and assertive wines and were said to have a "foxy" or wild-grape flavor. Early settlers in the Eastern United States found this flavor strange to their palates, and, dissatisfied with the musky wine the native grapes yielded, imported and planted European grape varieties. (These varieties are known as the species *Vitis vinifera,* or the wine grape, and have been cultivated for centuries in Europe.) In fact, attempts were made to grow European grapes in the East from 1619 on by a great number of people, William Penn and Thomas Jefferson among them.

Every attempt failed. Since the native vines flourished in the Eastern United States, early vineyardists in the East were unable to understand why imported European vines slowly sickened, why their fruit turned colorless and their leaves yellowed, and why the plants eventually died. Some of the more determined vineyard owners even tried importing European soil. Nothing worked.

Early grape-growing in California was far more successful, however. The first man said to have planted vines in California was Padre Junipero Serra, who is supposed to have brought vines from Baja California and planted them at Mission San Diego around 1769. In succeeding years, the mission fathers planted vines to make sacramental wine at their various missions as far north as the Sonoma Valley. These Franciscan fathers planted a grape variety (the Criolla) that came to be known later as the "Mission" grape. The Mission is not a native American grape, but a *vinifera* variety, apparently first introduced into Mexico by the Spanish about 1520. This bountiful variety yields only undistinguished wine. Its greatest drawback at the time, however, was that it would not ripen properly in cooler climates, and although the padres soon resorted to distilling brandy from the poor vintages, their vineyards at Santa Cruz, San Francisco, and Santa Clara were the first failures in California viticulture. But, through a half-century of endeavor, they had established winemaking in California.

The many winemakers who followed them experimented with varieties more suited to cooler climates and finer wines. Although it has been estimated that in 1870 the great majority of the vines in California were still of the Mission variety, by 1890, ninety percent of the state was planted in better *vinifera* varieties.

Phylloxera

While the potential, if not the actuality, of American wine had been noticed as far back as 1862, when French viticultural experts reported that California was capable of "entering serious competition with the wines of Europe," America's first impact on world wine production was not exactly applauded. America turned out to hold the secret of both the cause and cure of phylloxera, the worldwide nineteenth-century vine blight.

The story of phylloxera is indispensable to understanding the history of every wine-producing country. The wine vine has numerous enemies, from beetles, mites, and grubs to little red spiders, to various rots and mildew (including a virulent form known as odium), not to mention frost, hail, rain, wind, and other weather problems. But the greatest enemy is *Phylloxera vastatrix,* the American root louse, which nearly destroyed every vineyard in Europe and California between 1870 and the turn of the century before a radical solution was discovered.

Phylloxera vastatrix is a species of aphid which lives upon the roots and sometimes the leaves of the grape vine. Native American grape vines are immune to this nasty little bug, which can be found in Eastern U.S. soil. *Vinifera,* however, are not immune, which of course explains the early Eastern viticulturalists' failure to grow this species of vine. The early California vineyard growers had no problem with their *vinifera* as there was no phylloxera present in the soil—at first.

The horrifying discovery that *vinifera* were not resistant to a hitherto unsuspected blight did not dawn on the wine-growing world until some native American vines carrying the heartless pest were brought to Europe for experimental purposes. The first outbreak was noticed in botanical gardens in England, and had spread to France by 1864. A decade later, it also spread to California. Not until the 1880's did anyone think of the drastic but obvious solution of grafting European *vinifera* onto the hardy native American root stocks,* but the replanting of entire wine regions could not be accomplished overnight, and nearly every vineyard in Europe was destroyed by the turn of the century. California's vineyards were also devastated, but its industry recovered more quickly than Europe's—which did not recover for decades.

Throughout this period winemakers east of the Rockies had been developing an industry based on native American varieties and hybrids that were unaffected by phylloxera. By 1859, for example, Ohio produced almost half a million gal-

---

*Now, grape-growers all over the world first plant the "root stock"—a native American grape variety that is resistant to phylloxera—and then when the root stock catches hold, graft on the more delicate variety of *Vitis vinifera* that will bear the fruit. Once the graft buds, the rest of the root stock plant is cut off, and the shoot becomes the grapevine. (There are other grafting methods as well, but all accomplish the same purpose.) Virtually all the vineyards of Europe (including the famous ones) and California always graft *vinifera* on American root stock, although direct planting of *vinifera* has been undertaken recently in some areas of California and Washington.

lons of wine a year, and many Eastern states produced more wine in the nineteenth century than they have ever since.

The California wine industry began to prosper as well. In the first decades after the ravages of phylloxera, the state made great strides in enological and viticultural research, and had established statewide regulations to raise the standards of the industry as a whole. The California wine industry had only begun to realize its potential when it suffered its worst blow, the one obstacle that no American winemakers were able to overcome: Prohibition (1920-33), or as its proponents liked to call it, the Great Experiment.

Prohibition and Its Effects

The history and background of what appears in retrospect to have been an exercise in national lunacy makes fascinating if head-shaking reading today. What is of interest here, however, is its impact on the wine industry, not its sociology. The impact was immediate and far-reaching: the growing achievements of the American wine industry from 1895 to 1918 were wiped out in the Prohibition period, which saw most wineries go out of business and vineyards plowed under or replanted to table grapes. A number of wineries managed to continue to make wine, but their ambitions were reduced to making "cooking wines," "tonics," grape concentrates for home winemaking, or the humble task of the mission fathers over a century before—making sacramental wine.

Thirteen years of Prohibition resulted in the loss of nearly all winemaking talent. There were hardly any remaining vineyards planted to fine wine grapes in California, no cooperage to age the wine, no distribution system, and, worst of all, no market for fine wines. The wine industry in California and the East was generally moribund, wavering, and occasionally severely depressed in the thirties and forties. Although a few exceptional wines were made (mostly California Cabernet Sauvignon), the general quality of American wine was very low.

The first post-Prohibition wines were frankly terrible. In the rush to get into the market, vast amounts of poorly made wine from unsuitable grapes were bottled. This was not surprising, since very few vintners had anything in the way of vineyards planted to varieties that would yield creditable wine, adequate stocks of aged wine, or skilled help. Those who were already enophiles turned to imports, and it was years before American wines were taken seriously by most wine lovers.

An additional unfortunate result of Prohibition was the legacy of a crazy-quilt of local laws that left regulation of "intoxicating liquors" up to states, counties, and municipalities. Local prohibition still exists in one county or another in over thirty states, and there are still eighteen states that regulate the distribution and sale of alcoholic beverages through state-owned stores—the so-called "control states." There is also a pattern of discriminatory taxation in some states on wines not made from that state's grapes.

Perhaps worst of all, state legislatures, the federal government, and various regulatory agencies crank out or hand down literally thousands of laws, regulations, and directives each year governing the sale and distribution of beer, wine, and liquor. Consequently only the largest producers of wine in the country are equipped to handle the blizzard of paperwork necessary to distribute their products nationally. Since postal laws prevent the mailing of alcoholic beverages, and since it often requires an importer's license for an individual to get wines made in another state shipped to him, few fine California wines were ever shipped outside the state until recent years.

While these laws hampered the distribution of post-Prohibition wines in the United States, another significant factor kept the industry moribund. An entire generation had grown up with the attitude that alcoholic beverages were illicit if not illegal, imbibed solely for effect, and whose experience had been limited to bootlegged liquor, bathtub gin, and 3.2 beer. The idea that wine was a wholesome, natural beverage—in fact, a food—was unknown to a nation of drinkers who thought of wine as just another (and rather weak, at that) form of booze. Before Prohibition, table wines outsold dessert wines three to one. But by 1935, the reverse was true; consumers were more interested in alcoholic content, and a flood of ports, sherries, tokays, and muscatels found ready acceptance as the cheapest intoxicants. (Not until 1968 did Americans again consume more table wine than dessert wine!)

Prior to World War II, table wine consumption was at an all-time low: Americans drank only a half a gallon per capita per year. It was clear to the larger wineries that if Americans were to adopt the habit of drinking wine with their meals, they would have to be persuaded that wine was an everyday, uncomplicated, unmysterious—and tasty—beverage.

As a result, for the past few decades the largest wineries have produced and marketed wines to appeal to the consumer who feels uncomfortable with the vagaries and variety of wine and distressed at the thought of choosing among vintages. This has meant packaging and advertising that stresses a minimum of fuss and bother: no vintage dates, no worry over matching certain wines to certain foods, no trace of sediment, nothing that requires aging, often no corks—just a pleasant, reliable, bland drink for any time or any meal. The giant California and New York firms have even gone so far as to concoct flavored blends to appeal to "the American taste," which, judging from the products designed for it, must be something like a great passion for fizzy fruit punch.

While this marketing approach has been successful in one respect (in trebling wine consumption since Repeal), it has not introduced wine drinkers to fine American wines. It has, rather, fostered an image of California and New York State wines as jug wines and sweet, fruity blends, and has left many wine lovers with the erroneous impression that only European wines represent quality. This complicated and far-reaching effect of Prohibition on the American wine industry only began to change in the late sixties—when prosperity for fine American wines began to reign.

The U.S. Wine Industry Today

During the period from Repeal in 1933 to the 1960's, when American wine came into its own, there were enormous strides in technology and research, and many efforts to make fine wine were undertaken. It is true that fine and even great wines were made from time to time during the thirties, forties, and fifties, but the greatest accomplishments during those decades were not so much the wines themselves as the extraordinary advances in viticulture and vinification. By the 1960's, groundwork in these fields was laid that enabled an astonishing amount of fine and great wine to be made in America.

Two themes in this growth of quality are, perhaps, typically American: first, the belief in the efficacy of science in

clarifying the hitherto mysterious processes of fermentation
and aging; second, the pioneering efforts of winemakers who
believed it was possible to make great wine on American soil.
Both are consistent themes in American winemaking and
continue to be among its great strengths.

Since 1880, the University of California has been conduct-
ing research into viticulture and enology, and by the 1950's
its campus at Davis had become one of the world's greatest
centers of wine research. Much of this research is too technical for the average wine lover to appreciate, but the effects
of such research—at Davis and other centers in the country—on almost every aspect of wine has been to enable good
grapes to be grown in places long thought inhospitable, and
fine wine to be made where formerly only passable wine was
the rule. The development of new grape varieties for specific
climates, the selective breeding of stock, heat-treating of root
stock, mechanical harvesting, drip irrigation and frost protection, cold fermentation, and hundreds of other technological
improvements have enabled the grower and the winemaker to
have better control over grape quality and the winemaking
process.

Some of the more interesting and important advances will
be touched upon later in the appropriate sections. For now, I
simply want to point out that the dominant idea behind these
efforts to improve the technology of wine production is that
in winemaking there is no virtue in leaving quality to chance.
Rather, to the extent that stages of growing and steps in
winemaking can be controlled, to that same extent the winemaker can make decisions affecting the quality of his product
and does not have to trust to luck. In almost every case, the
appropriate use of technological advances has led to better
wine, not blander wine; and, even where the wine is a mass-
produced product, the quality has improved markedly.

Of course, advances in quality have not been the sole prov-
ince of the professors. Wineries themselves have been and
still are in the forefront of experimentation in the United
States, and have pioneered advances on all fronts, and on all
levels of quality, from researching the best color of glass for
wine bottles to handpicking grapes berry by berry, to experimenting with dozens of different types of wood for aging.
As far as experimentation at the highest levels of quality
goes, a great deal of credit must also go to the pioneering efforts of winemakers at the small fine wineries of California
such as Hanzell, Stony Hill, and Heitz Cellars, who showed

that it is possible to make a number of great wines in California; and to men like Philip Wagner, whose work with French hybrids in Maryland has sparked efforts to grow better wines all over the continental U.S. east of the Rockies; and to Dr. Konstantin Frank, who grew *vinifera* successfully for the first time in the East, and showed that superb wine could be made from it.

In accomplishing these feats, American wine-growers have managed to knock holes in a number of notions long hallowed in wine lore. Europeans have long claimed that great wine could only come from a few blessed patches of soil in France and Germany. Americans have shown that what it takes to make great wine is the right grapes grown in the right location, the cooperation of the weather, the skill to realize the potential of the grapes in the wine, and devotion to quality. It had long been supposed that many of the subtleties found in the finest European wines were due to the soil. Enologists now suspect that such differences in taste which are commonly attributed to differences in soil may really be attributable to the influence of yeast flora. Research has uncovered nothing so far which indicates that soil composition directly affects wine quality; rather, the effect of soil on the vine appears to be indirect, in terms of how it affects drainage, growth, temperature, and the like. Long-cherished notions, such as "the best wine comes from the oldest vines," now appear less than satisfactory truisms when winemakers have made great Chardonnays from three-year-old plants. The world of wine has long been one in which new developments and reputations are the products of centuries, not decades, of cultivation, and therefore the enormous distance that American wine has come in such a relatively short time is simply startling.

In the past decade or so, these achievements have met with an enthusiastic response from wine consumers. Total United States wine consumption has doubled—from 163 million gallons in 1960 to 367 million gallons consumed in 1975. Impressive as this seems, Americans barely consume eight bottles of wine per capita per year, while the French and the Italians, for example, put away upwards of one hundred and fifty bottles per capita annually. But all predictions see American wine consumption continuing to gallop ahead in the years to come; by 1985, many assume Americans will consume fifteen bottles per capita. These rosy prognostications have resulted in tremendous growth of the industry: a rapidly ex-

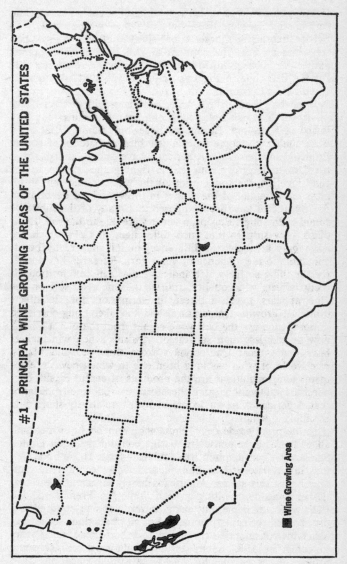

#1 · PRINCIPAL WINE GROWING AREAS OF THE UNITED STATES

■ Wine Growing Area

panding amount of vineyard acreage, a host of new wineries, and increased production in the industry as a whole.

The United States has some 700,000 acres of vineyards, about one-fortieth of the world's total. However, there is plenty of prime potential vineyard land left. In fact, in the early 1970's, 50,000 acres of vineyards were being planted each year in California alone, and the state now has more grape acreage than it did in the record year of 1926, when it had 630,000 acres of vines. The proportion of better-quality wine grapes is much higher now than it was then. Before supply matches demand, Californians may continue to set out up to 30,000 acres of vines a year into the late seventies, and these figures become even more impressive when one considers that there are only 22,000 acres of vineyards in the entire Cote d'Or region of Burgundy. New York State has under 40,000 acres of vineyards, and other states half that or less, but they too are expanding acreage.

The United States is now sixth in world wine production, behind Argentina and the USSR as well as France and Italy. There were 1,310 bonded wineries in the U.S. in 1936, but only 395 in 1965. In 1976 there were still fewer than 600 wineries in the country (almost 300 in California), yet the industry has increased its production dramatically, and this is because fewer and fewer firms produce more and more. While today there are new small wineries coming into existence every year—many of them devoted to fine wine production—the majority of wine continues to be produced by a few giant firms.

The list of big American producers is headed by E & J Gallo, which produces more than one out of every three bottles of wine drunk in the U.S.: a staggering 125 million gallons. United Vintners, the giant wine-producing division of Heublein, Inc., seems tiny by comparison with its fifteen percent share of the market, a mere 50 million gallons. Guild, Almadén, Mogen David, and Taylor follow in order with lesser but still huge chunks of the wine market.

The better U.S. wines amount to roughly ten percent of the total production; these are termed "premium" wines. "Premium" wines are defined by the industry, however, not on the basis of quality *per se*, but usually as any table wine sold in regular fifth bottles for $1.50 or more, a category which necessarily includes the expensive-to-produce better wines. The giant premium wine producers—Almadén, Paul Masson, and Christian Brothers—account for approximately three-quarters of the premium wine trade. While decent table wines and some very good wines are made by these large producers, none is noted for fine wine.

The rest of the premium wine trade is mostly taken up by large producers about a tenth of the size of the three premium giants. Louis M. Martini, Wente Bros., Charles Krug, and Beaulieu Vineyards are some of the well-known names in this category, producing from around 150,000 cases to 500,000 cases per year. Good wines and, on occasion, outstanding fine wines can be found among their large, varied, and not always distinctive offerings. The production of some of the fine wine producers, in contrast, ranges from around 2,000 to 20,000 cases of wine per year, with some aiming for an eventual annual production of 30,000 cases. One realizes that fine wine, only a fraction of premium wine, is but a trickle in the annual American flood. It ought to be remembered, of course, that fine wine is always a tiny fraction of any wine country's output. The total production of all the classified growths of Bordeaux, for example, is only three percent of the total Bordeaux production.

American wine enthusiasts are liable to be misled on this, since the great majority of American wines they see are the everyday wines in jugs that line supermarket shelves. They tend to forget that the imported wines they see are almost always the best wines of the exporting country. It is just as distorted a picture of French wine to assume the wine of a great château is typical of most French wine production, as it is to assume that there are no American wines better than screw-top Mountain Red.

Chapter 3
Grapes and Wine

Climate and Grape-growing

It comes as a surprise to most people that practically the entire continental United States is suitable for the cultivation of wine grapes of one variety or another. With the exception of the northernmost areas of the country, where severe winter temperatures may kill the vines, and the hottest Western and Southern regions, the majority of the states could support a wine industry. Whether fine wines—much less great wines—could be produced in most of them is another matter. Certainly it has been demonstrated that superior *vinifera* varieties can be grown and do make fine wine outside California.

Even in states where the overall conditions do not seem suitable, there are usually small areas where the conditions of sun, weather, nearby bodies of water, or local effects such as fogs create microclimates that can support a small vineyard and allow excellent wines of various types to be made. The enthusiastic experimentalists who now tend such small patches of hybrids and *vinifera* in places like Idaho, Kentucky, Connecticut, New Hampshire, and other surprising locales are bringing nearer the day when it might be possible to ascertain areas where particular grape varieties might do better than where they are now grown.

For the present and the foreseeable future, California remains the home of the vast majority of ordinary, good, fine, and great wines of America. It has the historical precedent, the most acreage under cultivation, good overall conditions for grape-growing, and is a center of viticultural and enological research. Not surprisingly, more research has been done on grape-growing climates in California than elsewhere in the U.S., and each of its principal wine districts has been roughly divided into "regions" according to careful heat-summation studies undertaken by the University of California at

Davis. Briefly, the ratings are based on the fact that grapes do not grow and ripen when the average daily temperature is under 50°F. By taking the average daily temperature during the typical growing season (April 1st through October 31st) and subtracting 50°, one gets a daily figure, and the total of, these figures gives one the "degree days" of the grape-growing season. The various districts of California are subdivided into five "regions" on the following scale:

   I: 2500 degree days or less
   II: 2501 to 3000 degree days
   III: 3001 to 3500 degree days
   IV: 3501 to 4000 degree days
   V: 4001 degree days or more

In terms of degree days, Region I is similar to the Rhine and Moselle districts in Germany and the Champagne district of France. Region II matches that of Bordeaux. Region III is similar to Northern Italy, Region IV is like Central Spain, and Region V is similar to North Africa. Since *vinifera* varieties were adapted over centuries to specific conditions found in European wine-growing districts, one's first guide to the suitability of a given grape variety to a given region is how closely the degree days match the grape's traditional district. Thus, German and Alsatian varieties like White Riesling or Gewürztraminer and Burgundian varieties like Chardonnay and Pinot noir are recommended for Regions I and possibly Regions II; Bordeaux varieties like Sauvignon blanc, Sémillon, and Cabernet Sauvignon, while excellent in I and II, can be grown in Region III, though Cabernet is not thought to do as well as it does in cooler locales. Italian varieties like Barbera do best in Regions III and IV, while Portuguese varieties used in dessert wines, like Tinta Madeira, do best in the hottest areas, or Region V. The major grape-growing districts and their various region ratings are shown in Figure 2.

There are, however, a number of other climatic factors which can have considerable effect on the actual growing conditions, which may account in part for the sometimes wide differences in wines made from the same grapes in various parts of the world with similar degree days. Vineyardists in California are always quick to point out the advantages (or disadvantages) of their particular patch of ground and its individual conditions, or microclimate. Elevation, exposure, fogs, wind, drainage, rainfall, and dozens of other effects can

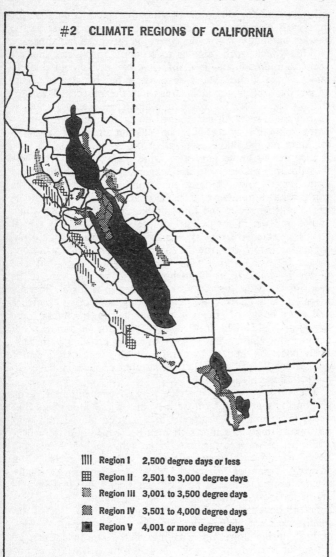

#2 CLIMATE REGIONS OF CALIFORNIA

|||| Region I   2,500 degree days or less
⊞ Region II   2,501 to 3,000 degree days
▦ Region III   3,001 to 3,500 degree days
▨ Region IV   3,501 to 4,000 degree days
■ Region V   4,001 or more degree days

either accentuate, diminish, or alter the actual conditions for the vines. Nonetheless, such ratings are clear guides to the *general* suitability of growing certain grapes in certain areas.

While much work remains to be done on regions and, especially, microclimates in California, research on suitable climates in the United States as a whole has just begun. Wine grapes have been grown in areas like the Finger Lakes District in New York since the mid-nineteenth century, but recent climatic research has opened up promising new areas for grape-growing in places like the Yakima Valley of Washington State and the Willamette Valley of Oregon.

In order to understand why wine grapes can grow where they do, it is necessary to understand something about *how* a grape vine grows. Among the fruit-bearing plants of the world it has a number of unusual characteristics. It can flourish in soils so rocky and inhospitable that other plants would wither and die in them. Part of the reason it can is that it boasts an extensive root system that seeks out water and nutrients far below the ground. Another reason is that what one means by a fine wine vine "flourishing" is not what one means by most fruits flourishing. In grapes that are to be used for fine wine, less is more. If grown in rich soil, liberally irrigated, and allowed to put out long wandering branches and every bunch of grapes it is stimulated to, the finest grape varieties would yield fruit suitable only for mediocre wine. Only if the vine's yield is kept small by growing it in relatively poor soil, and/or by careful pruning, can the vine produce a small crop of fruit concentrated enough in flavor to produce fine, intense wines.

The life span of a grape vine may cover a hundred years, and during that time it will turn from a wispy little shoot that needs to be staked for support to a gnarled old veteran with a trunk as thick as a man's. It may be pruned and trained in a number of ways to facilitate its growth, yield, or harvesting (even to aid mechanical pickers). Its yearly cycle has a growing season of 90 to 195 days. In the spring, usually around March, the vine puts out buds, and small, quite undramatic flower-clusters emerge with the shoots. These bloom about 45 days later, and small hard green berries "set" if the weather has not visited such plagues as early frosts or rains or heat during flowering. The rest of the season consists in letting the berries ripen, which is why a long, warm (but not scorching hot), dry summer is ideal. Careful pruning must be done to match problems of weather—for example, thinning the foliage to let the berries have more sun, spraying to prevent mildew, and the like.

There are differences between grape varieties, too, in their tolerance for specific climates and vineyard conditions, their yield (whether they are "shy-bearers" or "high-yield" grapes), their growing season (some are "early ripeners," some "mid-season varieties," others "late ripeners"), and their fussiness. Some are much easier to grow than others; some are more resistant to some diseases and prey to others; and all alike can fall victim to a host of soil and root pests, molds, mildews, caterpillars, bees, birds, and deer. In short, to nurse a vineyard of fine wine grapes through a season even of perfect weather is still a task calling for never-ending vigilance.

The grower of fine wine grapes anywhere in the world is particularly concerned with two things in the mature, ripe grape: sugar and acid. In the northernmost areas of Europe and in New York State, for example, a grower's principal concern is whether the grapes will fully mature or ripen to the point where the sugar content is high enough to allow the conversion by yeast of these fruit sugars to a sufficient level of alcohol to make a wine. In California, on the other hand, and in many other wine regions, the vineyard owner's principal worry is that excessive heat during the final stages of ripening and harvest will cause the natural fruit acids simply to respire right out of the grape. In a year that is too cool, one may end up with thin, acidic wines; in a year that is too hot, one can end up with coarse, heavy wines that lack acidity—the crisp, fruity tang without which any wine seems flat, flabby, or dull.

The grape is unique among fruits in that its sugar content does not increase in even increments during final stages of ripening, but wavers as the harvest approaches because sugar during cool days retreats back into the stalk. This is one of the reasons that deciding the exact time of harvesting is so critical for the wine-grower. Once the proper balance of sugar and acid is achieved in the grapes—barring other mishaps of weather and grape pests—they are picked.

Winemaking

The enjoyment of many things in life is not dependent on knowing how they came about. Nonetheless, a little knowledge of the materials and processes that are used in the creation of a given product helps one to appreciate it, whether that product be venison with chocolate sauce, a Gothic cathedral, or a glass of fine wine. For that reason, and because there are a number of variations employed in wine-making that can profoundly affect the wine and add a number of subtleties to it, it's worth taking a brief look at how wine is made.

I hasten to point out that wine drinking no more qualifies one as a winemaker any more than eating makes one a great chef. The following account is therefore appropriately simplified. I frankly do not understand the conversion of pyruvic acid to acetaldehyde and its catalyzation by the enzyme alcohol dehydrogenase, etcetera; such matters far transcend my ability to explain them, and doubtless transcend the average reader's interest as well. I suspect that most wine lovers, like myself, have their vinous attention focused almost exclusively on the contents of wine bottles and, ultimately, wine glasses.

There are issues, however, which do intrigue the wine lover, because they have to do with the quality of wine and often have a noticeable effect on the taste; matters such as aging whites in oak, or making tannic reds, or whether Zinfandel or Chenin Blanc ought to be made in a "big," "little," "soft," "bone-dry," etcetera, style are the sort of things that are of great interest to the consumer, and they are the result of decisions that are made in the winery, and, before that, in the vineyards.

Wine is the fermented juice of grapes. It is possible to make a mildly interesting fermented beverage from other fruits, but only grapes, and then only a very few kinds, make outstanding wine. The making of wine is a very simple and natural process at bottom, which of course accounts for its early discovery. (In fact, *Vitis vinifera* has been cultivated for over five thousand years.) The nutshell explanation of this process is that there are particular yeasts found on grape skins, which, when grapes are crushed, come into contact with the grape juice and convert its fruit sugars into alcohol and carbon dioxide. This is fermentation. This carbon dioxide is given off as a gas and causes the seething and bubbling of the juice during fermentation. After the yeasts have gobbled up all the available sugar and/or created enough alcohol—roughly fifteen percent by volume—to kill themselves off, or at least render themselves dormant, they fall to the bottom of the fermenting vat as sediment. The juice has now been turned into wine, and can be drawn off the dregs and be put into barrels for further aging, or bottled right then, or drunk. However, a clean, well-made wine, much less a wine of interest, requires much more care each step of the way to ensure that it escapes spoilage, emerges without defect, and, hopefully, exhibits some character and complexity.

The winemaker controls and shapes this very natural process. All the complexities associated with it in a modern winery anywhere in the world are simply elaborations of the process to ensure that the wine the winemaker ends up with, and the quality he reaches, are a matter of conscious choice, and not an accident, whether fortunate or disastrous.

Although there is a great deal that is known about viticulture and vinification—growing grapes and making wine—there are few hard and fast rules about when to do something and how to do it. There are thousands of choices and decisions to be made, beginning with the questions of where to plant, what to grow, and what sort of quality one is aiming for. A winemaker must also decide what sort of role he wants to play: does he picture himself as a midwife to the vineyard, one who attempts to bring forth the flavor and character of the grapes he grows on that soil, or does he think of himself as an alchemist, transforming, by his wizardry in the cellar, the mere potential of the grapes into the magic of a superb wine? Doubtless some winemakers regard themselves as chemists in a food-processing plant, just as some vineyard owners think of themselves as farmers, and would just as soon grow prunes. But making fine wine requires artistry.

Regardless of the winemaker's outlook, he must always take into consideration the limitations that the grape variety and the weather impose; he may want to make a great red wine that will last and improve for thirty years, but he is not likely to do it with Gamay in a wet, cold year. Within the framework of his materials, the winemaker must make a great many decisions on taste alone, and these decisions all have a profound influence on the end product.

The first significant decision in winemaking is what sort of wine to make. There are two basic types of wine—table and dessert—that can be made, and several variants. The simplest, and most basic, is table wine—red and white. With table wine, a winemaker is concerned that the sugar and acid content in the grape be in balance. When to pick, therefore, is a critical decision. As it is difficult to retain acidity in the grapes as they reach maturity (ripen), grapes for dry table wine are picked as soon as the sugar content is sufficient to produce the proper alcoholic content. Grapes for dessert wines, on the other hand, have high sugar and low acid.

Of course, the winemaker may have had nothing to do with the growing of the grapes; in all wine-growing areas of the world, there are growers who sell each year's crop to wineries, and many wineries in the U.S. do not have vineyards of their own. The winemaker may shop around for grapes, but often he has long-term contracts with growers to buy their produce, and works closely with them. Depending on the grape variety, viticultural methods, and climate, an acre of vines yields anywhere from a single ton to twenty tons of grapes, and a ton of grapes yields around 175 gallons of juice, usually less for quality wine.

Once the grapes are picked, they must be crushed, and crushed quickly. If too much time elapses between picking and crushing, some spoilage of the fruit can occur, and this can diminish the quality of the wine. Some U.S. wineries have gone so far as to initiate crushing operations in the field with excellent results, but the majority of them simply try to shorten the length of time between picking in the field and crushing at the winery.

The picture of happy peasants jumping on grapes may be part of the folklore of winemaking, but it has long since been replaced almost everywhere by simple or elaborate crushers which also de-stem the grapes. The resulting mass of crushed grapes and juice is called "must." Before fermentation and pressing take place, this "must" is sulphured. Because in the U.S. (and many other regions of the world) the wild yeasts naturally found on the grape skins are neither sufficient nor of the right sort to ensure reliable fermentation, the must is inoculated with sulphur dioxide. This kills off the wild yeasts and any microorganisms that might damage the wine.

Fermentation and pressing are the next step. White wines are pressed before fermentation in order to remove the juice from the skins, while reds are pressed after fermentation. The reason for this is that the juice of all grapes (with a few exceptions not worth noting here) is white. Neophyte wine enthusiasts are often confused by this, since it is true that most red wines come from red grapes, and most white wines come from white grapes (although most wine grapes are actually some shade of purple or green). But the reason why red wines are red is that the juice is allowed to remain in contact with the dark skins during fermentation and thereby picks up color, whereas white wine is removed from the skins immediately after crushing and pressing. Rosés, unless they are ordinary blends of red and white wines, are made from red grapes where the clear juice is allowed to remain in contact with the skins of the grapes only long enough to pick up a pink hue. It is perfectly possible, in other words, to make a white wine from red grapes, and it is a common procedure in districts like that of Champagne, where the clear juice of the red Pinot noir grape is used, along with other varieties, to make Champagne. In New York State, reds, whites, and rosés may be made from the same red variety.

The same kind of press is used in making both red and white wine. While basket presses, looking something like an upright barrel with every other stave missing, combined with a screw-down plate or piston, are still in use, especially in smaller American wineries, most use the larger pneumatic presses which inflate a rubber bag that presses the must against a cylindrical wall. Basically the idea is to squeeze out the juice without crushing seeds and stems and allowing an excessive amount of bitter tannins to be added to the wine. "Free-run" juice refers to the juice obtained from light or no pressing, and is generally considered to yield the best wine. Press juice—or that which is yielded by a harder pressing—yields less fine wine, but is sometimes used in the production of fine wine to add additional flavor.

The juice of white wines and the entire crushed grape mass for reds is now fermented. After these have been transferred to a fermenting container (anything from a simple barrel to a stainless steel vat), a cultured yeast is added to start fermentation. The action of fermentation gives off heat; reds are fermented in open vats, while whites are fermented in closed containers because of their susceptibility to acetification (spoilage which eventually turns wine to vinegar) when they come in contact with air. They are also fermented at cooler temperature than reds to preserve delicacy. Controlling the temperature of fermentation is important (especially in white wines) as fermentation that becomes too hot can coarsen flavor and may even stop halfway through the process or become "stuck"; the methods used to start it again are liable to result in diminished quality. Jacketed fermentors in which cool water can be circulated allows the fermentation to proceed at a rate and rhythm the winemaker selects to retain all the elements that contribute to aroma and flavor.

After the initial phase of fermentation—usually one to two weeks—wines are typically removed to storage tanks to complete their fermentation, which may take months, especially if kept cool. Reds intended for long aging are allowed to stand on the skins up to two weeks before draining and pressing in order to pick up sufficient tannin to allow them to age and develop over a long period of time. Most table wines are dry to the taste because the yeasts consume all the sugar that is available before they also produce so much alcohol that they become dormant. A sweet table wine, however, is one in which a small amount of residual sugar is left in the wine because the yeasts are filtered out of the wine at, say, eleven percent alcohol (something that might be done for a semi-sweet, fruity white wine), or the grapes contain such an excess of sugar that it cannot be "fermented completely dry."

The next step in the winemaking process is aging, and what wines are aged in is known collectively as cooperage. Traditionally, such containers were wood; however, today a good many wines (even the finest whites), may never touch wood at all but spend only a few months in a glass-lined tank before being bottled. Other wines may be aged in neutral cooperage, such as redwood tanks of large capacity. The finest reds, and some whites, are often aged in small oak barrels, some as little as 50 gallons in capacity. Wine aged in wooden cooperage comes in contact with the air and actually "breathes" through the wood; enough is evaporated to develop an air space, or ullage, that must be "topped up" or replenished every few weeks with more wine to prevent spoilage—principally acetification—from occurring because of *excessive* contact with air. Certain varieties of oak, particularly French oak, impart their own nuance of flavor to wines, and this added subtlety is much in vogue now among some California winemakers. The smaller the container, the more contact there is between the wine and the wood, and it is almost true to say that the finer the wine, the smaller the barrels used for aging—and the longer the aging, up to two or three years, for wines like Cabernet Sauvignon. White wines are another matter, depending on the winery's idea of what it wants its wines to taste like; there are wineries which feel that a maximum of fruitiness and clean taste is retained by keeping the wine in glass-lined tanks before bottling, and those which feel that some contact with wood adds complexity to the wine.

The processes of clarification of wine begins with settling

and pressing; after fermentation, wine can be clarified either by patient "racking" (or transferring wines from one container to another), filtering, or fining, or—usually—some judicious combination of all three methods. Racking is time-consuming and involves a great deal of labor, as the wine is simply allowed to settle naturally and precipitate, or throw off, its heaviest sediment into its cooperage. This requires a good deal of careful cleaning of barrels, as well as caution in seeing that the wine does not come into excessive contact with air. For troublesome material that will not settle out but persists in hanging suspended in the wine, winemakers can "fine" the wine. Fining is the addition of various materials to the wine, such as clays, egg whites, gelatins, and various synthetics, which act as a kind of net to draw these materials to the bottom of the tank. The wine is then racked off the sediment. Filtering is just that, the pumping of the wine through pads of various materials of differing fineness, in order to remove harmful microorganisms and to clarify the wine.

The problem with both filtering and fining is that quality can be adversely affected. American wineries, especially large ones, are often concerned lest consumers discover one speck of sediment in their wines. While a great many consumers a decade ago would have been convinced that anything looking like dirt in the bottom of a bottle of wine was *prima facie* evidence of a rotten bottle, nowadays a good many consumers know that to see such material there is actually evidence that the wine has not had everything stripped from it, including flavor and much of its ability to age.

Unlike spirits, wine is always in a constant state of evolution. It evolves because it is a food, and just as grapes come to maturity on the vine, so too wine comes to maturity in the cask and bottle. Throughout its life, it naturally precipitates a deposit of one sort or another.

Of course the impetus to overfilter comes not only from a zeal to remove all traces of sediment, but from a general desire to make wines designed for immediate drinking. Much Cabernet Sauvignon is now removed from its skins as soon as it has picked up a passable color, so that it need not contain any more tannin than necessary and is further smoothed out by filtration and fining. This of course makes Cabernets more pleasant to drink when young, but shortens their life span and potential development. However, instability in a wine can alter it for the worse, even more dramatically than the misuse of filtering or fining. The danger of spoilage from microorganisms is the other major reason why winemakers resort to these stabilizing techniques.

Filtration has become so advanced that winemakers have been able to dispense in some cases with further sulphuring of wines as a guard against spoilage, which is very desirable, since oversulphured wines can have a most unpleasant volcanic odor. Others argue that it is not necessary to filter and fine to any great degree to make a stable wine. One promising development in the technology of clarification is the increasing use of centrifuges, which clarify wine without the flavor loss that filtration and fining may cause.

The last step is bottling. Very, very few wines gain by additional aging in the bottle, which is why a great many are simply closed with screw-tops. Few wines topped with a cork benefit by long keeping either, but for the ones that do, some wineries have adopted the practice of holding the wine for extra bottle aging themselves.

There are any number of other processes and pieces of sophisticated equipment, such as ion exchangers, rota-tanks, heat-exchangers, etcetera, as well as additives which the modern winemaker can employ. All are designed to help insure that the transformation of grape juice to wine goes without a hitch, but, as in other natural processes of this sort, the less fiddling that is done with the wine, the better. The cures for various problems and imbalances often correct the problem at the cost of diminished quality.

Winemaking in the Eastern U.S. differs from winemaking in California in that sugaring of musts is often a necessity if wine of an average alcoholic content is to be made, a process known as chaptalization. This is partly due to the fact that the cold climate of areas like the Finger Lakes makes it unlikely that grapes will fully ripen every season, and because most native American grape varieties are typically too low in sugar to ferment into wine without additional sugar. The addition of water is also allowed outside California, and Eastern winemakers claim they must add it in order to counteract the great acidity one has in grapes grown in that climate. It ought to be pointed out that in Germany and Burgundy, the addition of sugar, at any rate, is common and necessary in order to make wines at all in certain years. Other Eastern wineries feel that adding sugar and water is often overdone, and amounts to stretching the product.

A final note on table wines: It is popularly supposed that all inexpensive U.S. wines are pasteurized, or subjected to a heating process, in order to insure stability. This process is no longer used as it once was, having largely been replaced by very fine or "sterile" filtration. Not that there was anything wrong with pasteurizing a wine of ordinary quality anyway; such careful practices with jug wines in the United States have made them the most reliable ordinary wines in the world. It is extremely rare to find an unopened, screw-top American wine that is spoiled.

Dessert Wines

The process of making table wines results in wines that normally range from ten to fourteen percent alcohol. "Dessert" wine, on the other hand, is a category employed by the U.S. wine industry to refer to any of the higher alcohol (sixteen to twenty-one percent) natural wine products, such as sherry or port. Thus, "dessert wines" in the U.S. are fortified wines and are not, as the name would imply, always sweet; their production involves the addition of small amounts of brandy (this is why such wines are called "fortified"), which brings up their alcoholic content to a range usually of seventeen to twenty percent. The simplest process used, at least in outline, is that employed in making port, because it is a variant of making red table wine. In the case of port, a heavy red wine is fermented until half its sugar is converted into alcohol, at which point grape brandy is added to bring the alcohol level above fifteen percent (the point at which yeast activity, and thus fermentation, stops), usually to twenty percent. Such wines are almost always blended products, and their quality depends on the grape varieties used as well as the care taken in the process. They are normally aged in wooden cooperage, but cheaper varieties may not be.

Sherry in the U.S. is made by several methods, the most common of which is "baking." This process uses dry or sweet white wines fortified with the addition of grape brandy, and involves heating the wine from 120° to 140° for 45 to 120 days, normally in large tanks. The wine is also slightly exposed to air (or air is bubbled through it). This process turns the wine to the desired shade of amber or brown. It does not produce fine wine. It is interesting to note that in sherry-making, oxidation of the wine is an essential part of the process; this is possible only because the high levels of alcohol lessen

the danger of acetification. This, of course, is why dessert
wines keep much better after opening than table wines.

Variants on the baking method include "weathering," in
which the sherry is put in barrels and left outdoors for varying lengths of time. A product similar to this can be achieved
merely by lengthy aging in small cooperage for two to four
years. At best such products can be quite good, and have a
"nutty" flavor. Varietal-flavored grapes are of little advantage
in these processes, as the process itself provides what flavor
there is. This, in fact, is an advantage in the Eastern U.S., as
the process of baking or weathering removes much of the *labrusca* flavor of the native American grapes used.

Sherry can also be made by the *flor* method, which, although not widely used, approximates the classic Spanish
sherry-making method and yields good to fine wines. The
fresh, bready aroma and the flavorful tang of good Spanish
Sherry comes from an unusual form of yeast, *flor*, that forms
on the surface of the wine. In the U.S., the *flor* can be encouraged to grow on the surface of the wine in partially filled
barrels for several years, and yields a complex wine; since this
is time-consuming and cannot be easily controlled, new methods have been discovered which enable the winery to submerge
the *flor* yeast with aeration. The flavor that the yeast imparts
to the wine can thus be controlled much more exactly.

The solera system that one often associates with sherry has
to do with the blending, not the making of the wine, and is
often used in the U.S. Anywhere from several dozen to
several hundred barrels of wine of different age and character are arranged in tiers. Blends are produced by drawing
wine from the older stocks at the bottom, while new wines
are added to barrels on top; thus, a constant process of "topping up" older wine with newer wine of the same type in-
sures that the character of the blended product remains consistent, and yet always contains a portion of matured wine.

Sparkling Wines

Sparkling wines, or those which have a carbon dioxide content sufficient to appear effervescent when opened, include
mildly bubbling "crackling" wines as well as fully bubbling
champagnes. Champagnes derive their effervescence from a

secondary fermentation in a closed container, either bottles or tanks. The classic method—*méthode champenoise*—is employed for the finest sparkling wines. It will be remembered that when the juice of grapes is fermented to make wine, yeast is added as a catalyst in order to turn the grape sugar into alcohol. Carbon dioxide is given off as a by-product of the yeast's action, and simply escapes from the seething fermenting vat. To make a sparkling wine, one makes the finished wine undergo a second fermentation by adding yeast again, and some sugar for it to feed on; then one makes sure the carbon dioxide doesn't escape. In making wine, one is interested in the yeast converting sugar into alcohol; in making champagne from wine, one is interested in the yeast giving off carbon dioxide. In the classical method, one simply bottles already made wine with a certain amount of sugar and yeast to ensure that none of the gas ordinarily given off can escape until uncorked. Of course, there are problems to be met, and how they are met is what distinguishes one champagne process from another.

In the traditional method, the bubbles of trapped carbon dioxide are obtained by a second fermentation within the stoppered bottle. The process was developed in seventeenth-century France and is still employed there, as well as in a few American wineries. It is expensive and time-consuming, requiring a great deal of hand labor—some 120 hand operations. The wine for French and French-style American champagne is made principally from Pinot noir and Chardonnay grapes. Since the Pinot noir is a red-skinned grape, care must be taken to separate juice and skin before fermentation. In fact, although a blend (or *cuvée*) of both Chardonnay and Pinot noir is generally employed as the base wine in champagne, each must be crushed and fermented separately. Blanc de Noir (from red grapes only) and Blanc de Blancs (from white grapes only) are made as well. Fermentation of the base wine or wines proceeds similarly to the making of still white table wines, although aging in wood is generally minimal and great efforts are made to keep the wines brilliant and free from any off-odors, since the bubbles merely accentuate any unpleasant faults or flaws.

Some months after fermentation, the *cuvée* is made, the exact proportions of which are determined by tasting, and the "*tirage*," consisting of sugar dissolved in some of the wine of the *cuvée* and a specially selected yeast starter, is added; the amounts are carefully controlled, so that the carbon diox-

ide given off as a by-product of the yeast growth will result
only in a certain given pressure. (As this can amount to some
sixty pounds of pressure per square inch, this must be carefully measured.) The wine is then bottled in special heavy
champagne bottles, capped securely with a cork-lined crown
cap (something like an old-fashioned soda bottle cap), and
the bottles are stored on their sides. Three to six months
later, most of the second fermentation has taken place, but
the wine is left six months to three years longer to let the
yeast cells settle, die, break down, and impart both an interesting nuance to the wine and an attractive element to its
nose, often reminiscent of fresh bread. The next, and very
tricky, operation is to remove the sediment of dead yeast.

The problem is to remove sediment from the bottle without removing the wine. To do this, "riddling racks," in which
the bottles are placed slanting neck down, are used. These
racks look something like standing sandwich boards with
rows of oval holes. The bottles are given a sharp twist each
day by hand, about an eighth of a revolution daily, and grad-
ually tilted at a sharper angle, to startle the deposit away
from the glass and to shake the loosened sediment down onto
the cork cap. A splash of whitewash on the bottom of each
bottle is the traditional way to ensure no bottle is missed, and
each is given the proper number of turns. The process is called
"remuage" in France and "riddling" in California, and may
take as long as a month. Once the sediment is on the
corks, it is ejected by means of "disgorging." The bottle is
chilled, and the wine in the neck is frozen by dipping the
neck into a sub-frozen brine solution; the bottle is then expert-
ly opened, the plug of frozen sediment is pushed out by the
pressure of the gas, the wine is given the *dosage* that determines its sweetness, topped up if necessary, and quickly re-
corked with the traditional wired-on mushroom cork. All this
must be done very quickly, of course, so as not to lose pressure.

As might be expected, most American wineries have
devised means to cut down on hand labor while retaining the
individual treatment of each bottle. Automated riddling racks
have been devised, as well as conveyor methods which bring
each bottle neck through the freezing brine bath, disgorge it,
add the dosage, and recork it, all automatically.

The dosage added to champagne consists of sugar of varying amounts dissolved in well-aged wine or brandy, and contributes both flavor and sweetness. By tradition, the sweetness

of champagnes range from Brut (very dry), Extra Dry (less dry), Sec (sweet), Demi-Sec (sweeter), and Doux (very sweet). One can also omit the dosage, in which case the wine is extremely dry, or "Nature." After disgorging, the bottle rests a few more months, and then is "dressed" in its fancy foils and labeled for market.

So far I have been describing the classic method of making sparkling wine. Because such wines are expensive to make due to the great number of hand operations required in the process, two simpler processes for making sparkling wine are in much more common use in the U.S. These are the "transfer" method and the "bulk" process, or Chamat method.

The transfer method is similar to the *méthode champenoise*, but the principal difference is that the bottles are disgorged into a large vat where the sediment is filtered out (under pressure so that bubbles are not lost) and the wine is then rebottled in fresh bottles. This results in a more uniform wine, but inevitably some gas and flavor is lost during the transfer and filtration. The principal reason why transfer sparkling wines are not the equal of *méthode champenoise* sparkling wines, however, appears not to be so much due to shortcomings in the transfer method as in the fact that a winery using the transfer method to reduce costs will typically use less expensive grapes, shorten time on the yeast, and will employ other shortcuts as well. If good grape varieties are used, it can result in a very good product, however.

The "bulk," or Charmat, process is used for all inexpensive sparkling wines and is by far the most commonly used method in the U.S. The base wine is put into tanks where the secondary fermentation can take place. It is not, in other words, bottle-fermented at all. The wine is then bottled under pressure to retain its effervescence. Due to the use of undistinguished grape varieties and the lack of aging on the yeast, such wines are quite ordinary, although they can be good.

Flavored Wines

Flavored wines include vermouth, pop wines (or fruit-flavored wines), and even "retsinas" and "May wines." As none of these products are of especial interest to wine lovers (though there is more to say about pop wines later), there is little point in dwelling on their production, which consists basically of the use of neutral wines to which various ingredients from fruit concentrates to herbs are added to impart the desired flavor.

Brandy

Brandy is a spirit made from grape wine by distillation. Distillation is simply a process of concentrating the strength of any alcoholic beverage by removing the water. (Table wines, it should be pointed out, are about eighty-five to ninety-five percent water.) Since alcohol boils—vaporizes—at a lower temperature than water (as anyone knows who cooks with wine), heating wine removes the alcohol. Distillation is a method by which the "steam" given off is collected and condensed. There are two types of stills used in brandy-making: pot stills and continuous stills. The pot still is really a giant kettle, and as it allows the greatest control over the process, is used for the highest-quality brandy in both the U.S. and Europe. It is a slow and laborious method, however, and the continuous still—a process by which a continuous stream of wine can be heated by steam to separate the volatile alcohol—is much more widely used. After distillation, brandy is cut to approximately fifty percent alcohol by the addition of water, and a small amount of caramel sugar is added for sweetness and flavor, about one percent by volume. It is then aged in small oak cooperage for at least two years; often it is blended with older stocks, and cut further with water before bottling to about forty percent alcohol. Straight brandies, not usually seen, have no flavoring agents, and if aged four years and bottled at fifty percent alcohol, may be labeled "bottled in bond." White grapes of lesser varieties are used in brandy-making.

Grape and Wine Varieties

There are over 10,000 varieties of grapes from which wine can be made. Only a few dozen varieties, however, can be made into fine wine; of these, only about a dozen types have ever yielded great wines. Why this should be so is complicated, and the answers are not simple even when they are known.

Americans are more familiar with grape varieties than European wine lovers, because the finest American wines are labeled by the name of the predominant grape variety used in the wine. This is known as "varietal" labeling, and the wines as "varietal" wines. Wines labeled under generic names—"burgundy" or "mountain red"—of course consist of grape varieties as well, but not usually from a single predominant grape. Thus, to know something about fine American wines (and about fine wines made anywhere in the world), it helps to know something about the grape varieties after which (in the U.S., at least) they are often named.

While many of the constituent elements of wine have been subjected to exhaustive chemical analyses, the substances that are responsible for the characteristic aromas of certain grape varieties and that contribute to the bouquet and flavor of a mature wine are present in extremely minute quantities and have yet to be fully understood. In many cases, such nuances are not caused by the presence of single substances, but are the effects of whole hosts of compounds, esters, aldehydes, alcohols, acids, and other substances. It is precisely the distinctive individual scents and flavors of certain grape varieties, however, that allow some of them to yield great wines.

Some varieties, like muscat, have a characteristic smell even as grapes; what is significant about the few most important varieties is that they have a characteristic smell and taste of their own when made into wines. Thus, while there are thousands of varieties of grapes, only a few have an odor as wine that is *characteristically varietal*—that is, recognizable as belonging to a *specific* grape variety. It is possible, in other words, to detect, often by smell alone, the grape variety out of which many fine wines have been made. The most famous of these readily identifiable varieties are Cabernet Sauvignon, Pinot noir, Chardonnay, and White Riesling. A fine example of a wine made from any one of these grapes can be readily identified by an experienced taster. There are a few other grape varieties of which this can also be said, but these four are thought of as the "noble" varieties because they not only make wine of unmistakably individual character, but wine whose scent and flavor can be extraordinarily complex; they are capable of developing further nuances in the bottle and are the principal grapes out of which most of the world's great wines have been made.

The vast majority of grape varieties, on the other hand, cannot readily be distinguished from each other when made into wines, and are recognizable only as belonging to a general species of grapes—*vinifera, labrusca,* etcetera. Their smell is often simply "vinous." While such grape varieties can yield pleasant wines—sometimes even delicious wines—they do not yield superbly fine *complex* wines. Thus, they are often described as "not distinctive," or "undistinguished." To say that a wine is "undistinguished" is often not as derogatory as it sounds, because it refers to the fact that such wines often cannot be readily distinguished as particular varietals, have simple scents and flavors, and thus are rarely so constituted as to be capable of developing with bottle age. They are certainly not beneath a wine lover's interest, however, as there are many occasions in which a simple, pleasant wine is far more appropriate than an intensely distinctive one.

Fine wines from distinctive grapes are another matter. Why a fresh, young, well-made White Riesling smells wonderfully flowery is not easy to explain, but in brief it is the result of a number of constituent organic compound molecules volatilizing from the surface of the wine and being whisked up the nose by a good sniff. There these molecules tingle our sensitive nerve-endings in such a way as to give us a distinct sensation and impression—in this case, "floral."

Beginning wine enthusiasts are often surprised to find out that the smell of a fine wine rather than its taste is frequently its most attractive and revealing aspect. The opposite impression is often gathered from drinking very ordinary wine with little smell and a great deal of rough flavor. The sensitivity of the nose surpasses that of the palate (and besides, a great deal of what we think of as flavor is really smell, as anyone knows who has had the common experience of a cold rendering food tasteless), and almost all virtues and defects to be found in a wine's taste are first revealed in its smell—in short, what the nose detects, the palate confirms.

Naturally, enologists are anxious to track down these elusive substances, because the more that is known about what accounts for quality in wine, the easier it would be to devise methods to retain and enhance these nuances, from vineyard to bottle. At any rate, it is important to be reasonably precise about the terminology for these qualities, because it helps one to make clear distinctions in tasting.

The smell of a wine is often called its "nose." The nose, however, has two distinct sources, which are often imprecisely muddled as terms: "aroma" and "bouquet." *Aroma* is the odor that a young wine has; this is principally grape aroma, or the part of a wine's nose that is attributable to the grape. *Bouquet* is that part of a wine's nose which arises from fermentation and aging, including aging in wood, and from the development of the wine during bottle aging. Most fresh young wines made for immediate consumption don't exhibit bouquet—they only have aromas. Bouquet, in fact, is mostly (but not entirely) something found in fine red wines that have matured in the bottle, though hints of aging in oak cooperage are readily detectable in some fine young wines, white as well as red. Bottle aging appears to allow slow elaborate chemical transformations to occur in the wine, mostly reductions of one sort of organic compound into another. However such development occurs, it adds greatly to certain wines, and gives them subtleties in smell and taste not apparent in their youth.

In the following notes on the principal wine grape varieties, I am concerned with the characteristic aroma of the varieties (if there is one, and if it can be described), and the bouquet that may be expected from the manner in which the wine is typically made and aged. While I naturally dwell at length on the "noble" grapes, it ought to be remembered that a fine example of a "lesser" grape is a far more distinguished wine than a poor example of a "noble" grape.

I have listed only those grape varieties that one is likely to see bottled and labeled as a varietal wine in the U.S. Included in the lists are variant names of the grapes that are sometimes seen. Sauvignon blanc, for example, is bottled under at least five names, which is confusing and misleading to wine consumers, to say the least.

Most wine books make no attempt whatsoever to describe the aromas and flavors of various grape varieties and their wines. The reason is, of course, that it is notoriously difficult to do so. Even if the odor is distinct, it often doesn't resemble any others. Nonetheless, it is enormously useful to give the neophyte wine taster some metaphor which he can associate with the smell of particular varietals, and which will help him bring their odor to mind, even if the metaphor is inexact. Thus, Cabernet Sauvignon, when its odor is described, is often said to smell somewhat like blackcurrants or olives, even though there are some tasters who may find it reminds them of neither. What *is* important is that the would-be tast-

er be able to use these distinct impressions of, say, Cabernet
Sauvignon in later tastings of Cabernet, so that he can compare a given glass of the wine to his standard impression of
the kind of wine the grape can yield, and say with some ac-
curacy that it is or isn't typical, what is different or distinct
about it, whether it is an excellent or poor example of Cabernet Sauvignon, and the like.

Thus, readers should bear in mind that the following descriptions use metaphors which *I* find useful as *aide-
mémoires*. To think of Chenin Blanc as a "peachy," for example, is only helpful as an index to other impressions of
Chenin Blanc—most of which, I must confess, have not been
particularly "peachy," but "peachiness" is the only element I
sometimes find in the aroma of Chenin Blanc that reminds
me distinctly of another particular odor. The same is true of
most of the metaphors used here. Nonetheless, it is better to
suggest a general focus for the beginning taster than to avoid
the issue entirely by stating that a varietal's nose and flavor is
"unmistakable but indescribable." In short, don't be distressed
if you can't find "peppermint" in your Pinot Noir; the point is
to develop your own tasting vocabulary. (Readers who are
fuzzy on the basic rudiments of tasting may find it useful to
read the section on tasting in Chapter 4 before reading the
following smell and taste descriptions of principal U.S. grape
varieties.)

Note: When "blanc" or "noir" appears as part of a grape
name it is not capitalized if one is referring to the grape, but
is capitalized when one refers to the varietal wine. Thus,
Pinot Noir wine is made from Pinot noir grapes.

Principal U.S. Grape Varieties and Their Wines

Vitis vinifera—Red Wine Varieties:

BARBERA

Originating from the Italian Piedmont, this red grape retains acidity even in California's warmer regions, and is often
made into a not very distinctive, coarse, tart wine. If well-
made and well-balanced, however, it has sufficient tannin to

let it develop from a merely full-bodied, robust red to a fine, perfumed, expansive wine. At its best it retains a full, rich, earth-and-tar-scented nose and mouth-filling tart fruitiness. Its color is usually quite dark, sometimes even purplish.

CABERNET

A few years ago, wines labeled simply "Cabernet" were almost always Ruby Cabernet, not Cabernet Sauvignon, even though the latter is often shortened, as in this book, to "Cabernet." Label regulations no longer permit this practice. See *Ruby Cabernet*.

CABERNET SAUVIGNON

The Cabernet Sauvignon is thought by many to be the grape that yields the greatest red wines in the world; certainly it is one of the "noblest" of grapes in the sense that truly great wines can be made from it, which is true of only a very few varieties. Further, it has made great wines in a number of wine-growing lands. Cabernet Sauvignon is responsible for the character and distinction that one associates with the greatest wines of Bordeaux; while it is not the most widely planted grape in that region, it makes up roughly sixty to ninety percent of the grapes used in the finest Clarets; the rest of the grapes are usually lesser cousins of that grape, such as Cabernet Franc and Merlot, which yield softer, less pronounced wines and are blended with Cabernet Sauvignon to yield a wine of less austerity. Whether such blending also adds complexity as well is an issue much discussed among winemakers in California, who are now experimenting with adding small amounts of Merlot, up to twenty percent, to their Cabernet Sauvignon wines. Others feel that there is nothing which can be added to Cabernet to improve it, and continue to make one hundred percent varietal wine from it.

The majority of the outstanding Cabernet Sauvignons from California have all been one hundred percent Cabernet, and the wine it can yield on occasion has long been thought America's greatest wine and an equal cousin to Claret. It is not easy to describe its character, as it is complex and subtle at its best, and it is precisely for those reasons that it can make wines worthy of contemplation.

The aroma of the grape, apparent even in the wine when

young, is said to be reminiscent of green olives and often exhibits herbaceous nuances. I have sniffed specimens on occasion which were leafy, sometimes vegetative, sometimes earthy, sometimes "dusty." While Cabernet is not what one describes as a "fruity" wine, it often exhibits a strong blackcurrant scent, though this may not emerge unless the wine has some bottle age. Since it is typically aged in small oak casks for several years before bottling, it usually shows some woody traces of this; the strong cedar scent a well-aged Cabernet can have may be contributed in part by this. One shouldn't get the impression from these suggestions that the nose of a good mature example of Cabernet ever smells like a hodgepodge of these odors; it is rather that its pungent deep smell will often amount to a harmonious mélange of scents whose nuances will remind one of one or another, sometimes several of these. One may encounter hints of violets, roses, cherries; an old thin Cabernet can smell like tea.

Its flavor is distinct, and while substantial specimens are sometimes described as "packed with fruit," such phrases really refer to the intensity of flavor rather than any resemblance to a fruity, grapey quality. An olive flavor is often apparent when young, but the wine's most obvious component is its high tannin and good acidity, both of which give one an impression of chalky dryness, considerable dimension in the mouth, and a great length of flavor—sometimes so austere as to be quite hard, firm, and unlikable. With age, the tannin is transformed and precipitated, and the body of a mature Cabernet is velvety, even silky. It is never soft, but retains its dimensions for decades if the wine is well-balanced.

Of course, I have been talking about Cabernet at its best; or, to put it another way, when its finest qualities are apparent. The typical specimen will not show such distinction, and as the Cabernet, more than any other wine, needs considerable age, it is the one wine which is most victimized by a wine market uninterested in aging wine for several decades. Wineries are encouraged to extract color from the Cabernet grape skins without letting the wine pick up the excess tannin that will make it unpleasant when young but allow it to age magnificently and show its true capabilities. It is sometimes blended with more neutral wine like Petite Sirah, in order that it show a little more charm in its youth. Such a product costs less to produce, since Cabernet Sauvignon grapes are among the most expensive due to great demand and relatively low crop yield.

California Cabernet Sauvignons range from light red to ruby to purple red, the deepest colors usually indicating a "bigger" style of winemaking. The lightest specimens are sometimes so stripped of their character by overfiltering that they are thin and sharp after a half-dozen years; excellent specimens come into their own only after ten to twenty years of bottle age.

CARIGNANE

One of the most widely planted grapes in California, it is not distinctive as a varietal and is usually used in blending. If well-made, it has a pleasant vinous aroma, a full tannic body, a robust, sometimes bitter flavor, and a dark color to match, although lighter, fruitier versions are sometimes made.

CHARBONO

An Italian grape long confused with Barbera, it is produced as a varietal principally by Inglenook; it most resembles Barbera, and in its current light style can be enjoyable, but is not particularly distinguished. Older, more substantially made examples have aged well, however.

GAMAY

Long thought a variant of a similar grape, the Gamay Beaujolais, the Gamay (or Napa Gamay, as it is sometimes called), is now thought to be the genuine grape of Beaujolais. It produces a light, soft, grapey wine that often has the sappy, gulpable attractiveness one associates with Beaujolais, though it lacks the charm of Beaujolais at its best. It has a slightly spicy, very fresh-fruity nose when young and well made. At its best enjoyed young, some wineries now market it less than a year after vintage. Some wineries make it into a more substantial wine, in which case it is very good but often unexciting. Its color is light red to ruby.

GAMAY BEAUJOLAIS

Recent research has shown the Gamay Beaujolais grape to be a clone—a sub-variant—of Pinot noir. The Napa Gamay grape is actually the grape of Beaujolais, although until recently, the entire matter was muddled. In any event, the Gamay Beaujolais grape produces a wine very similar to the Gamay grape, with perhaps more distinction, though neither are complex wines. The Gamay Beaujolais, at least some examples, can age well, say up to five years, when it develops some complexity in the nose. In general it is to be enjoyed when young, and like the Gamay, is typically light in color.

GAMAY NOIR

See *Gamay*.

GRIGNOLINO

Italian in origin, the Grignolino grape is made into a wine by few California wineries. It is quite refreshing and distinctive, although not distinguished. Somewhat orangey in color, it can have an attractive, fruity, apricot-like, sometimes strawberry aroma, and its flavor is tart and intense.

MERLOT

This Bordeaux grape is grown in California, as it is in Bordeaux, to blend with Cabernet Sauvignon, which it most closely resembles. It is, however, more neutral in character and produces a much softer, less tannic wine. A growing number of wineries are bottling it on its own.

NEBBIOLO

The grape responsible for the great Barolos of Northern Italy, it is scarce in California. So far it has not made distinguished wine in the state, probably because the proper conditions for its cultivation have not been found.

PETITE SIRAH

Long used for blending, this grape is also bottled as a varietal. Recent research has discovered there are actually two similar varieties called by this name. One is derived from a common Rhône grape, the Durif, the other from a more distinguished Rhône grape, the Syrah. Both these grapes produce coarse to attractive wines in California's climate—soft, mellow, mouth-filling, quite tannic and spicy at best, and sometimes capable of gaining additional character with bottle age. They have a fruity-vinous, sometimes "peppery" aroma and their color varies from light red to deep ruby.

PINOT NOIR

Pinot noir is the great red grape of Burgundy and one of the principal grapes used in the making of French Champagne. In Burgundy it can yield wines of opulent richness, soft, almost bosomy in body, yet immensely mouth-filling and exquisitely lingering; unfortunately, this fussy grape rarely yields anything like that in the U.S., at least so far. I say "so far" because it appears that either the clones (special variants) of Pinot noir that are currently grown in the U.S. are ill-adapted, or that the right areas for its cultivation have yet to be discovered.

Nonetheless, while great American Pinot Noirs are rare indeed—some would argue there have only been a couple—a number of very fine ones are made from time to time which exhibit that expansive fine, grapey scent that reminds one of a sort of profound peppermint, and that luscious flavor and satiny body for which the wine is famous. It often has an attractive, if odd, rhubarb aroma in California and occasionally spicy nuances reminiscent of cinnamon or nutmeg. Others can be less attractively vegetative in aroma.

It is always less tannic than Cabernet (at least Cabernet as it should be) and matures more quickly, generally in four to ten years. Unsuccessful specimens should be drunk right away, as age will only reveal their defects. Such examples are usually overpriced, especially for something which tastes no more distinguished than Petite Sirah. It, too, ranges in color from light red to—rarely—a dark ruby.

PINOT ST. GEORGE

Said to be a distant relation of Pinot noir, it is sometimes labeled Red Pinot. It is not especially distinctive either in aroma or flavor, and is a robust, earthy, spicy red at best.

RED PINOT

See *Pinot St. George.*

RUBY CABERNET

Developed by the University of California as a cross between Cabernet Sauvignon and Carignane, this grape has
more finesse and flavor than Carignane and yet grows well
and abundantly in the California's warmer districts, which
makes it an excellent source of grapes for reasonably priced
wines with some character. It is tannic, has some character,
and a pleasant, sometimes weedy-leafy nose and flavor at best.

ZINFANDEL

Zinfandel is unique among grapes grown in the U.S. in that
for many years its origin was unknown; it is now thought to
be related to certain Italian varieties. In any event, it does
not resemble any wine made elsewhere, and is California's
contribution to the world of fine wines. Whether any Zinfandels have deserved the compliment "great" is perhaps debatable, though I think a few examples have. Certainly few would
deny that it has yielded on occasion superb wines, and that it
can do so comes as a surprise to those who are only familiar
with the light fruity wines that are usually made from this
widely planted red grape.

Its character is unique among red wines. It is often very
attractive and charming when young when it commonly exhibits a strong berry-like aroma, usually rather like raspberries, although sometimes like blackberries, and has a full
fruity flavor with berry-like hints as well. Yet surprisingly
enough for a red wine which is so charming in its youth, it
also ages very well, losing its berry-like character and becoming something reminiscent of a light old Cabernet. If made in
a "big," substantial style, however, with plenty of tannin, it
can age magnificently, exhibit a great deal of complexity, and
end up a big, rich, mouth-filling wine unlike any other in
character. Its fruit can be zesty, intense, and spicy, and good
examples often show hints of earthiness; Zinfandel also benefits by aging in wood. These qualities are only found in better
Zinfandel, of course; Zinfandels from California's warmest
regions are much less interesting. The color varies from

light red to deep purple-red, depending on the style of wine-making.

Vitis vinifera—White Wine Varieties:

BLANC FUMÉ

See *Sauvignon blanc.*

BLANC DE SAUVIGNON

See *Sauvignon blanc.*

CHARDONNAY

If the Cabernet Sauvignon is the greatest red wine produced in America, then Chardonnay is the finest white. Responsible for all French White Burgundies, and one of the principal grapes of French Champagne, the Chardonnay in California (and possibly elsewhere in the U.S.) can yield a white wine of tremendous character and magnificent flavor. It has the largest, most mouth-filling dimensions of any dry white wine. The greatest examples of American Chardonnay can sometimes be bigger and more overwhelming than the finest of Burgundy, and certainly equal in distinction. It is a viticultural puzzle why the red grape of Burgundy, the Pinot noir, seems to yield mostly coarse wine in California (which is warmer than Burgundy), while the white grape of Burgundy, the Chardonnay, yields rich, full wines in the same climate without sacrificing finesse.

In color it can range from straw-yellow to outright gold. Its aroma is often appley, if it can be said to resemble any fruit at all, especially when the grapes are fully ripe; when young it may exhibit hints of oak in the nose, as it is often (but not always) given some time in that wood to complement its flavor. It benefits the most of any American white wine from age, and superior examples keep and develop well in the bottle for ten years or more. It is always dry, sometimes steely, even austere, and has a great mouth-filling character at its best. It should always have good acidity and strong flavor; some examples can be incomparably rich and oily on the tongue. It is never simply fruity, and it can in fact lack fruit, but it should be able to stand up to any dishes calling for white wines. Some Chardonnays I have had exhibit slight spiciness, and sometimes a kind of floral quality in the nose; an earthy scent is sometimes encountered, but is not always harmonious, as is true of excessive wood character, which can range from a hint of vanilla to a burnt wood scent. The wine is also seen labeled as *Pinot* Chardonnay, which is superfluous, as the grape is no longer thought to be related to the Pinot family.

CHENIN BLANC

Chenin blanc is grown extensively in the Loire, which is why it is sometimes labeled Pineau de la Loire in California. This grape yields very attractive, soft, full white wines made quite dry or semi-sweet. While its aroma is not distinctive, it is usually pleasantly scented and fruity, and sometimes rather reminiscent of peaches. It is usually best as a semi-sweet wine, when it is often uncomplicated, fruity, and delicious, although outstanding dry versions have been made that reveal hidden potentialities of Chenin blanc as a fine wine grape. Often very light in color, sometimes nearly colorless and sometimes light gold, it varies a good deal in character depending on the winery and winemaking style.

EMERALD RIESLING

A white wine grape developed by the University of California for use in the hotter wine-growing districts, it is a cross between White Riesling and the Muscadelle. Light, fresh, often made slightly sweet, it is a simple and reasonably good wine when cleanly made, and very refreshing at best. It is very light in color.

FLORA

A light, spicy-fruity white developed by the University of California from Sémillon and Gewürztraminer, it is not yet widely seen. It is not distinguished, but can be pleasant.

FOLLE BLANCHE

This white grape is bottled as a varietal only by Louis M. Martini. Originally a grape used in Cognac for making brandy, it makes a very crisp, acidic, whistle-clean, and re-freshing wine at best. Very light in color, it has a fruity but not particularly distinctive aroma.

FRENCH COLOMBARD

Much used in blends in California, this grape is sometimes seen bottled as a varietal; light-straw in color, it is rather neutral in character but refreshingly tart, as it has good acidity; its aroma is not distinctive, but aromatic-vinous.

FUMÉ BLANC

See *Sauvignon blanc*.

GEWÜRZTRAMINER

Gewürztraminer means "spicy Traminer," and at its best, this Alsatian grape can be superbly floral-spicy, even clove-like, in aroma; more often, in California, it is merely aromatic-herby. It can be attractively delicate in flavor and light-bodied, but often lacks acidity. Its color varies, but it is often straw-yellow. Gewürztraminer is bottled in both dry and semi-sweet versions, both of which can be charming, uncomplicated, and delicious.

GREEN HUNGARIAN

A grape of obscure origin, it is mostly used for blending, as it does not yield a distinctive varietal wine; light and fresh at best, it is sometimes made slightly sweet.

GREY RIESLING

Not a member of the Riesling family at all, the grape yields a soft, spicy, pleasant wine at best. It was formerly thought to be related to the Chauché gris of France.

JOHANNISBERG RIESLING

See *White Riesling*. As the unprefaced name "Riesling" is used loosely on labels in the U.S., the true Riesling here is called White Riesling. White Riesling is commonly bottled under the legal but unfortunate label "Johannisberg" Riesling, after the famous Rhine vineyard of Schloss Johannisberg. It is an inappropriate and unnecessary nomenclature.

MOSCATO CANNELLI

A member of the Muscat family, this grape—sometimes called Muscat blanc—yields a very sweet white wine that has a strong fruity-floral distinctive scent. (It is also made into dessert wines under its French name, Muscat Frontignan.)

MUSCAT BLANC

See *Moscato Cannelli*.

PINEAU DE LA LOIRE

See *Chenin blanc*.

PINOT BLANC

A white grape secondary to Chardonnay in Burgundy, it is not commonly bottled as a varietal in California, though it can be quite distinctive. It resembles Chardonnay more than any other wine, but lacks the Chardonnay's ripe fruit quality. It often has a very weedy or leafy aroma, and an austere flavor, but ages well and has been made into superb wine. Sometimes quite acid, its color ranges from straw to light gold.

PINOT CHARDONNAY

See *Chardonnay*.

RIESLING

An ambiguous quasi-varietal name, it is most unlikely to be used in the U.S. for White Riesling; typically it is used for either Sylvaner or, rarely, Grey Riesling. However, *Riesling* used without quotes in the book refers to the true (White) Riesling.

SAUVIGNON BLANC

This white grape is grown in the Graves region of Bordeaux (where it is blended with Sémillon) and is the grape of Sancerre and Pouilly Fumé. At its best it produces in California a wine of equal distinction to the wines of its homeland. Certainly it can be superb; its aroma is complex and rather difficult to describe: it is fruity, perfumey, and herbaceous, and often has hints of olives or spice; its scent is aromatic or musky, and is quite distinctive. It often is quite earthy; sometimes this nuance is as mild as fresh mushrooms, and other times it can be somewhat like damp humus, or vegetative. It is, or should be, clean in smell, and its flavor should also leave one with an impression of cleanliness; as it is usually possessed of good acidity, it often has crisp taste dimensions and a fine finish. Intense in flavor, it is excellent with seafood. It is sometimes vinified sweet, which is usually a mistake; although it can make a fair sweet wine in California, it makes a much better dry wine. Its color ranges from pale straw to deep gold.

This wine is sold under a confusing variety of names: Blanc Fumé, Fumé Blanc, Blanc de Sauvignon, and the like, all of which apparently sound more attractive than its correct name.

SAUVIGNON VERT

High in acid, this grape is widely used for blending, and is rarely seen as a varietal. It is quite neutral.

SÉMILLON

A commonly bottled varietal wine, it is made in sweet and dry versions, and often lacks acidity. It most resembles the Sauvignon blanc in character, though without the Sauvignon's distinction. Its body is curiously rounded in texture, however, which gives it an attractive weight in the mouth. It is perfumey, aromatic, and often earthy, and said by some to be fig-like. It is often sold under labels employing some indication of sweetness (such as "Haut Sémillon" or "Château Sémillon"). Its color ranges from light to deep gold.

SYLVANER

Probably more often bottled as plain "Riesling" than under its own name, the Sylvaner is roughly similar to White Riesling but lacks its finesse and complexity, and lacks the true Riesling's crisp acidity. It is often bottled slightly sweet, can be quite refreshing, and is sometimes very good.

TRAMINER

Traminer is the variety of which Gewürztraminer is a subvariety; as Gewürztraminer is more interesting than Traminer, Traminer is not widely grown on its own in California. In the past, Traminer was sometimes confused with Red Veltliner, an Austrian variety close to Traminer. In any event, the wines are typically light and fruity, soft, and aromatic; refreshing at best, but not particularly distinguished.

UGNI BLANC

Also known as Trebbiano and as St. Emilion (under which it occasionally appears), the grape yields a soft, pleasant wine at best, and is usually used in blends.

WHITE PINOT

Has nothing to do with Pinot blanc. It is one of the more confusing labels of Chenin blanc.

WHITE RIESLING

This grape at its best produces some of the noblest white wines in the world, wines of such elegance and distinction that they are often much better on their own than they are with food. The White Riesling, of course, is responsible for the incomparable wines of the Rhine and Moselle in Germany, and is also grown in Alsace. In those areas it is simply known as the Riesling; in this country, use of that name for lesser varieties such as Sylvaner or Grey Riesling has resulted in most wineries referring to the true Riesling as Johannisberg Riesling, although its proper name here is White Riesling.

Until recently, most wine lovers would have agreed that, like the Pinot noir, the White Riesling in the U.S. did not yield wines of the distinction that it does in Europe, but recently examples of it from the Pacific Northwest, New York State, and California indicate that this grape can yield wines here with the same delicacy and subtlety for which it is famous in Germany.

The aroma of White Riesling at its finest is always lively, fragrant, and expansive, both fruity and flowery, sometimes with hints of pine or wintergreen. Its flavor is tart, due to its refreshing acidity, sometimes even citrusy or pineapple-ish, exquisitely balanced by a rich, ripe, luscious fruitiness. It is never, unless a poor specimen, soft, but on the contrary is rather austere, sometimes even steely; as this is usually balanced with a sweetish (or outright sweet) quality it can have a character that ranges from charming to fascinating. Under certain ripening conditions it can make an extraordinary sweet wine, with a honey-apricot scent and flavor. Such conditions in the U.S. are not as rare as once thought. Its color ranges from pale straw with a greenish tint to deep gold. Depending on how it is made, White Riesling can gain considerably with age, though it is commonly enjoyed young.

In California, White Riesling is successfully grown, but its wine, while often fine, tends to be bigger in body and strength than its old-world counterpart (often twelve percent or more in alcohol, compared with nine or ten percent in Germany), and thus often lacks delicacy even when its fine, flowery character is retained. As light, delicate White Rieslings are not easy to make in California, some vintners have tried to make a virtue of the climate's effect and have made Rieslings of considerable power and bigness, bone-dry and rather alcoholic, or else rich and heavy. Interesting as such wines can be, they do not have the charm and appeal of the low-alcohol, delicate Rieslings which a few California wineries are now able to produce. Since superb light Rieslings have also been produced in other states, it is probably safe to assume the grape could be grown successfully in many parts of the U.S.

Note on whites:

Since the juice of almost every red grape is white, it is possible to make a white wine from red grapes. This is comparatively rare, although white wines have been made in California from Pinot noir, Zinfandel, even Cabernet Sauvignon. So far, white Pinot noir appears the most appealing.

Vitis vinifera—Pink or Rosé Varieties:

Since a rosé is made by removing the juice of red grapes from their skins as soon as the juice has picked up a light pink color, it is possible to make a rosé out of any red grape. (Of course, it is possible to make a rosé just by blending red and white wines, too, and this is sometimes done for ordinary wines.) Varietal rosés have been made from the following grapes among others: Grenache, Cabernet Sauvignon, Zinfandel, Petite Sirah, Grignolino, and Gamay. While the Cabernet Rosés can be very good, most wineries consider it a waste of good Cabernet grapes and the same is true of Pinot noir; Zinfandel can yield a very attractive spicy rosé, and Petite Sirah, Grignolino, and Gamay, interesting ones. The Grenache is the most widely used rosé grape. It yields very attractive, almost strawberry-scented rosés; Grenache rosé is usually bottled rather sweet, and is rather simple and refreshing at best.

Vitis vinifera—Dessert and Sparkling Varieties:

Grapes used in the production of American dessert wines include the classic Palomino grape used in Spanish Sherry and in some American sherry and the classic Portuguese varieties Tinta Madeira, Tinta Cão, Alvarelhão, Souzão, and Touriga used in a few American ports. Most American dessert wines use, however, quite undistinguished grapes. Varietally named dessert wines are rare, and there are no regulations governing which grapes may be used in making them. Grapes sometimes seen as dessert varietals, in addition to the classic varieties above, include Muscat Frontignan, Aleatico, and, under "Black Muscat," the Muscat Hamburg grape. Some of these last mentioned can be very good, distinctive, crisply sweet wines.

Also seen on occasion is the Malvasia bianca, which is sometimes made into a table wine, but is usually made into a sweet, golden dessert wine of Muscat flavor. It is also made into a light sparkling wine on the order of an Asti Spumante by a few wineries.

Sparkling wines made from vinifera are rarely made into varietals, although there are occasionally Sparkling Chardonnays, and "Blanc de Pinot" (or some such variant), indicating the use of the classic grapes of Champagne, Chardonnay, and Pinot noir. More often other grapes are blended in to increase acidity—usually Pinot blanc and French Colombard. Depending on the quality of sparkling wine sought, almost any sort of white grape can be used. Chenin blanc makes an attractive sparkling wine, but often much less distinguished grapes are used, right down to the humble Thompson Seedless. Thompson Seedless, by the way, as it makes a wine which is perhaps the ultimate in blandness, is often used as the base wine for flavored "pop" wines.

Native American Grape Varieties and Hybrids

These varieties, and their hybrids with *vinifera,* are unique among wine grapes in that they are the only non-*vinifera* varieties commonly made into wine. They do not make great or even fine wine, but they do make, at best, good wine. It is possible that superb wines will eventually be made from some of the French hybrids; so far this has not been the case. Many wine lovers who are familiar with the *vinifera* wines of Europe and California find these wines strange, or even unlikable. The reason is that they are quite different in character from *vinifera,* and can be very unattractive. They are often so strong in smell and taste that they make the normal tasting vocabulary used in describing *vinifera* seem quite overblown. Next to many wines made from the Concord grape, for example, a so-called "fruity" *vinifera* will seem downright ethereal. Most of the prized aromas and flavors found in *vinifera* wines are quite subtle compared with wines from native American grapes, which are quite simple, strongly scented in a powerful and unmistakable musky way, and can be quite cloying to the palate even if not made sweet—which they often are.

The scent of native American grape varieties, of which the species *Vitis labrusca* is by far the most widely grown, has long been called "foxy." The origins of this term are obscure and puzzling, but inasmuch as none of the other terms used to describe the aroma and flavor are any more descriptive, it persists. To say that these varieties have a *"labrusca"* flavor is less offensive-sounding than a term which falsely suggests a zoo scent.

Unlike the aromas of *vinifera* varieties, which arise from hundreds of odiferous elements, the scent of at least one *labrusca* variety, the Concord, arises from a single substance, the ester methyl anthranilate. Esters are organic compounds and contribute fruity odors to wines, and sometimes rather solvent-like smells, such as those of wine vinegar or nail-polish remover. The ester methyl anthranilate in Concord is the strongest odor found in any grape; other *labrusca* scents have a similar smell, but are composed of more than one substance.

At one time Eastern winemakers argued that these "foxy" scents did not have their origin in the grapes, but the soil. This idea is, strangely enough, still repeated in print, in spite of the direct evidence that *labrusca* odors originate in the grape itself of *labrusca* varieties, regardless of where they are grown. There is no evidence for the long-hallowed notion that soil composition directly affects the taste of wine made from grapes grown on it, and in any event, *vinifera* grown in the East hasn't a trace of "foxiness."

In spite of the fact that many consumers are attracted to the grapey zing that an out-and-out untamed Concord wine can give them, it's common for connoisseurs of fine *vinifera* wines to grimace openly at the thought of drinking *labrusca*, or to hint that only someone with a peanut-butter-and-jelly palate could find *labrusca* wines attractive. This blanket dismissal of any and all *labrusca* wines as beneath serious enophilic consideration is as unfair as it is uninformed. There are considerable differences in the wines produced from native American varieties, and it must be said that a good many of the wines—particularly whites—produced in the heart of *labrusca* country (the Finger Lakes region in New York State, for example) are quite drinkable, much subtler than the strongest examples of *labrusca* would lead one to suspect, and even, in some instances, quite good and palatable with none of the defects just described. However, wines such as these are typically achieved at the cost of blending, often with California wines, the liberal use of sugar and water to balance the excess acidity often found in *labrusca* grapes, and a good deal of processing. It is true that the sparkling and dessert wines of the Finger Lakes are the least "foxy" wines produced in the area and consequently among the most attractive. The adroit use of processing in producing sparkling and dessert wines, especially the use of heat and oxygenation, seems to aid the wines in getting rid of most of the *labrusca* character found in the varieties used.

In recent years there has been a great deal of research and interest in the Eastern United States in French hybrid grapes.

These were developed, following the devastation of the French vineyards by phylloxera in the late nineteenth century, as an alternative to grafting *vinifera* onto phylloxera-resistant native American root stocks. After innumerable attempts, a good many hybrids were developed which yielded reasonably good wine, and of course, could be planted directly into the soil without danger of destruction by phylloxera; grafting, it ought to be remembered, is both expensive and time-consuming. In fact, a considerable amount of French wine production now comes from these hybrids, although none is allowed to be used in appellation-controlled wines. (The French call these varieties "American hybrids.")

In the Eastern U.S., wide planting of these hybrids have allowed wineries to produce not only wines of better quality than is possible from native varieties, but has allowed them to produce their wines without excessive reliance on blending wines brought in from California. These hybrids, unlike *vinifera*, are often much hardier in the colder Eastern climate, and much less problematic viticulturally.

Interestingly enough, the origins of some of the native grapes of the U.S. are obscure; some may not be pure *labrusca* but may be hybrids themselves, the result of accidental crosses with *vinifera* due to extensive experimentation by early growers with hundreds of varieties in their search for good grapes. Delaware, for example, which is the least "foxy" of the *labrusca* family, may well have some *vinifera* somewhere in the background. Certainly most of their parentage is native, as many of these are crosses between several wild varieties and seedlings of chance crosses.

The French hybrids, however, are quite deliberate efforts to cross *vinifera* with *labrusca* and other native varieties in order to achieve, ideally, disease-free and hardy vines that would produce quality wine with *vinifera* characteristics. In fact, these hybrids derive from every sort of *vinifera* from Pinot noir to Folle blanche as well as the entire range of native American varieties. Unfortunately, in almost every cross between *vinifera* and *labrusca*, *labrusca* characteristics dominate the scent and flavor. Thus, with rare exceptions, hybrids fail to produce fine wine. Most wines produced from hybrid varieties are ordinary in quality, whether free of *labrusca* characteristics or not. At best they produce good wine and, less often, very good wine. Experimentation with them, however, has really just begun. New hybrids are being developed in a number of countries, and there are examples of some of these wines which are promising indeed. The best hybrid wines at the moment are mostly blends of a number of hybrid grape wines, and vinified with great care. A number are produced as varietals, as are a number of native American grapes.

While it is not possible to say a great deal about the characteristics of native and hybrid varieties—most, especially native grapes, are not markedly individual—on the other hand, many (again, mostly native grapes) are quite striking to the nose and palate, and it is worth saying something about the odor and flavor characteristics they have in common. Even superb *vinifera* wines may not have an expansive nose, though certainly some do. But a good number of *labrusca* and hybrid wines, even poor ones, have "high," perfumey scents that reach right out of the glass. The flavors also are, as a whole, much more aggressive than *vinifera* flavors, which often expand only in the lingering finish of the wine, revealing their subtle complexity after the wine has been swallowed or spit out. *Labrusca* and hybrid flavors assert themselves "up front" in the palate, with an effect on the taste buds that ranges from crisp to striking to startling. There is little or no depth of flavor, and the finish is always quick—usually instant, in fact—and what flavor does linger in the mouth may not add favorably to one's overall impression of the wine. This last family characteristic is why white *labrusca* and hybrid wines are best drunk stone cold and most of the reds are better cooled. Such temperatures numb the flavors of *vinifera*, but severe chilling has a beneficial effect on *labrusca* and hybrid wines and keeps the aftertaste neutral—whatever "foxiness" is evident in the wine tends to emerge as it warms.

These comments on the quality of native and hybrid wines may appear overharsh. But it does these wines, some examples of which are interesting, unique, and worth sampling, no service to overrate their virtues and claim, as some of their zealous advocates do, that they can be the equal of superb Chardonnay and Pinot Noir. Anyone familiar with such fine *vinifera* would be gravely disappointed, to say the least, if such quality were expected out of, say, Seyval Blanc or Baco Noir.

Of course, it is quite true that superior Seyval Blanc, for example, is certainly better wine than inferior Chardonnay. But I think it is far better to admit that all native and most hybrid wines rank, at best, on a par with or below *vinifera* wines in the ordinary class. (If it weren't for the fact that most U.S. wine producers, East and West, describe even their simple table wines as bottled wonders, no one would think that to describe a family of wines as typically ordinary, sound, table fare implied anything derogatory.) That way, with no overblown expectations, the curious wine lover will appreciate the number of pleasant surprises to be found among native and hybrid wines rather than spend his time looking for a level of quality that isn't there, and indeed, isn't there in the vast majority of *vinifera* wines.

The following principal native varieties are primarily of *Vitis labrusca* origin. Many are bottled under varietal labels. Since a good many of the red varieties are made into white wine, both red and white varieties are listed together here. Where appropriate, some description of the wines made from these varieties is given. The most readily identifiable wines made from native American grapes are not necessarily the most successful in terms of quality.

Native American Varieties—Red and White Wine:

CATAWBA

Known since 1823 when it was found growing on the banks of the Catawba River in North Carolina, this large pale red grape is made into whites, reds, and rosés that typically vary from semi-sweet to very sweet. Although quite native in scent and flavor, its "perfume" is more pleasant than that of most native varieties, and, like its flavor, can be attractive in its own way. Its high sugar and relatively low acid, coupled with its simple, pleasant character, allow it to be made into a very distinctive, unusual, and palatable sweet white wine. Its clear juice is also widely used in Eastern sparkling wines.

CLINTON

A red wine grape type, perhaps of *Vitis riparia* origin, it is also used as a root stock.

CONCORD

Rather low in sugar, this small dark red grape is the most widely planted and easiest to grow of the *labrusca* family.

Eighty-five percent of New York State's vineyards are planted in this variety. Introduced in the 1840's, it yields a strong,
pungent, and intensely grapey wine; its scent is familiar as
the grape widely used in concentrates, grape juice, jellies, and
preserves, as well as in Kosher wines, of which it is the prime
source. It is made into very distinct red and white wine, and
is also widely cultivated as a fresh table grape. Those who
are not fond of *labrusca* scents and flavors will probably find
Concord wine objectionably strong in this respect.

DELAWARE

The small, light, red grapes of this variety yield the least
labrusca-scented wine of native American grapes. It apparently has considerable *vinifera* in its genetic background. It
rarely needs sugaring, unlike most native grapes, as it ripens
well. Introduced in the 1840's, it is made into both reds and
whites—principally whites—and is widely used in Eastern
sparkling wine. It is also grown as a high quality table grape.
At its best it yields a palatable ordinary wine, golden, aromatic, and somewhat individual in character. Some examples
have a pleasant fruity, ciderish quality.

DIAMOND

See *Moore's Diamond*.

DIANA

A seedling of Catawba, this juicy red is used for making
whites. It was first introduced in the 1840's.

DUTCHESS

Of Concord and Delaware origin, this light-green grape
yields a neutral wine. It apparently has some *vinifera* in its
parentage, and can be made into a light, fruity, palatable
wine with some *labrusca* character. It is often made in a
rather sweetish style.

ELVIRA

Introduced in the 1860's, this grape is also known as the "Missouri Riesling" and has *Vitis riparia* parentage. It is not extensively planted, though it is said to be subject to improving molds such as Botrytis.

ISABELLA

Introduced in 1816, it is quite strongly scented and flavored. Its dark grapes are made into fruity rosés and reds. It is now largely supplanted by Concord.

IVES

The dark "black" grapes of this variety are used in red wine blends as *teinturier* (tinting) grapes; by itself, the variety makes a powerful, pungent *labrusca*-flavored wine.

MOORE'S DIAMOND

A Concord and Iona (another *labrusca*) cross, its greenish-yellow grapes yield one of the best native white wines, light-colored, dry, clean, intense, and individual, with an aromatic scent and gravelly, flinty undertones to its spicy-fruity flavor. A clean-tasting wine, often with "foxy" traces, it ranks with Delaware as a native wine most likely to appeal to *vinifera*-accustomed palates.

NIAGARA

Introduced in the 1870's, Niagara is a Concord-type white grape and is used for both dry and sweet wines of a very "foxy" and somewhat individual character. The grape is also used for eating. As a wine, it is somewhat individual in character.

NORTON

Also known as Virginia Seedling and Cynthiana, it yields red wines from its dark grapes. It is not considered particularly "foxy."

SCUPPERNONG

While there are a number of varieties of *Vitis rotundifolia*, the Scuppernong is the best known. Its grapes are made into an amber, musky-scented wine.

VERGENNES

This *labrusca* grape is thought by some to make one of the better dry native white wines. It is not widely planted.

Vitis labrusca—Dessert Wines:

The typical baked and weathered Eastern sherry-type wines are made primarily from Concord, Niagara, Elvira, and Catawba, or blends of these. Most exhibit little or no *labrusca* character and are, on the whole, successful products, well-made and ranging from ordinary to good in quality.

French Hybrids

Most of these carry the name of the hybridizer and a number, and some have been renamed. "Blanc" and "noir" are often added to the commercial names given some of these grapes to help identify them as white or red varietals; for convenience I've done the same here. Only a few hybrids are listed, principally those of current interest in the U.S.

French Hybrids—Red Wine Varieties:

BACO NOIR (BACO NO. 1)

Capable of developing a bottle-nose with age, wine from this hardy and successful hybrid has great acidity, dark color, and a light body. It is often blended, but is somewhat individual in character and can be made into ordinary to quite good table wine on its own. It has a pleasant, vinous nose.

CASCADE NOIR (SEIBEL 13053)

Used for better Eastern rosés and red blends, this variety yields a light-colored wine.

CHANCELLOR NOIR (SEIBEL 7053)

Widely grown in France, it yields full-bodied wines, and is now used in several successful Eastern red blends.

CHELOIS (SEIBEL 10878)

Important commercially in the Eastern U.S., it yields a lighter, fruitier red than Baco noir, with a faintly *labrusca*-like spicy nose.

COLOBEL (SEIBEL 8357)

A *teinturier* grape (its juice itself is red), it is used to darken light red blends.

DE CHAUNAC (SEIBEL 9549)

A very promising hybrid, it may yield fine reds. Some samples are reminiscent of fine young Zinfandel.

FOCH (KUHLMANN 188-2)

A vigorous Alsatian hybrid, it makes a tart but pleasant red wine, with an attractive berryish nose.

LEON MILLOT (KUHLMANN 192-2)

Similar to Foch.

ROUGEON (SEIBEL 5898)

Yields good-colored wine for blends or light reds. It has high acidity.

French Hybrids—White Wine Varieties:

AURORA BLANC (SEIBEL 5279)

Most widely planted hybrid in New York. It yields ordinary to good soft, fragrant, simple whites with leafy-green overtones, and is used in making Eastern sparkling wine.

RAVAT BLANC (RAVAT 6)

Yields good, full white wine.

SEIBEL 10868

Yields a clean, acidic wine. Said to be "stony" in character.

SEIBEL 13047

Makes good quality but neutral wine.

SEYVAL BLANC (SEYVE-VILLARD 5276)

A promising variety, it makes white wines that vary from pungent, heavy-flavored, and ordinary to crisp, appley, fruity, and good. It may have a sharp green, apple-skin flavor accent as well, but is still the most promising white hybrid at the present. At its best, it might be mistaken for a good *vinifera* wine.

VERDELET (SEIBEL 9110)

Yields delicate, aromatic wine; acidity is moderate.

VIGNOLES (RAVAT 51)

Makes crisp white full-bodied wine.

Chapter 4

Labels and Tasting

*American Wine Labels**

The language on U.S. wine labels is governed by federal law and reflects federal regulations concerning permissible practices in winemaking. Individual states abide by these regulations except where their own state requirements are more stringent; California, for example, has a number of important additional regulations.

Because of the increasing quality and sophistication of American wines as well as the public's increasingly sophisticated wine consciousness, it has become obvious to many observers of the wine industry that a number of improvements could be made in current labeling regulations. The Bureau of Alcohol, Tobacco, and Firearms, a branch of the U.S. Treasury that regulates the U.S. wine industry, began holding hearings in 1976 and 1977 to iron out a series of changes in label laws—some proposed by the Bureau, some by the wine industry, and some by other groups—which would give the wine-consumer more specific information on the source and content of the wine in the bottle. No changes are likely to take effect until the late seventies or early eighties, however, so current label laws are discussed below, along with probable areas of change.

Current or future laws notwithstanding, wine lovers should remember that with wine regulations it is not really what is on paper that counts, but what is done in practice. Demand for quality wine is the only thing that finally ensures quality wine, because there will always be winemakers willing to go to the trouble to make fine wines if there is an appreciative market willing to pay a commensurate price for them. If the public doesn't care what it drinks, there will always be those who won't care what they make.

*The sample U.S. wine labels reproduced here (see pages 64, 70, 71) illustrate the language and legal terminology discussed in this section.

63

1972

EMIGRÉ

RED

*This dry, red dinner wine is made
entirely from French hybrid grapes grown
by us in our own vineyard at Augusta, Mo.*

ALCOHOL BY VOLUME 12%
TABLE WINE

ESTATE BOTTLED BY

*Mount
Pleasant Vineyards*

AUGUSTA, MISSOURI

*A Selected Bottling of
California*

Riesling Spätlese

Vintage 1969

*Produced from a late picking
of Johannisberg Riesling Grapes
from our Arroyo Seco Vineyards
and bottled by*

*Wente Bros.
Livermore, California
Alcohol, 12% by volume*

Label Name or Trademark

As in most wines from all over the world, this means a great deal, sometimes almost everything as far as quality goes, because it is the trademark that carries the reputation, whether ignominious, splendiferous, or mediocre. On most American wines, it is the name of the winery; large wineries, however, market wines under a number of different label names or trademarks.

Note: The word "vineyard" or "vineyards" in a winery name is not regulated; just because a winery calls itself "X Vineyards" does not necessarily mean that the firm has any vineyards whatsoever, or even if it does, that the wine in its bottle came from its vineyards. Future label laws may require such winery names to be clearly designated as brands or trademarks.

Vintage Years

The use of vintage dates on American wines is strict. Regulations require that ninety-five percent of the wine in the bottle come from the year stated on the label: This is not likely to change. Many U.S. wines, of course, carry no vintage date, as they are blends from a number of different years. There are, it should be noted, both vintaged and non-vintaged varietals, and both vintaged and non-vintaged generic wines.

Geographic Origin

The most commonly seen geographic designations are of states ("California") or wine-district areas ("Finger Lakes") or counties ("Napa"). One sees sub-district designations as well: Alexander Valley (in Sonoma County, California) or Naples Valley (in the Finger Lakes), etcetera. Federal regulations require that seventy-five percent of the wine in the bottle must be produced from grapes grown in the stated district on the label. If more than twenty-five percent of the grapes used in the wine come from elsewhere, a broader appellation must be used. A wine labeled New York State, for example, must contain at least seventy-five percent New York wine; if the blend does not, the wine must be labeled "American." California wine, however, must be one hundred

percent from California grapes; if a county name appears on
a California label, at least seventy-five percent of the grapes
used must have been grown in that district, and ninety-five
percent if it is a vintage-dated wine.

Specific vineyard names are now beginning to appear on
labels, especially when the winery gets its grapes from a
source it is proud to mention. It is a practice which ought to
be encouraged for fine wines, as it enables wine lovers to
become acquainted with the distinct character of grapes
grown in a particular location. If the label states only "Napa
Valley," the grapes could be from Regions I, II, or III in the
valley. A wine lover would be unable to compare Cabernet
Sauvignon from, say, Rutherford, Spring Mountain, and
Calistoga (all different climatically) in the Napa Valley if
the label gives no further information on the specific region
in which the grapes were grown. Because of increasing consumer interest in (and the high prices that can be obtained
for) wines from specific districts and individual vineyards
within counties, there is a need for the formalization of the
use of sub-county appellations and vineyard designations. At
the present, some sub-county appellations of origin are permitted ("Alexander Valley") while others ("Spring Mountain"), perhaps equally worthy of recognition, are not. It
would be reasonable to require wines bearing vineyard appellations, and perhaps also sub-county appellations, of origin
to be ninety-five percent grown in that vineyard or district.
In any event, future regulations will have to address themselves to this issue.

The designation "estate bottled" is supposed by many to
pinpoint the source of grapes precisely, but as currently used,
is far less informative in this respect than most wine lovers
are aware. Most assume it indicates that the grapes used to
make the wine come from the winery's home vineyards,
which are obviously adjacent to the winery. For a number of
reasons the designation has now been stretched considerably,
and need only mean that the grapes used in the wine come
from vineyards owned, controlled, leased, or under contract
to the winery. Such vineyards may be scattered over many
miles, and may not even be in the same county. A number
of small wineries that are estate operations, however, do
employ the designation, while others consider the term much
abused, and instead employ a phrase such as "Grown, produced, and bottled at the winery." Other wineries who could
use "estate bottled" refuse to use it. Since it's reasonable to

require that wine labeling be rational and defensible, phrases used on labels should mean what a reasonably intelligent consumer would think they meant. In this regard, the requirements for the use of the phrase "estate bottled" will doubtless be made far more stringent under future regulations than they are at present.

Varietal, Generic, and Proprietary Wine Names

The contents of the bottle are described by a name which is either varietal (the name of the predominant grape used), generic (intended to convey a type or style of wine), or proprietary (a trade name used by a single winery for a particular blend or style of wine).

A varietal wine contains at least fifty-one percent of the grape named on the label; at present, *there are no stronger percentage requirements* for varietal labeling in the U.S. It is a commonly held notion, repeated in print, that a vintage-dated varietal must be seventy-five percent of the named grape. This is just not the case. In practice, however, most of the better varietals produced are seventy-five to one hundred percent of the named variety. This is because many fine grapes cannot be blended without losing their character, and it is that character which consumers justly assume they are buying when they buy a varietal-labeled wine. It is quite true, as a number of people have pointed out, that it would be a mistake to insist that every varietal wine be one hundred percent of the grape named. While there is doubtless nothing that can be added to Chardonnay, White Riesling, or Pinot noir that would improve them, the same may not be true of Cabernet Sauvignon; although some winemakers are advocates of one hundred percent Cabernet, others are experimenting, with considerable success, with adding small amounts of Merlot. No winemaker would be hamstrung, however, if the percentage requirement for varietal-labeled wines *were* raised to, say, seventy-five percent of the stated grape. Such a requirement would merely standardize the practice of the better U.S. wineries, and for that reason, is likely to be adopted. Current regulations ignore another important requirement: that the percentage of varietal content be linked with the appellation of origin percentage. It is now permissable to make a varietal wine that meets the seventy-five percent content requirement for wines carrying a county appellation as well as the fifty-one percent varietal require-

ment in such a way that, say, a "Napa Valley Cabernet Sauvignon" need contain only twenty-six percent Cabernet from Napa Valley! Even if no vintner of repute would dream of taking advantage of the regulations in this way, such loopholes will doubtless be closed.

An unfortunate and growing practice in varietal labeling that future regulations should control is the misleading proliferation of variant names. Sauvignon Blanc has been marketed under five different names, including "Pouilly Fumé!" Currently, wineries are permitted to label varietals under almost *any* of the variant names used for a given grape in European districts, a practice that undermines the informative function of varietal labeling, and makes it into a quasi-proprietary marketing gimmick.

A generic wine is one which is labeled with a name intended to convey a type of wine, one that is supposedly associated with the original place name. There are seventeen such names which are permitted on U.S. labels, including burgundy, claret, chablis, champagne, chianti, malaga, madeira, moselle, port, rhine wine, hock, sauterne, sherry, tokay.*

Since there are no legal requirements as to the grapes that must be used in the making of generic wines, or any restrictions on the processes that may be adopted, any resemblance between a generically labeled U.S. wine and its European namesake is extremely rare. In Europe these districts are regulated as to the grapes that may be grown, and often the wine-making processes. A French Chablis, for example, is made from Chardonnay. Thus, the U.S. counterpart to it is a wine labeled with this varietal name, and not something labeled "chablis." Generics may contain any sort of blend of grapes, and in practice contain less distinguished varieties, as anything which can be sold at a higher price under its own grape name will not be used in a blend. It is perfectly permissible, in fact, for a winery to label the same red wine "burgundy" or "claret," or the same white wine "chablis" or "sauterne." The name used usually depends on which name the wine sells best under. Since a good deal of these perfectly honest everyday blends of wine are sold under simple names like "Mountain Red," it is unfortunate that this inappropriate

---

*To avoid confusion here, these generic names are not capitalized unless they actually refer to wines with geographic place names. Thus, "Burgundy" in this book refers to the French wine, while "burgundy" refers only to American generic wines produced under that name.

nomenclature continues for wines that ought to be allowed to stand on their own unpretentious merits. Nothing could more emphatically announce to the world that American wines have come of age than an industry decision to drop the use of those generic names associated with European place names, but because of economic considerations, this is unlikely to happen.

Proprietary names are ones coined by wineries to differentiate their blends from others on the marketplace. Examples of this are: "Ruby Chablis," "Baroque," "Emigré," "Lake Country Pink."

Note: In California no addition of sugar or water to wine is allowed; wines must be one hundred percent natural grape wine and any additional material must be pure grape brandy or pure condensed grape must. Federal law allows wineries to add sugar and water to the wine so long as the volume is not increased over thirty-five percent. The reason for this is that many wineries in the East need to resort to chaptalization to ferment low-sugar grapes, and to add water in order to balance the very high acidity of native grapes. Flavored wines must carry a description of additional fruit flavorings on the label (apple, pear, etcetera).

Bottler and Address

Every label must at least carry the name of the company that bottled the wine and the location of its cellars or offices, and the words "Bottled by." Some large wineries are quite vague about where the bottling is carried on, preferring instead to list corporate headquarters or even addresses adopted for the purpose. "Cellared," or "perfected," and so on, along with "bottled by," indicate that the wine was purchased, aged, finished, and bottled by the firm; "made and bottled by" indicates that the bottler does produce at least ten percent of his own wine, and blends or changes the wine in the bottle in some way. "Produced and bottled by" indicates what most consumers presume, that the winery has fermented, aged, and bottled the wine in the bottle—at least seventy-five percent as a minimum must be its own.

Alcoholic Content

Unless the wine is labeled "table wine" or "light wine," in which case it is understood to mean that it is not over four-

RIDGE
CALIFORNIA
ZINFANDEL
GEYSERVILLE
1969

TRENTADUE VINEYARD GRAPES (SONOMA COUNTY)
BOTTLED JAN 1971 ALCOHOL 12.9% BY VOLUME
PRODUCED AND BOTTLED BY RIDGE VINEYARDS
17100 MONTE BELLO RD, CUPERTINO, CALIFORNIA

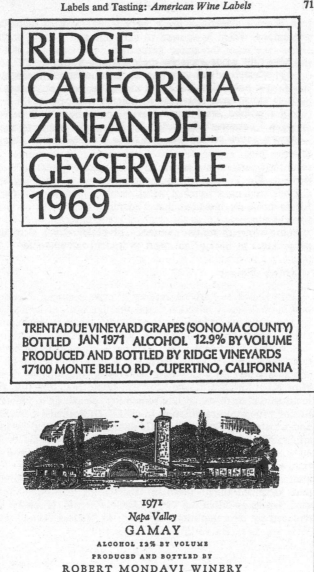

1971
Napa Valley
GAMAY
ALCOHOL 12% BY VOLUME
PRODUCED AND BOTTLED BY
ROBERT MONDAVI WINERY
OAKVILLE, CALIFORNIA

teen percent alcohol, it must carry a statement of alcoholic percentage, which is allowed to vary one and a half percent either way from the stated percentage, and must fall within the range of ten percent (for white) or ten and a half percent (for red) to fourteen percent alcohol in California for standard wines. Dessert wines are those wines above fourteen percent alcohol (and taxed accordingly) to an upper limit of twenty-one percent alcohol. Most dessert wines fall within the eighteen to twenty percent range, and their stated alcoholic content may not vary more than one percent either way. Sherries must now have a minimum alcoholic percentage of seventeen percent in California; other dessert wines, eighteen percent. The Federal minimum in any wine is seven percent alcohol, and most flavored wines (such as pop wines), California products included, have no more than eight or nine percent alcohol.

Some wineries make a practice of giving exact alcoholic percentages as part of an effort to inform the customer.

Other Terms

Terms such as "private reserve," "private stock," "limited bottling," "special selection," and the like are not controlled by law and merely indicate the winery's effort to distinguish either higher-priced wine from lower-priced, or individual lots of wine from each other, or what is thought to be better wine, or to entice sales. Such terms may appear on all a winery's wines, in which case there is no meaning to them. "Lot X," "Bin X," "Cask X," "*Cuvée* X," and the like are intended either to sound like something special, or to indicate lots of wine that are different in character, bottled separately, and which can be compared. These are not controlled by law either. Neither is the word "mountain" which is simply evocative, one supposes, of hillside vineyards. The proliferation of rich, sweet White Rieslings in the past few years has called attention to the need for future changes in the label language that identifies them; German label terms now sometimes used (such as "Spätlese" and "Auslese") will probably be replaced by clearer phraseology such as "Late Harvest" and "Selected Late Harvest."

Sparkling Wines

The term "fermented in *this* bottle" is used by champagne

makers who want to make a distinction between the original *méthode champenoise* they employ, and the "transfer process," which allows the wine to leave the bottle for disgorging and rebottling. Transfer champagnes do not have to be labeled as such, and their labels often state "fermented in the bottle." The Charmat process, whereby sparkling wine is fermented in large tanks and bottled under pressure, must be labeled "bulk process." All three processes can be labeled "naturally fermented." Some of the better producers of bottle-fermented sparkling wine do not state the process on the label. There are no definitions legally of "natural," "brut," "extra dry," and the like, other than the tradition that "natural" is the driest, brut next, and so on.

Back Labels

Since false, misleading, or disparaging claims are not allowed, the statements such as "matured in oak," etcetera, on back labels must be accurate.

Back labels, in fact, can sometimes be very informative, giving the grape varieties in the blend, or even giving one such unnecessary but encouragingly forthright information as picking time, sugar/acid ratios, and even fermentation charts! Usually, however, back labels are less informative than they are opportunities for wineries to state their pride in their product, and, all too often, to make preposterous quality comparisons.

Other Information

Future label laws will have to address themselves to the vexing question of ingredient labeling; most of the wine industry is strongly opposed to any such labeling requirements on the grounds that most materials added to wine during processing are removed before bottling, and that imported wine, if not held to the same requirements, would falsely appear "purer" to the consumer. All this has served to deflect discussion from the central issue, which is whether the list of permitted additives—some fifty substances—needs to be as long as it is. Privately, most winemakers will admit that given sound grapes, only a few natural substances (such as sulphur dioxide, which has been used since winemaking began) are really necessary in the production of fine wine.

Tasting American Wine

As with many art forms, appreciation is easier and more rewarding if one can be discriminating. Developing a critical wine palate is essential to the appreciation of wine. Unfortunately, many people assume such a skill is hopelessly arcane, the sort of thing passed on in secret rites in cobwebbed cellars over a glass of Tokay Essenzia. Well, it isn't. Having a critical wine palate simply means you can say something intelligent (and accurate) about any wine—identified or not—poured into your glass. It isn't difficult to detect and describe a wine's characteristics, roughly assess its age and quality, and, with many fine wines, recognize the predominant grape variety from which the wine was made. Unless you're cursed with a dead nose and a wooden tongue, you can develop a fair palate in a surprisingly short period of time. To assess wine critically, however, you have to develop a memory for wine smells and wine tastes and that takes a lot of careful and comparative tasting. There are few skills that are as pleasant to acquire as they are to possess, but a critical wine palate is one of them!

One of the happiest aspects of American wine is that it is the most useful upon which to develop a critical palate, because it is possible to taste varietals unblended, from an incredibly wide variety of areas and climates, and made in a great assortment of styles. White Riesling, for example, is grown in California, New York, Washington, Oregon, and even Arkansas. This permits the wine neophyte to soon learn which odors and flavors in his glass are due to the grape, and which are due to the winemaking. It is comparatively easy to find examples of particular varietals that are made in cool or warm climates, with or without aging in oak, vinified in a light or heavy style, etcetera. Also, the fact that so many American wineries produce so many different wines makes it difficult to generalize in many cases about their quality; wine lovers cannot rely upon labels in the uncritical way they often do with European wines. Instead, one has to taste, and this forces one to pay attention to what he puts into his mouth instead of what he reads on the label. These sorts of skills are enormously useful and are, of course, easily and rewardingly used on wines from anywhere in the world.

Many people persist in having the most ludicrous view of what it means to be able to taste wine. They picture monocled old gentlemen sniffing the Port after a dinner party and proclaiming something like "Hmmmmm! Quinta do Noval '31, I perceive."

Such things have little to do with wine tasting. Assessing wines blind is common in wine tasting; identifying them blind is a stunt. To *identify* wines is not the point of tasting, appreciation, or even connoisseurship. The point is *evaluation*. Yet it is astonishing how many people think something like the above is what having an excellent palate is all about.

There are actually several different kinds of wine expertise. The most basic kind is the ability to assess any glass of wine put in front of you. This is not an enormously difficult skill to acquire. A more difficult skill is that of judging a young wine's potential; this involves not merely assessing a wine for what it is, but for what it may become with further age. To do this well takes considerable experience, and it is not hard to be fooled. The third kind is the sort of skill a winemaker needs, and this is a profound skill indeed.

Making fine wine (as opposed to just making wine in your basement) demands a well-developed palate as well as considerable technical knowledge and experience. Many critical decisions which make the difference between mediocrity and magnificence in a wine are made on taste alone. Deciding how long a wine should mature in wood, what kind of wood to use, what size barrel to employ, whether to separate or discard various lots or casks of wine, when to bottle, etcetera, is all done on the basis of sniffs and tastes of the wine at various stages, when the effect of certain kinds of aging and the like are assessed. I certainly would be terrified to make the expensive decisions of taste that all wineries are dependent upon. Standing there and tasting from several thousand-gallon lots and announcing, "Let's give the Cabernet a light egg-white fining next Tuesday; then rack it off into the Nevers oak, top it up every three and a half weeks, and I'll check it in two months; the Chenin Blanc needs another week before bottling, but let's put lot number fourteen of the White Riesling aside until we see how the batch in the glass tanks does by the week after next . . ."—this requires a certain kind of experience and expertise few non-winemakers have.

Developing a palate discriminating enough to appreciate the nuances of fine wine is not so difficult, fortunately. What it requires is first, to become familiar with the dimensions of taste, second, to learn to distinguish the principal grape varieties, and third, to learn the principal virtues and defects one is likely to encounter in tasting. The neophyte also needs to develop a reasonably precise vocabulary to describe wine smells and tastes, so that he can develop a memory for the basic aspects of wine. This last, a sort of set of mental vinous standards for various types of wines, is essential if one is to be able to make quality comparisons.

The best way to begin to gain the necessary experience is by doing what the professionals do: taste wines directly against each other. It's not difficult to notice, isolate, and compare even slight differences in wines tasted together, but it's another thing to remember clearly a wine tasted months ago. That requires a memory, and such a memory can only be developed with considerable experience. If at first one tastes wines against each other, later one can taste against his memory, so to speak—though serious comparisons must always be direct.

The four aspects of wine that are easiest to identify are acidity, acescence, sweetness, and tannin, because it is possible to use non-vinous examples of these tastes. This makes it easy for the neophyte to pick them out when tasting wine. Lemon juice in water will illustrate acidity quite easily and a little wine vinegar in the same illustrates acescence. Sugar dissolved in water of course demonstrates sweetness, and a very strong cup of tea at room temperature conveys tannin readily.

It is less easy to pick out wines which illustrate these aspects, as the best examples of these are imbalanced wines in which these aspects predominate. It is not, however, difficult to find crisply acidic whites, sweet wines (again whites are best), and young, tannic reds, although excessive acescence is a sign of spoilage and not likely to be encountered in dramatic display save in a spoiled wine. Wines which contrast these—i.e., flabby whites, assertively dry wines, and fully mature, softened reds can be found; lack of acescence is, as might be expected, a characteristic of fresh sound wines.

After some initial experience with these basic wine dimensions, the beginning wine enthusiast ought to make himself acquainted with at least the four "noble" varieties—Cabernet Sauvignon, Pinot Noir, White Riesling, and Chardonnay—and try to fix their characteristics in his mind. After some practice, it is fairly easy to identify major varietals, at least in good representative specimens.

It ought to be remembered that the differences in varietal characters, even though obvious to the nose and mouth, require metaphorically descriptive tasting terms. These refer to the presence of flavor constituents which bring to mind other non-wine examples of certain smells and tastes—"flowery," "peachy," "fruity," "berry-like," "spicy," "flinty," "appley," "nutty," "earthy," "smoky," "weedy," etcetera. The important thing is to use them if they help to fix the major varietals in your mind; if they don't, discard them.

As far as learning about wine nuances goes, lists of tasting terms always include dozens of terms like mousey, corked, moldy, etcetera, which are fortunately not frequently encountered. Besides, a wine lover is more interested in virtues than defects; unlike a winemaker who is interested in prescribing a treatment to correct a wine's condition, a wine lover simply stops drinking a problematic wine. I couldn't tell you that a "rubbery" odor in a wine was due to the fermentation of high-Ph musts, for example—I would simply note it as an off-odor and reject it. Virtues are something else. I would only suggest to the budding wine lover not to err on the side of caution out of timidity in trying to find words to express subtle nuances. Merely to mumble something about "breed" over every other wine tasted is totally unimaginative and uninformative. It is far better to free-associate and talk about cigar butts, cedar chests, wet herb gardens, fruitcakes, vegetables, etcetera; often these metaphors hit on the very aspect that is so apparent and yet so difficult to describe. At the least, tastings become more interesting.

Some comments are in order on tasting wines for their potential. While it is not difficult to develop a palate critical enough to assess wines as they are, it takes a much greater degree of skill and experience to judge wines on what they can become. A number of fine wines develop in the bottle for years, and judging the potential is a skill which is not only much esteemed in wineries and among buyers and shippers of wine, but is one which is useful for a wine lover to have, if he expects to buy wine to put away for several years to a couple of decades in his cellar.

It is frankly not easy to see hidden in the harsh tannin and raw power of a young Cabernet Sauvignon the silken smoothness, the layers of flavor, and the long perfumed finish the same wine may have in fifteen to twenty years. While it is true that a wine which shows nothing from the start is unlikely to turn into a champion, many wines show better in the barrel than they do after bottling, sometimes for a year or two. It is not always true that one can simply aerate a young

Cabernet, for example, to catch a glimpse of what it might be like in the future: sometimes the wine simply goes through a period of several years in which it is extremely difficult to see what is contained in it. I've had the experience many times of tasting wines when young that I thought very little of that astounded me six years later. Some seemed to have had very little tannin and flavor, and in general lacked "stuffing," causing me to think them poor candidates for the long haul; but later tasting showed them to be supple wonders with superior balance. Every hard, tannic young wine, on the other hand, is not necessarily a frigid princess. Some never come around and amount to anything, but always remain rather hard and uncompromising, lacking both fruit and charm. In short, it is easy to be fooled, and I've been fooled many times, especially with American wines, because it is difficult to gain enough experience with the wines from a given area to have a definite idea how they will behave in future years. Part of this is due to the fact that winemakers in places like California constantly experiment with different styles and, typically, shop all over the landscape for grapes for their wine, or to supplement their own production. The result is that one winery's wines may be very different from one year to the next. Complicating the situation even further is that wineries will sometimes put out two different batches of a given vintage-dated varietal with no indication of this on the label. I once tasted an astonishingly good wine and later bought some from a different source, only to find it entirely different in character. When I later had a chance to talk with the winemaker, he blithely told me there had been two different lots. Personally I suspect this happens more often than might be imagined, as I have often been surprised by the abrupt changes in character I have found in wines from time to time, and for which it would be hard to find any other explanation. This kind of occurrence may have something to do with the rather surprising differences in opinions given on many wines in various rating competitions.

On Comparing Wines

One of the best ways to come to know a wine is to taste it against another wine. In order that the comparison be meaningful, there has to be some similarity between the wines.

One of the most obvious bases of comparison is the grape variety; in fact, unless the grape varieties used in the wines are the same or related, it is very difficult to compare wines. The age of the wines should also be close, unless you are purposely contrasting the effects of differing ages. An old Cabernet Sauvignon cannot be meaningfully compared with a fresh young White Riesling, for example, although one can find one better than the other, in the way that one can say after a succession of different wines during a meal what the best one was. But in that case one is not comparing them directly against each other.

In other words, the trick in comparing wines is to pick ones which are similar enough that you can contrast their virtues and defects. Wines that are being compared in this fashion are best tasted blind, and all this means is that the labels are hidden or kept from view. The reason for not looking at the labels is to prevent one's expectations from influencing one's impressions.

Not every wine enthusiast realizes how potent his impression, expectation, or image of a wine can be. The poor reputation of American wine until recent years was due to a good number of factors, but I suspect an important one was simply that the notion of "California wine" or "New York State wine" did not radiate a particularly glorious and glowing image in the typical wine drinker's mind, unlike the image of for example, French wine, even where quality was equal. The image of California wine is still often regarded as unintriguing and unromantic, so much so that its fine wine reputation can appear lackluster as well; for many wine lovers who are aware of the better California wines, even the best do not elicit the fascination that lesser wines of other countries do.

Of course, the great reputations of Europe's best wine regions rest on the deserved fame of their greatest wines, and this doubtless accounts in part for the popularity of their less noble efforts. The fame of the finest wines of Europe adds stature, in the wine drinker's mind, to their lesser cousins and even poor relations.

Every wine enthusiast knows how one's expectations color one's appreciation; there is a profound difference between approaching an untried wine with anticipation or with trepidation. A wine preceded by a noble reputation alerts one to every nuance the wine can offer; a wine without repute is often drunk without attention.

A wine's reputation, whether resplendent with honors or under a cloud of ignominy, must be accurately based on the smell and taste of the wine, if its reputation is to be founded on fact. But reputations have a life of their own, and we often put as much trust in them as in our own taste. In becoming acquainted with the reputation long before the wine (as we often do), we run the risk of prejudging a particular wine long before we even swirl a glass of it. In adopting a snobbishly narrow view of what kinds of wines possess an alluring and romantic image, we run the risk of ignoring whole categories of wines whose appeal may be as unique and fascinating as any of the world's wines.

In this regard, American wines have often been hastily and quickly dismissed. No one would think it reasonable to judge, say, French wine by its merest *vin ordinaire,* yet until very recently American wine was commonly assessed, at least in print, on the basis of nothing more than a sampling of its least ambitious table fare.

Not the tables have been turned, and the finest American wines are not only receiving their share of recognition, but are also being compared with the finest of Europe in blind tastings. What astonishes a good many wine lovers is that American wines sometimes win rather easily! The reputation of European wines is so potent, however, that many people assume that if a panel of tasters finds a California Chardonnay better than Montrachet, they must have been "fooled," instead of assuming the obvious—that the California wine must have been better.

This brings up the question of whether American wines can be meaningfully compared to European wines. Of course they can; in fact I advocate doing it (blind) as a useful and enlightening exercise for the palate. The best wines to compare with each other in this fashion are ones that cannot be *easily* distinguished from one another as being from different geographic locations. One American wine which fits these requirements quite easily is Chardonnay; due to the prevalence of aging in French oak nowadays in California, it is very hard in many cases to tell them apart from French White Burgundies. This makes tasting them together a fascinating exercise, since they can all be rated on quality irrespective of one's suspicions about their origins. (Not that it isn't quite illuminating in many cases to unveil the bottles after the tasting!)

But tasting wines like California Cabernet Sauvignon

against Red Bordeaux raises a more difficult problem: that it is not always meaningful to compare a California Cabernet Sauvignon with a French Bordeaux, merely because they are both made from the same grape. This is not just because Bordeaux wines are usually blended wines, using grapes like Merlot, Malbec, Cabernet Franc, as well as Cabernet Sauvignon, while fine California Cabernet Sauvignons are almost always unblended. (Fine Bordeaux range from around half Cabernet to ninety percent, though some—Pomerols, for example—are about three quarters Merlot.)

It is not always meaningful because the comparison is usually not very well thought out. The implicit assumption is that the Cabernet Sauvignon is supposed to resemble the Bordeaux style, and if the California Cabernet doesn't, then it is considered out of character and therefore flawed.

Given the history of wine, it is natural to take the European as the standard simply because it is the traditional style of wine made from certain grape varieties. But there is no necessary reason why great wines of a different style or character could not be made with the same grapes. It is obvious that a comparison between two kinds of wines in which one kind is taken as the standard is hardly a straightforward comparison of quality, irrespective of wine style. If the California wine has its own particular nose and body, it may be impressive in its own right, even if it would be out of character for a Bordeaux wine. It is certainly prejudging the issue to assume that what is done with the Cabernet grape in Bordeaux is the only worthwhile thing to be done with it. If the comparison is undertaken in the spirit of seeing what sort of things can be accomplished with a particular variety of grape grown in different climates and with a variety of methods, then one can appreciate what a California wine can do. Otherwise one would end up giving an unimpressive Claret high marks simply because it distantly echoed a first-growth, and a magnificent Cabernet Sauvignon low marks because it lacked Bordeaux character. To do that would be to hold a wine's own unique character against it as if it were a defect. (In fact, this sort of thing is a common error in tasting American wines, to my way of thinking—a wine that is "untypical" cannot be said to be poor on that ground alone. To insist that every wine adhere to a ideal notion of type and style would force one to mark down a number of magnificent wines merely because they were unusual.)

Nonetheless, there are differences between a good many

American wines and European wines; these differences may
well diminish when more fine American wines come from
states other than California. Conditions in California are often warmer than in Europe, so that many of the differences
that one notices between California wines and European
wines appear to be due to the difference in climate. California wines often have less acidity than European wines—at
least the ones from the northernmost districts—and because
of its superior grape-ripening conditions, more sugar. It is not
surprising that in blind tastings, especially among wine drinkers in general, the softer, fruitier, more agreeable California
wines are often preferred.

White Rieslings and Pinot Noirs may well do better in
other states than in California, though some superb examples
have been made there; at this point, American White
Rieslings are not equal to the best of Germany and the best
American Pinot Noirs are not equal to fine Burgundy. Cabernet Sauvignon becomes an extraordinarily powerful, direct,
assertive—and magnificent—wine at its best. It is often more
alcoholic than Claret, and like most California reds, can
show a warm, full character, even "roasted" at times, that is
more characteristic of the wines of southern Europe. Chardonnay, however, seems to do magnificently in California. It
is true that America does not produce sparkling wines equal
to the better Champagnes, nor does it produce a first-rate
sherry-type, nor anything to equal fine vintage Port. On the
other hand, superb things have been done with grapes like
Sauvignon blanc, Zinfandel, Chenin blanc, Pinot blanc, and
others, and really surprising things have been done with
grapes like Barbera and French Colombard.

Until recently there were few interesting American sweet
wines produced, due to vintner disinterest in the conditions
suitable for the growth of *Botrytis cinerea*, the "noble rot"
of Sauternes that is also responsible for the sweetest fine
wines of Germany. Out of the dozens of foul diseases that
can attack a grape on the vine, botrytis is a benevolent mold
that in certain conditions can shrivel the skin of grapes and
allow moisture to escape, concentrating the flavors and
sugars and adding a flavor of its own. Wines made from such
grapes have an excess of natural sugar, so that not all is
used up in the process of fermentation; the result can be a
luscious, complex sweet wine. The specific conditions of high
and low humidity necessary for botrytis to take hold aren't
as infrequent in American wine districts as previously sup-

posed. The quality of the luscious natural sweet wines that have been made make it likely more will be attempted in the future.

But comparing wines to discover "the greatest" is not by any means all there is to drinking and tasting wines. What is interesting about wine is its variety. An exclusive interest in the "greats" is the mark of a snob. It is at least as interesting to discover the simple charm of the first wine from a new wine district, or to recognize the quality in a hitherto little-known wine, as it is to have one's umpteenth glass of first-growth Claret. There is more to the world of wine than meditating over a glass of some legendary vintage. Magnificent as a bottle-aged Claret or Cabernet Sauvignon can be, I sometimes think that a fresh, fruity Chenin Blanc is all that one can ask of a wine. Hard as it may seem to those of us who lack the wherewithal to indulge such a fancy, a constant diet of first-growths and grand-crus would be boring, in the same way that never listening to anything but a handful of symphonies, no matter how great, would be boring.

Very great wines, like great works of art, demand certain settings to be appreciated, and always demand all our attention. But not every excellent wine, or even superb wine, demands to be studied to be appreciated; some are just gulpably delicious.

One should also realize that the greatest wine is not the most ideal drinking on every occasion. Great wines do not gracefully take a back seat to food; they are often too powerfully scented and overwhelming in taste to be enjoyable with or complementary to many dishes. Sometimes a wine not wholly harmonious alone will do a better job with food. A lightly acid wine may be perfect with some seafood, a young tannic red may nicely balance a rich oily duck. So too every occasion is not necessarily the one for a momentous wine; an old vintage Port may be just the thing by a winter fireside, but hardly the wine for a summer garden stroll that a happy, spicy, young Gewürztraminer would be.

It is the supreme wine, of course, that commands our attention and respect. But we should remember that America's claim to be a great wine country is based on more than its production of a few wines that can be drunk with reverence; its importance lies in its remarkable variety of wines of all types, its spectrum of wine styles, and its vast production of sound, reliable, and interesting wines that represent good value for the money.

A Note on Wine Prices

I have purposely avoided the topic of price so far in this book because (1) wine prices are a thoroughly depressing topic these days and (2) the rapidly changing economic picture in regard to wine in the U.S. makes it very difficult to say anything specifically useful about prices that wouldn't be instantly dated. Grape prices for the finest varieties have soared over a thousand dollars a ton in some cases recently in California, which works out to something like one dollar a bottle just for the juice! When you add in the cost of running a winery, processing, aging, packaging, marketing, and distribution costs, one shouldn't be surprised to pay around five dollars a bottle for a good many interesting American wines; there are, however, excellent values to be found at one to two dollars a bottle, and one can find fine wines that repay further aging as low as three dollars. One should remember that the smaller wineries in the U.S. often cannot afford to sell wines to distributors for less than what they would sell it for retail at the winery; this means many wines from small California wineries may be priced at seven to ten dollars or more by the time they appear in the East. While in general, one gets what one pays for, it should be remembered that in some cases the price may reflect the wine's rarity rather than its quality.

There is no hard and fast rule about wine value. I myself would rather drink more interesting wine less frequently than mediocre wine constantly, and therefore I don't wholly subscribe to buying wines on the basis of price/quality indices. While in many cases it makes great sense to purchase wine for one's table this way, it is difficult to put a price on the opportunity to try a special bottle. Nonetheless, for everyday drinking, it makes perfect sense to sample a single bottle—or sample a mixed case with friends in a blind tasting and share the cost—and rate the wines on a suitable scale, say, a twenty-point scale. Afterwards, divide each wine's price by the points each wine earned, and you have an index of what each point of quality costs. Remember that it may be worth it to pay a few cents more to get those few extra points of quality, as it sometimes spells the difference between a boring and an interesting wine.

Buying and Storing Wine

Wine books often instruct the novice to find a good wine merchant and follow his advice on purchases. This is strange advice indeed, since if you don't know anything about wine, it is rather difficult to judge a merchant's advice; in short, there is no substitute for knowing something about wine yourself. Wine merchants who are capable of dispensing sage advice are few and far between; these days many merchants are more enthusiastic about the wine boom than they are knowledgeable about wines, and far too many know more about imported wines than American wines.

Wine stores in the U.S. can be divided into three basic categories: posh emporiums, typical liquor outlets, and places-to-be-avoided. In the first category are some of the best-stocked and most knowledgeably run shops, often with reasonably competitive prices, as well as those who put most of their effort into a pretentious carriage trade atmosphere instead of their selections. A request for something inexpensive in the latter type of store is liable to be treated with as much enthusiasm as a request for cooking wine.

Typical liquor outlets range from vast wine supermarkets to neighborhood stores. Their selections can be excellent or limited, their prices may be bargain-basement or buyer-beware, and their staff may be knowledgeable and enthusiastic or blissfully ignorant. Such shops are the mainstay of the average wine lover and his moderate wine budget. The shops in the third category look like a lot of the shops in the second category, but can be distinguished chiefly by their ten-year-old window displays and/or their hostility to browsers. Their main business is hard stuff, as evidenced by the dusty rows of spoiled Mountain Red standing in the sun.

The wine enthusiast, unlike the buyer of gin or Scotch, needs to be concerned about the storage conditions and handling of wines where he buys, and even if knowledgeable, will have to rely on his merchant's advice at least occasionally. Differences in wine stores are important to any wine buyer; there are few wine lovers who, at one time or another, haven't been stuck with an off bottle, been given bad advice, or paid outrageous prices. Because there's a lot more to rating a wine store than trying a few of their recommendations, wine lovers need to look for and ask about the quality of advice, the selection, and the storage.

Unfortunately, many wine merchants make no distinction between rendering advice and giving a sales pitch. It is quite easy, however, to detect stores whose sales tactic is based on outright snobbery; these are the places where the salesman will answer your request for an excellent and reasonable wine with something like, "Well, if you don't want the best . . ." somehow implying that you have little right to a palate if you have to ask how much. The merchant's knowledge can often be tested by asking his opinion of American wine, or, if his state or a neighboring one produces any, about the wines of those states. If he knows nothing about them, or repeats only the most obvious or outdated (or discredited) information, a great lack of curiosity on his part can be suspected, and chances are his shop will have made no effort to carry anything but the most obvious and best advertised choices, rather than the hard-to-get but interesting wines that are produced in small quantities in all price ranges.

By far the worst problem a wine enthusiast encounters in wine stores, however, is storage. It is simply outrageous how many stores, even otherwise very good stores, fall down in this respect. Perhaps it is because most wine shops in the U.S. are still largely liquor stores that they tend to treat wine as if it were spirits. Hard liquor, at forty to fifty percent alcohol, is largely impervious to normal ranges of heat and light, and must be stored upright lest the alcohol eat away the cork. But wine, as should be obvious by now, is a different matter altogether. Its alcoholic content is not sufficient to protect it from harmful exposure to air, and it is in a constant state of development in the bottle. It would be far better if merchants thought of it as a sturdy but still perishable form of food. A bottle of wine must be stored on its side so that the wine remains in contact with the bottom of the cork, keeps it swelled, and thus keeps air out. A bottle stored upright will eventually have a shriveled cork, and that means that air will be admitted. This means, of course, that one will eventually have an expensively packaged bottle of vinegar. While it is true that corks will sometimes hold up for an incredibly long length of time, the average life of a cork standing up is three months before it will begin to dry out. Some last only a month.

There is a great deal of damage that can be done to a bottle of wine short of having it spoil completely. It need not have a sun-bleached label or several inches of ullage to have been unduly affected. The cork, for example, may only be partially dried out, but it is ridiculous to purchase wines for laying down in such condition, when the life span for the cork—lying down, twenty to thirty, even fifty years—has been so drastically shortened. Screw-top wines are not designed to be laid down, and will be perfectly sound stored standing. But wine lovers have a right to expect that wines costing up to ten dollars or more have been treated as the expensive items they are. Do not accept the argument, "Oh, we move our stock so rapidly we've never had any problems . . ." Rubbish. It is the expensive items that move the slowest, and you should make it clear you don't care to buy wine that has been subjected to suspect storage. It is still the case in many areas, too, that all American wines are subjected to upright storage while the ninety-nine-cent imports are accorded the honor of lying down!

Do not buy older wines from stores where storage is not impeccable for another reason as well: temperature. Wine should not be subject to temperatures above 75°, and is better off at a constant temperature under 70° with only a few degrees variance. Around 55° is ideal for long-term storage. There are only a few wine stores that have adopted the ingenious solution of air conditioning the entire store to a much cooler temperature than usual, allowing them to display enticingly their best stock without harm. (A word of warning: do not buy wine that has been stored in a refrigerator, i.e., chilled wine. Wines go downhill in as little as two weeks at such excessively cold temperatures.)

The reason why temperature is so critical to quality is that it affects the development of the wine. The warmer the temperature, the faster the evolution of the wine; wines stored at high temperature age rapidly, become fatigued, and mature poorly if at all. Wines stored at fluctuating temperatures literally get worked to death. The longer and cooler (to a point) the storage, the more gradual the wine's development will be and only wines stored in this fashion ever come to their full flower. Disturbing a wine excessively, either by constant movement or vibration, is also damaging, as is excessive light, which can alter the color of wine.

Fortunately, the great majority of wine produced is neither fine enough nor requires lengthy aging to be at its best, or we would all, merchants included, have more problems than we do over storage. I don't mean to suggest by all this that it isn't possible to find merchants who store their wine properly (some even store it for their customers). But it is a problem that wine lovers should be aware of and about which they should be vocal.

Having proper facilities in the home is a more difficult problem. The ideal thing to have is a wine cellar. For many wine lovers the phrase "wine cellar" is laden with images and fantasies: stepping softly down creaky stairs into the cool dark silence of a stone *cave*; browsing among rows and stacks of cobwebbed bottles; bin tags revealing by the light of a sputtering candle the roll call of great vintages stretching back decades; selecting from the vast array a precious old bottle.... Well, most of us have neither the space nor the wherewithal to make such fantasies realities, but that isn't to say a "cellar" of much more modest proportions can't furnish some of the same keen pleasure, convenience, and economic advantage an enormous one affords.

Besides, as almost everyone knows, buying the wine when it is first offered is a good way to save money. Ten years later it may cost ten times as much—if there is any to be had. Even if one is not buying in sufficient quantities to lay away cases at a time for drinking years later, the sheer convenience of having even a few cases of wine stashed in a closet avoids a great many problems. A last-minute dash to the local liquor store just before the guests arrive is a good way to get stuck with high prices and a poor selection. And certainly no fine wine, especially one that throws any sediment, is at its best immediately after the excessive agitation it gets from being jiggled and jostled from store shelf to your table (though most whites and young light reds are not affected by mild handling). It is much better for most wine to be retrieved gently from your own cupboard, closet, or cellar, where it has been resting quietly.

But where does one store even a small amount of wine—say, ten to twelve cases for drinking within a year and a small collection of wines, perhaps accumulated over several years, laid down for future drinking? Let us assume such a cache amounts to perhaps two dozen cases in all. Two dozen cases of wine take up a lot of space, about twenty-four cubic feet. That's about the size of a small closet. Actually, short of having basement corner or fruit cellar which can be pressed into use, a closet is probably the best bet, as it offers darkness and a place to keep the wine undisturbed. Make sure that the area is free from vibration and sudden changes in temperature. If unsure, determine the temperature range with a minimum-maximum thermometer; this will show you the highest and lowest temperatures reached since you last set it. There should be no more than a few degrees variance during any twenty-four-hour period, though a slow rise and fall of temperature in a slightly wider range from summer to winter should not harm most wines. The closer you can get to 55° as a constant, the better, but steadiness of temperature is important as well. There are such things as temperature-controlled air-conditioned units, but the cost is very expensive—around five dollars for each bottle stored. Unless your wines are worth a lot more than that, it isn't worth it, and chances are there's a relatively cool spot somewhere in your living quarters.

The last requirement for proper storage—undisturbed rest—can run into money. Even if you buy wines in full case lots only, eventually you'll end up with a good number of miscellaneous bottles, and these need to be stored in individual bottle racks so you can get at, say, that '64 Cabernet Sauvignon, without disturbing your '70's. Bottles laid on a flat shelf invariably roll around, assorted bottles stacked on each other in a bin are never the right order, and it is less than satisfactory to have to stir up an entire pile to get at a particular wine on the bottom. Wine racks vary considerably in price. They run from fifty cents per bottle slot up, usually because they're more decorative than functional. There's little purpose, of course, in paying for such stylishness when your rack is going to sit in a dark closet or cupboard.

In looking for economical racks, remember that large wire metal racks have a tendency to vibrate. Wooden ones are more satisfactory in that respect, and if you have the space and can take the weight, terra cotta drain tiles—foot-long cylinders with a four-inch-diameter hole—stack well, insulate the wine against rapid temperature changes, and provide rattle-free rest. Of course, if you're adept at carpentry, there are a number of designs which can provide near to ideal convenient storage, from diamond-shaped bins to stacking units. Remember, however, to avoid racks that store the wine slanting neck down. Some people obviously have the impression that if wine is better off on its side, then it's best nearly upside down. This is a bad idea for wine that throws sediment, as it will collect right behind the cork, in the worst possible place for it to be when you want to decant it.

You might consider cardboard. Wooden shipping cases suitable as racks are rare indeed, as almost everyone ships in cardboard cases now. While they cost nothing, they're unsteady when stacked on their sides. It's rather upsetting to have a stack of several such cases collapse on you like a house of cards. Further, a case will sometimes collapse inside when you remove bottles from the bottom slots first, unless you're using whiskey cartons. Single, unmixed cases of wine can be stored in their own cases, however, as long as they're not stacked and bottles are removed from the top. It's an excellent way to make use of an odd corner or shelf.

While it is enormously convenient to have wines on hand, the principal reason for buying American wines to keep for future consumption is that the best are still in very short supply and rarely last long on the shelves. Older, properly matured California Cabernet Sauvignon from top producers is harder to find than old Bordeaux; if one wants to taste a twenty-year-old Napa Valley Cabernet, then there is usually no solution but to buy some and put it away—even if it is only a case or two.

PART II

A Brief Guide to the Wineries and Wines of the United States

Chapter 5
California Wine

If wine lovers in California have a favorable impression of their state's wines, it is not simply because California produces three-fourths of the wine consumed in the country, and far and away the majority of fine American wine; it is because of what they have tasted and seen in their wine districts. It is quite easy for a Californian to gain an accurate and even intimate view of California fine wine production, for most of the large and some of the small wine producers offer formal or informal tours and tastings. Premium wine centers like the Napa Valley north of San Francisco, with its picturesque countryside and historic sites, have become, at least on weekends, something of a tourist attraction. People drive around from one winery to the next, sampling fastidiously or with gusto; some take careful tasting notes; some load their trunks by the case; others pick out a bottle for the day's picnic, and in the process, all of them learn something about wine.

While a tour of the larger wineries gives one an excellent idea of the size of California winemaking on the larger scale, in a tour of the smaller producers one has the opportunity to see fine winemaking at its best. Most of the small fine wineries can be visited, although often by appointment only, and a visit is like being given a tour of someone's garden, rather than his business. The big wineries with their huge tanks, clanking bottling lines, and miles of vineyards dwarf the imagination; in the small wine estates even the most urban visitor begins to picture to himself the satisfactions of drinking a glass of his own wine while surveying the small plot from which it came.

The romance of wine is understood in California, and if it is little suspected to be there by most wine lovers, it is instantly appreciated when discovered by them. I remember coming upon old gnarled vines in a showcase plot carved out of a forest on a mountaintop with spring thunderheads over-

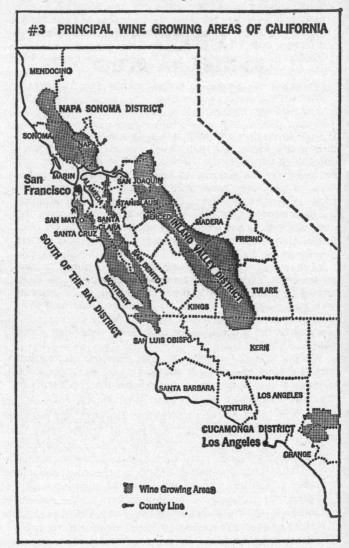

#3   PRINCIPAL WINE GROWING AREAS OF CALIFORNIA

head; walking on the soft red earth of a vineyard in a hot
early fall, inspecting the dusty tight bunches of Cabernet Sauvignon grapes and chewing a few astringent berries; sampling
a flowery cool White Riesling from the cask in a dim, ramshackle cellar; uncorking a magnificent old Zinfandel that
seemed to taste of the chalky hillside cave in which it had
been aged. One begins to understand the pull, the romantic
allure of the north coast valleys of California for the early
wine pioneers. In these valleys they saw something which reminded them of the wine-growing districts of Europe; some
came for gold, and stayed to make wine; some had never
made wine, and some brought years of skills and winemaking
traditions.

Jean Louis Vignes—so far as anyone knows, that is his genuine name—a native of Bordeaux, was the first man to im-
port *Vitis vinifera*—the European wine grape—to California,
some time in the 1830's. His was the first large-scale commercial winery in the state, and his first vintage was not later
than 1837. In 1840 his wines were regularly shipped to other
parts of California. (Believing a sea voyage improved their
quality, he often shipped his wines to Boston and back before
selling them.) By 1843, his El Aliso Vineyard covered one
hundred acres in what is now a considerably less pastoral setting, downtown Los Angeles.

Vigne's only major competitor was William Wolfskill, an
unsuccessful trapper from Kentucky, who did very well as a
winemaker. Up until the late 1850's the Los Angeles area
was the foremost viticultural region in the state, although
George Yount had a small vineyard in the Napa Valley north
of San Francisco as early as the 1830's.

While there was great interest in winemaking and viticulture, what these pioneers needed was a market, and the Gold
Rush of 1849 provided it: thousands of miners drank California wine. When gold proved elusive, some of the miners,
primarily the French and German ones, turned to winemaking, thus expanding the industry still further. The immi-
gration of European winemakers, like the importation of European vine cuttings, has continued down to the present in
California, so that traces of nearly every Old World winemaking tradition are found in the operations of its wineries.

Many large premium wineries in California today date
from the post-Gold Rush era: Paul Masson and Almadén
date from 1852; Mirassou followed in 1853; Charles Krug

and Inglenook began in 1861 and 1870, respectively; Wente Bros. and Concannon, among others, began in the 1880's.

As early as the 1850's, the California press began referring to California as the greatest wine country of the world, in spite of the fact that at that time California wine was not highly regarded elsewhere. And apparently much of the wine, even those wines made from European grape varieties, had problems: the winemakers did not take into account the fact that California growing conditions were different from those of France and Germany; all wine (good, bad, indifferent) was sold at the same average price; because of taxation wines were sold before they were properly aged; and last, but most important, the best California wines were often sold under foreign labels to command a higher price, while cheap, poor-quality European wine was bottled with California labels. Whatever prejudice still exists against "domestic" wine could probably be traced back to this unfortunate practice.

While initially the ravages of phylloxera in Europe were a great stimulus to the California wine industry, the inevitable spread of the disease to California in the 1860's had similar drastic consequences, and necessitated the same drastic solution. A severe depression in the wine market, caused by over-production and poor wines, hit the California industry from 1876 to 1877. Wine at ten and fifteen cents a gallon could not find a market, and many wineries failed. The industry soon revived by concentrating on finer varieties, and men like Leland Stanford planted more than a million vines between 1881 and 1883. These zealous efforts, however, brought about another severe depression, and the market was flooded with wines at six and eight cents a gallon from 1886 to 1892.

Vineyard production expanded rapidly in California up to 1900, in spite of the 1876-77 and 1886-92 depressions in the market. These economic swings led to the formation of state boards, private associations, and programs at the University of California to improve viticulture, conduct research, encourage suitable legislation, and, in general, promote the industry.

After that, the market for California wines improved, and until the devastating setback of Prohibition, good wines, recognition, and a share of the world's markets were California's. In fact, some pre-Prohibition wines were undoubtedly great (or at least very fine); there are a few remaining nineteenth-century specimens still living in the bottle today.

Perhaps it is California's historical situation—or perhaps it is something peculiarly American—but whatever it is, a tradition of bold enterprise and experimentation has characterized California winemaking from its beginnings. Even Old World winemakers who migrated to California experimented with their traditions in a way they would have never done in Europe—or perhaps it is just that California only attracted the bolder ones. In any event, experienced winemen and total amateurs alike acted as if they believed that California was the vineland of the future. Perhaps because of the unwavering faith, they brought California to the forefront of world winemaking not once but several times, rebuilding as readily from ruins of economic busts and the ravages of phylloxera as they were to build again after Prohibition.

Such eager adventurism on the part of inexperienced winemakers has had its price. For every success in winemaking, scores failed utterly to make even a drinkable product. Probably no wine region but California has a history of so many great glorious enterprises swept into almost total obscurity. The example of the great success of Haraszthy (there is more to say about him later) and others attracted fortune-seekers, speculators, foreign winemakers, and total amateurs to California, and the low price of land, cheap Chinese labor, and the small investment then required (it cost about fifty dollars to set out an acre of vines in the 1860's, and now, a hundred years later, over three thousand), not to mention the potentially high profits, brought about a scramble for vineyard land and some remarkable enterprises, the vast majority of which faded away as rapidly as they bloomed.

Once-famous names like Drummond of the Valley of the Moon, or Nouveau Medoc, whose wines were favored in Boston and New Orleans, exist today only as footnotes. The utopian community and winery-vineyard of Anaheim is now buried beneath, of all things, Disneyland. The famous Vina winery that once boasted three million vines in its vineyard is now forgotten, as is Charles Kohler, who made and shipped wines to South America, Europe, and China. There are ghost wineries scattered throughout California, some weed-grown ruins, some put to less romantic uses.

It seems that from the beginning of its wine history, California especially has attracted those bold enough to try not merely to produce a passable wine but to attempt to make a

great one—this in spite of the unknowns of the soil and climate, the investment of years of labor, the uncertainties of
an unsteady market, or even lack of knowledge about winemaking. But without this tradition of boldness, California
winemakers would have been much less ambitious than they
have been, and doubtless would not have achieved what they
have. A passion to make great wine can hardly guarantee
success, but the "amateurs" who have succeeded in California
have done so because they have been as eager to learn as
they have been to try out their new ideas. They have trans-
lated their ambitions into the necessary skills, equipment,
methods, experimentation, and grapes, and if they didn't
know the answers, they found out. If there were no answers,
they took risks.

In the nineteenth century, most (though not all) California
wine was terrible; most winemakers were simply too inexperienced, their grapes unsuitable, and their winemaking haphaz-
ard. While the wine industry itself was dealt a heavy blow
during Prohibition, viticultural and vinification techniques had
advanced to the point where the knowledge and means to
make fine wines was generally available to post-Prohibition
winemakers. Unlike the early winemakers, they could draw
on a fund of advanced techniques, use superior grape varieties, and match them better to climate and soil. But they still
suffered from the uncertainties of the market—in fact, in the
1940's there was no market for fine California wines at all.
Short of subsidizing one's own winery, the only recourse open
to a would-be maker of fine wines was the slow growth of local customers, and perhaps a mailing list of wine enthusiasts
interested in the effort to make fine California wine.

Californians will tell you that in some respects their industry is only forty years old, that they had to start from zero
after Prohibition in terms of labor, skills, and markets, but
one senses they don't mind it that way—at least not now.
They are happily unencumbered by any winemaking tradition
other than dauntless adventurism, and in spite of all the recent work on matching grapes to soil and climate, no one has
yet convinced anyone else that he has the best plot of land
for any specific grapes in all California. Thus, winemakers
are free to be their own men, devise their own methods, find
their own great soil, and make their own great wines. The
creative freedom, the attractions of working with the land,
the participation in an ancient ritual, the role of an indepen-

dent winemaker—all these are irresistible attractions to a variety of personalities, temperaments, imaginations, and ambitions.

California Wineries

A "winery," first of all, is simply a place where wine is made, probably named in keeping with "distillery" and "brewery." Many, but not all, wineries have their own vineyards, and, of those that do, many also buy grapes to supplement their own production. There are many vineyard owners who do not make wine but only grow grapes to sell to wineries. Many wine lovers are surprised to find out that a great many California wineries (and for that matter wineries elsewhere in the U.S.) do not grow their own grapes, but get them from a variety of sources. This is, in fact, common practice for many California wineries, and one would be mistaken in assuming that those wineries that grow their own grapes necessarily produce better wine than those wineries who buy some or all of their grapes from other growers.

A winery may grow grapes, buy grapes, sell grapes, buy and sell wine in bulk, or any other combination of buying and selling grapes and wine that suits its needs. With few exceptions, nearly every winery in California, large or small, utilizes all these sources of grape supply at one time or another.

There are, in other words, very few small vineyard estate operations in California (and again, elsewhere in the U.S.) which produce and bottle only the grapes grown in their vineyards. Most California wineries are closer to Burgundy shippers or *négociants* than Bordeaux châteaux; in Burgundy and in California the producer buys grapes or wine from growers and makes or finishes it in his cellars and bottles it under his own name, and sometimes the name of the vineyard. The infrequent use of vineyard names in California often means that a winery may produce a number of different vintages of a varietal under his label that have come from a different vineyard source each year; this often means that there is little continuity of character, save for the style of winemaking, from year to year. Many wineries do have their own vineyards, of course, and their production does ex-

hibit both a continuity of character in the grapes used and in
the style of the wine. Others find it irresistible to experiment
with different sources of grapes, varietal styles and methods,
which, while it makes generalization about their production
almost impossible, is an endless source of surprise for wine
enthusiasts who enjoy discovering special lots and batches of
outstanding wine from various producers.

The different styles of winemaking used in California are,
if anything, more varied than the sources of grapes. In the
various wineries I've visited, I've met with attitudes on wine
and winemaking that ranged from pre-industrial purism to
belief in the efficacy of scientific analysis and technology, and
from staunch traditionalism to experimentation bold enough
to border on the zany.

Debates continue over whether or not to fine and filter
wines, what style best suits Zinfandel, Chardonnay, White
Riesling, etcetera, whether to age wines in French oak or
not, and if so, how long. Whatever the winemaker's opinions
may be, the one thing that is certain is that he is not the least
daunted by anyone else's accomplishments. The most successful winemakers in California, however, have been those who
were willing to adapt their methods to fit the conditions they
discovered, rather than those who sought to impose methods
developed elsewhere to fit different viticultural requirements.

Juxtaposed with the bright machinery of modern winemaking, the ancient presses, historic buildings, and carved cooperage still in use remind the visitor of the California winemaker's
successful eclecticism. He frequently sees no contradiction
in combining the skills of laboratory research with the skills
of traditional winemaking, and simply adopts ancient or
modern tools with the techniques that will work to make the
best wine.

Visitors unacquainted with modern winemaking are liable
to find the gleaming panoply of modern equipment in most
wineries rather sterile, and may have their doubts over
whether the use of this sort of technology isn't really employed as a labor-saving shortcut that bodes ill for the quality
of the wine. It is certainly true that one can use modern
winemaking equipment for that purpose, but it is equally true
that it can be of enormous help to the winemaker who seeks
the highest quality. Because it gives him the tightest control
possible over the processes of winemaking, the less quality has
to be dependent upon happy accidents; in other words, the
more it is possible for the winemaker to make conscious deci-

sions that affect the wine's quality. It is for reasons like these that great wineries in Europe, such as Château Latour, now have a cellarful full of stainless steel fermentors. In short, quality in wine is not dependent on whether you use modern equipment or not, but rather on what you do with it. In this respect, the most interesting developments are coming these days from the small wineries devoting their production to fine wine. While nearly any winemaker in California will tell you that his concern for quality is unqualified, at the smaller wineries one encounters people with something like a sense of mission to make great wine that in some cases borders on the messianic.

Large vs. Small Wineries

The question of the effect of size on quality is one which occurs to wine lovers who are aware of the dramatic differences in size among California wineries. While the Napa Valley, for example, is certainly not the home of the giant California firms, some wineries there produce a thousand times more wine than others. There are wineries in the valley whose production is so small that bottles are filled and labels are pasted on by hand, while others have tour guides taking crowds into vast bottling rooms where the whir and bang of conveyor belts and mechanical arms bring corks, bottles, labels, and thousands of gallons of wine together as so many cases of wine per hour.

One can't assume, however, that smaller necessarily means better. The elaborate modern technology employed in production and bottling at the larger wineries means that one rarely encounters "off" bottles (typically acetic or musty-smelling wines) as frequently as one does from many smaller wineries. The principal problem that larger wineries have with quality is not control, but approach.

A large winery, because it's rarely one person's concern, is more susceptible to purely business considerations—that is, the pressures of the market. A very large operation tends to produce wine which fails to reach the ultimate peaks of quality possible in a good year, because its tendency as a business is to reach consistent quality from one year to the next. This naturally affects its methods. A large winery crushing many tons of, say, Cabernet Sauvignon, will simply throw the best lot of the vintage into the general batch rather than keeping it separate, or will hesitate to change a style of wine to take advantage of a particularly good year.

On the other hand, a small winery can assume that its customers are wine enthusiasts who will hardly be alarmed at the sight of sediment, and who expect to lay down their Cabernet for ten or twelve years before sampling it. This kind of audience enables one to make wine without inhibitions, and it often shows. The smaller winery can afford to take the time and trouble—and chances—that can produce great wine. It is one thing to ruin several hundred gallons of Chardonnay by aging it too long in wood; it is another to ruin many thousands of gallons in some unsuccessful experiment.

The other area where smaller wineries have an advantage is in their ability to concentrate on a smaller number of wines. It has been common practice for all California wineries, but especially large ones, to offer whole family trees of wines, sometimes a dozen varieties or more of red, white, rosé, still and sparkling, dry and sweet, fortified and distilled wines, both varietals and blends, vintage and non-vintage, under their label. Much of this was done simply to get shelf space on retailers' racks in the days when there was not much of a wine market. Doubtless this marketing approach was also useful in encouraging brand buying among customers of every taste and little discrimination who could—and would—rely on a given label for all their wine needs. The rapidly increasing sophistication of the wine-buying public, however, is rendering such an approach less attractive. It is obvious to most wine enthusiasts that no winery can produce first-rate wines in *every* category. Some degree of specialization is necessary if a winery is to be able to take the time and care it needs to with any given wine.

In this respect, the better premium California wineries—Beaulieu, Charles Krug, Inglenook, Louis M. Martini, Concannon, Wente Bros., and a few others whose production ranges from about 150,000 to 300,000 cases a year—are in a curious historical position. Since the repeal of Prohibition in 1933, they have been the principal source of good and fine wine from California. The four major premium wineries of the Napa—Beaulieu, Inglenook, Charles Krug, and Louis M. Martini—have produced some of California's greatest wines, especially Cabernet Sauvignon. In that respect it is ironic that general recognition of California's greatness should wait until the sixties. But it was not until then that California showed what she could do with most of her wines, especially white wines.

These middle-size premium wineries, some with long distinguished histories, came to maturity in the decades when the market for and interest in fine California wine was dormant. For a public uninterested in varietals, these wineries diversified their production to meet every taste, adding a long line of generics, "burgundies," "clarets," "sauterne," even "chianti," branched into sparkling and dessert wines, sacramental wines, and brandies, so that today they offer an average of two dozen different table wines each.

These wineries have played an indispensable role in the creation of the California wine market. Without them, and their even larger cousins, there would be no California wine industry. But they find their role as producers of the finest wines supplanted more and more by the smaller wineries with far more concentrated production.

Yet it would be a grave mistake to write off the middle-sized wineries as possible sources of fine and even great wine. At their best, their Cabernet Sauvignons are still among California's finest, and there is no question of their ability to produce from time to time wines of unquestionable nobility. I recall a 1967 Cabinet Gewürztraminer from Buena Vista that would be difficult to equal in sheer lusciousness. Wente Bros. is more noted for its white wines, but its special bottling of 1963 Pinot Noir was a perfumed beauty by 1971. Concannon's 1968 limited bottling Sauvignon Blanc was superb. Beaulieu's 1968 Pinot Noir was extraordinary. Most of the middle-sized wineries are like that; one or two of their wines every few years will be as successful as any in California. Such outstanding exceptions in the long, always well-made but often undistinguished lines of wines put out by these wineries make one regret that such skilled producers seem to have grown to such a size that they are locked into their markets, or at least are highly reluctant to abandon them. One wonders what they would accomplish if they concentrated their considerable abilities and resources on a few wines instead of spreading their energies over too many wines of purposely varied ambitions.

Not surprisingly, the newer fine wineries are specializing in one to four wines, and many of the older smaller ones are thinking of cutting back their lines. The larger premium wineries seem stuck on a never-ending extension of their wine families, sometimes with a corresponding diminution of quality.

There are two paths open to these larger wineries: either trim their lines and concentrate on their best products, or start down the slippery slope to mass market mediocrity. None have started down the first path, but I suspect some are starting the slide down the second. One hopes that most are at least standing fast. Many seem headed for eventual absorption by large corporations.

There have not always been happy results with many of the new small wineries either. Many of them are run by amateurs, and while this is sometimes a good thing, sometimes it is not. Most of the wine made in California, whether good, bad, or great, has been made by men who grew up in vineyards, who came from winemaking families, and whose lives revolved around vines and winemaking. But a surprising amount of *great* wine has been made by "amateurs," people who dropped other careers, sometimes late in life, to take up the difficult, risky, and laborious career of a winemaker, with all its demands of labor, investment, and years of time. Some have made fortunes in other businesses and traded it all for dawn-to-dusk tasks in the cellar or vineyard, because California can offer them not just the chance to own a winery, but a chance for a unique kind of achievement. The 1960's saw a tremendous surge of interest in wine and fascination with the vision of wresting a great wine from an untried plot of ground. This vision is as old as the wine industry itself in California, and one of the sources of its strength and creativity.

In fact so many new small fine wineries have been started recently that it would be difficult to keep track of them all, much less their latest developments. I will be mentioning a few of them in the following chapters to indicate the extent and variety of changes California will undergo in the years ahead. There are some whose efforts are spotty in quality, which, after all, is only reasonable to expect from brand-new operations whose methods, sources, and, often, winery buildings have only recently come into being. And because some of these enterprises are run by amateurs whose ambitions for their products overreach their winemaking expertise, some of their wines may exhibit impressive virtues and careless defects in the same bottle, defects which would never be found in the less exciting but reliable wines of larger wineries.

Thus, some of the new small wineries will not live up to their early promise; others will surely become important in the next decade. No doubt there are wineries in this category I have not discussed that will come to the fore among the great California wineries of the future. That, of course, is as it should be; there has always been room in California for a new fine winery, and it is part of the excitement in California today that a winery not yet founded could be producing the state's best Cabernet in ten years' time.

California Vintage Years

Almost all of the finest wine in this country, as in every wine-producing country, is vintage-dated. This is as it should be; fine wines are purposely made to accentuate their individuality, which is why they are usually made from one predominant and distinctive grape variety, and typically show the character of their climate and soil. One of the most obvious ways to accentuate this individuality is to distinguish between each year's crop of grapes, so that each such batch of wine will exhibit the marks of that season's weather.

This individuality of vintages means that among wines that are drunk soon after vintage (most whites and some light reds) some will be better than others—fuller, richer, finer—and others, the products of not so fortunate years, will be thin, sharp, flabby, or dull, as the case may be. Most will fall in between these extremes of quality, just as the weather in most years is neither perfect nor disastrous. Among wines that must be aged in the bottle for years after vintage to bring out their full character, these differences will be even more accentuated. Among Cabernet Sauvignons, for example, not only will the wines of stronger years take longer to mature, but the wines of lighter years may well have reached full maturity long before other wines do, even though they might be much younger. There are '67 Napa Valley Cabernet Sauvignons that are fully mature now, while some of the '64 Cabernets from Napa are still not ready, to give but one example. In other words, the commonly offered theory that the only function of a date on a California label is to tell you how old a wine is, is complete rubbish. Some wines which need aging mature in five years; others need twenty-five. Winemaking styles apart, it depends on the vintage.

The importance, meaning, and validity of American vintage years is a vexed topic, and is peculiarly controversial. As vintage years do make a difference, however, I'd like to make some attempt here to straighten out the issue.

The word "vintage" is used in a number of ways, and has several distinct meanings. A "vintage" is simply a harvest of the grape crop, and therefore a given vintage refers to the crop of that year. Many wine-producing regions of the world date each year's production; thus, the appearance of a vintage date on a wine from those regions has nothing to do with quality *per se*; some of the dates shown may stand for poor years and poor wines, and others for outstanding years and outstanding wines. The idea that a wine which carries a vintage date is superior to one which doesn't carry it actually applies only to Champagne and Port. Since both these are normally wines blended from several years' vintages, they normally carry no date. But in outstanding years, a "vintage" may be declared, which basically means that the producers feel that the crop of a given year is outstanding enough to be bottled on its own, without blending from other years. Thus, a vintage date on a bottle of Champagne or a bottle of Port carries with it a presumption of superiority, as only superior vintages will be bottled on their own (at least, this is the theory). But if wines from Bordeaux, Burgundy, the Rhine, California, etcetera, all carry dates year-in and year-out—as in fact they do—obviously it is not the appearance of any old year on the bottle that indicates quality, but what the year was like. Some dates may well mark a disastrous year, a terrible crop, and meager wines.

This, of course, is why there is such a thing as "vintage charts" for European wines: these little cards are supposed to tell you at a glance what to buy or order and what to avoid from twenty years' production of a dozen wine regions. They can be quite misleading; wines on them are rated according to their potential but often do not indicate when the wines will reach this last bit of maturity, and this information is all-important. Many wine drinkers do not realize that a wine rated "10," if opened long before its prime, is liable to be far less satisfying than a wine rated "7" but now at its full maturity. The difference in ratings is supposed to mean that at its peak the "10" will be a greater wine than the "7" will be at its peak. This is why highly rated vintages fetch the highest prices, and are often foolishly drunk long before they have had the opportunity to develop and justify their perfect and near-perfect ratings. This fact is unfortunately often ignored, mostly because wine lovers persist in assuming that the "poorest" years mean undrinkable wine. While this may have been true decades past, modern techniques of vinification have improved to the point where all that a "poor" year usually means is very light wines, wines that ought to be consumed within a few years after the vintage. The use of numbers in giving ratings to wines tends to obscure this fact, as it makes people assume that all the wines are identical in general character, and some are a lot better than others. The fact is that each year's vintage produces a wine of different character.

But, one may legitimately ask, are all the wines of a given area the same for a given year? Obviously not; in the poorest years, someone will make a good wine, and it will doubtless be better than the worst wine of an outstanding year's vintage. But, nonetheless, such ratings are roughly true of the wines of a given area, because they are based on European wine districts where often there is but one grape, or one family of grapes grown, and one typical style of winemaking employed. The differences that do exist within the region can be averaged out to arrive at a consensus of what the general quality of the wine of that region was in a given year.

The situation, however, is quite different when it comes to assessing California vintages. Take the Napa Valley as an example: first, the climate is extremely complex; the area ranges from Region I to Region III in degree-days, and vineyards there are found at levels ranging from the valley floor to over two thousand feet elevation. There are dozens of different grape varieties grown, scattered in different locations and microclimates in the valley, and last, there is an extraordinarily wide range of winemaking styles employed, again with every grape. Given the fact that it is impossible to count on Cabernet Sauvignon from the Napa Valley being made in a given style, and the variety of vineyard sources used, it is extremely difficult to generalize meaningfully about the quality of the wines of a given grape variety even from a district as small as the Napa Valley. Even if most American wine regions are not as complex climatically as the Napa Valley, they are all planted, for the most part, to a whole range of grape varieties, and experimentation with different winemaking styles is taken for granted. What may be perfect weather during the picking of an early ripening grape may turn into a heat wave or rainstorm before another variety is picked, and so on. Any winery producing dozens of different varieties will have some success with some grapes one year, and others the next. The result is a muddled picture, to say the least.

There is another factor which has tended to obscure the importance of differences in American vintages. While climatic conditions in many wine-growing areas of the U.S. are as varied and dramatic as in Europe, in California's wine districts—the source of most American wine—the climate is much more regular than in many parts of Europe. Grapes always ripen sufficiently to make sound wine. Add to this impression the sort of advertising many large California wineries commonly engaged in a few years ago, stressing that "every year is a vintage year in California" in order to demystify wines for the public. This is a phrase that is semantically ambiguous and viticultural nonsense to boot, and almost everyone but the grape-growers are left with the idea that California vintage years can be ignored.

Strangest of all factors in maintaining this false impression of American vintage years are the claims of some of the larger wineries, who persist in fostering the idea that blended wines are superior to vintage wines. It is obviously true that the light, thin, acid wines of poor years are much improved by blending with heavier, dark, flabby but flavorful wines of years which were too warm and vice versa; but the wines of a perfect season are just plain watered down by adding anything to them. Wineries that aim to produce reliable, consistent, and good table wine are obviously predisposed to blending vintages; but to blend year in and year out to maintain a consistent product levels off the peaks just as it fills in the dips in quality from vintage to vintage.

Wineries that aim to produce finer, more interesting wine, obviously lean toward vintage-dating as one of the ways to accentuate the individuality and character of a wine, even if in some years that wine will not have as full and exciting a character as it will have in other years. It is the individuality of wines that is the source of their fascination; it is the mark of fine wines. What is expected of good table wine is merely that it be reliable. Part of the interest that vintage-dated wine holds is that it has the element of surprise about it—will it be great? poor? or just mediocre? Such risks are not what one wants in everyday wine, but they are part of the adventure of fine wine.

One last argument that is sometimes heard for non-vintage wine is that blended wines allow one to produce a non-vintage wine that is ready to drink now. There is a place for this in the production of good wines, but there is also a place for fine wines that consumers should age themselves, just as they do the finest European wines. If American wines are good enough to treat seriously, then they can be purchased the same way. Anyone who buys a recent first-growth Claret of a good year for immediate consumption is cheating himself, and he is doing so if he expects to be able to purchase fine California Cabernet Sauvignon and experience the best it has to offer without waiting.

Dessert wines, however, do not lend themselves to vintage dating, because the way they are made usually necessitates blending, and it is the process which gives the wine its character, not so much, as in table wines, the grapes. Here one is often only concerned with how old the wine is, and often one year's release is as good as another to lay down for aging.

After having come this far, I can hardly not offer specific information on what the better years in California are. Some of the difficulties presented by differing winemaking styles, different grapes used, and the complexities of climate and weather should make it apparent I'm not going to offer anything as rash as a chart. However, the following notes on recent years should provide some useful information. If the notes seem inadequately sketchy, bear in mind that ratings on European wines are largely arrived at by consensus of growers, buyers, shippers, writers, and the marketplace. These notes are based on what little there is in print, what I've been able to extract from winemakers (many of whom stoutly claim all their progeny are of equal stature), and my own tasting notes. I am hardly in a position, therefore, to deliver the last word on a subject that ought to be aired more frequently than it is.

The following notes necessarily apply principally to the Napa Valley. In spite of the variety of climatic conditions, grape varieties, and winemaking methods used in the Napa, the concentration of wineries in the area makes generalizations about vintages—risky as they are—easier in that area than elsewhere in California, where wineries producing vintage-dated varietals may be scattered over many square miles. If the vintage picture is muddled in the Napa, it may be missing or incomplete in other areas, where all one has to go on are the successes or failures of the one or two wineries some regions have. What has been true of a given year for the Napa Valley isn't always the case for the other fine wine districts of the state—the regions from Sonoma to Mendocino, and the regions stretching from the Livermore Valley to Monterey. They may, for example, have escaped the frost and drought conditions experienced in the Napa Valley. Since roughly similar weather conditions are fairly common in these districts, however, these notes on the Napa can be used as a *rough* guide to North Coast wines in general.

Remember that most whites are intended to be consumed when young and fruity, though some varieties can gain with bottle age. Fine, well-balanced Chardonnay peaks in about five to eight years, and may last fifteen if well-stored. White Riesling, Sauvignon Blanc, and Pinot Blanc can be long-lived as well. "Best reds" refers principally to full-bodied Cabernet Sauvignons, tannic Zinfandels, a few Pinot Noirs (most are rather short-lived), occasional Barberas and other red varieties. These are rarely at their best when young, and need sufficient bottle age. Other reds, and light-style wines made from the above varieties, are, on the whole, best consumed within five years after the vintage. Rosés should be consumed within a year or two.

1976: Drought conditions and erratic weather resulted in a short crop, but high sugar and acid levels promised good to fine whites and at least some very concentrated, powerful reds.

1975: A cool spring, August heat, a cool autumn, and late rains produced mostly light wines, but a few early-ripening varieties—notably Chardonnay and Pinot noir—may prove outstanding.

1974: A cool summer and warm, dry fall resulted in long, slow maturation; this coupled with near-perfect harvest conditions produced good whites and outstanding reds, notably rich, concentrated Cabernets.

1973: Lack of frost, heavy spring rains, and favorable summer weather resulted in a huge crop. Reds and whites both very good; the best are beautifully balanced rather than rich or deep.

1972: Spring frosts, drought, heat waves (up to 110° in

Napa Valley), and heavy rains at harvest resulted in lowest yields in thirty years. Early-ripening varieties like Chardonnay fared well, much better than late-ripeners like Cabernet, of which some crops were washed out. Overall, a poor year with light wines.

1971: Spring frosts, cool summer, poor harvest weather; light to average wines. Early varieties best, including some fine Pinot Noirs. Most Cabernets thin and light.

1970: Worst frosts ever wiped out fifty percent of the Napa Valley crop, but warm summer and mild autumn yielded good sugar and great acidity in the remaining grapes; whites very good to fine and best reds may be among greatest ever, concentrated in flavor and very long-lived.

1969: Hot August and September yielded big heavy reds (some have an almost "cooked" or "roasted" quality) and substantial whites. Best reds need years, best whites should be enjoyed now.

1968: Cool summer and vintage into late October yielded fat, fleshy wines, some lacking in acid; best reds are outstanding and need several more years. A few whites still superb.

1967: Moderate conditions. Reds light and largely ready now.

1966: Cool year and small crop; wines light to big, but well-balanced. Most reds ready now; others need time.

1965: Very fine year; good full wines all around. Reds nearing maturity.

1964: Severe spring frosts; small crop, warm summer and cool harvest yielded some hard tannic reds, the best of which are superb and need several years at least.

1963: Late harvest with rains resulted in light wines. Best reds mature, others past it.

1962: Cool season; good acidity; poor to light wines. Best reds mature, others over the hill.

1961: Bad frosts, cool summer, small crop and light wines. Best reds mature, others past it.

Older years than '61 are likely to be only of academic interest to most consumers; as occasional bottles do turn up, however, I will add a few brief notes on the best and worst years. These apply to reds, principally Cabernet:

- 1958: Outstanding year; best reds are wonderful now, nearing maturity, but should hold their plateau of quality for some time.
- 1957: Considered a poor year.
- 1951: Outstanding year; best reds stunning.
- 1948: Considered a poor year.
- 1947, 1946, 1941, and 1934 produced some extraordinary wines, the best of which are still developing in the bottle.

One should also remember that these comments are very general, and cannot apply to each and every wine produced in a given year. To take two examples, the Robert Mondavi '68 Cabernet was well-balanced and fruity, but light compared with the Heitz Martha's Vineyard Cabernet '67, a big dark, tannic, rich mouthful of a wine that needs years yet to mature. There are, in other words, plenty of exceptions to the claim that '68 was a much better year for reds than '67; and one can find unusual wines that defy the expected. Like any generalizations about vintages, the above are merely a rough guide; the only surefire guide is your palate.

Chapter 6
The Napa Valley

The Napa Valley, like most of the premium wine districts of California, can be reached within a two-hour drive from San Francisco. The valley lies north of San Francisco Bay in a cool climatic zone somewhat similar to that of Bordeaux. The valley's reputation as a fine wine district, however, is not so much due to the excellence of its climate or soil—other areas in California match or possibly better its grape-growing conditions—as it is the result of its concentration of major premium wineries. Miles of vineyards and a gauntlet of producers, large and small, border the highway that runs the length of the narrow mountain valley as it curves to the northwest from the city of Napa to Calistoga, some twenty-five miles to the north.

Out of almost three hundred bonded wineries in California, Napa County has over fifty. Many of the wineries are uncompromisingly modern, with no romance or allure, save in the bottle; some perch in spectacular settings, and some have a ramshackle, carved-out-of-the-wilderness look about them. Only five miles across at its widest, the valley is hemmed in by the rounded Howell mountain range on the East, and the forested peaks of the Mayacamas mountains on the West. The climate is the reverse of what one might expect; the coolest area (Region I) is found in the southern part of the valley, near the town of Napa in the Carneros district; Oakville, farther north on the highway from Napa, is slightly warmer, Region II; Rutherford, two miles farther north, is also Region II; near Calistoga, however, at the upper end of the valley, the climate is Region III. A good deal of the valley floor is covered with vineyards, dotted every so often with huge tall fans, used, along with sprinkling systems, to ward off frosts. Vineyard work goes on all year long, and pickup trucks are constantly bumping down dirt roads between the plots to drop off vineyard workers in cowboy hats. The wine vine can grow in notoriously poor soil, but it is a sensitive

113

plant nonetheless. The vines in a vineyard, like children in a classroom, demand individual attention if they are to yield their best, and in the Napa Valley, they get a great deal of attention. The vineyards scattered among the hills and nestled in the mountains are harder to work than those on the flat valley floor, but their advocates claim the quality of the grapes compensates for the difficulty of cultivating slopes sometimes over two thousand feet high.

Grapes have been grown and wine has been made in the Napa Valley since the 1840's. By the late 1800's, there were 142 wineries in operation and by 1891 some eighteen thousand acres of vineyards. Before phylloxera and Prohibition, wines from the Napa Valley had already gained a great reputation and were shipped to Eastern cities and London. The valley and the surrounding hillsides are still dotted with Victorian mansions and old stone wineries that date from that era, some of which have been revived and had their vineyards replanted. When visiting some of them it is not hard to imagine what it was like in the days when Robert Louis Stevenson visited the Napa Valley in 1880 and wrote about it in his *Silverado Squatters*. Snippets from his chapter on "Napa Wine" are often quoted in books on early California viticulture, and some of his more poetic quotes even appear on a billboard welcoming tourists to the valley. But his most famous paragraph is worth repeating:

> Wine in California is still in the experimental stage; and when you taste a vintage, grave economical questions are involved. The beginning of vine-planting is like the beginning of mining for the precious metals: the wine-grower also "prospects." One corner of land after another is tried with one kind of grape after another. This is a failure; that is better; a third best. So, bit by bit, they grope about for their Clos Vougeot and Lafitte. Those lodes and pockets of earth, more precious than the precious ores, that yield inimitable fragrance and soft fire; those virtuous Bonanzas, where the soil has sublimated under sun and stars to something finer, and the wine is bottled poetry: these still lie undiscovered; chaparral conceals, thicket embowers them; the miner chips the rock and wanders farther, and the grizzly muses undisturbed. But there they bide their hour, awaiting their Columbus; and nature nurses and prepares them.

The smack of Californian earth shall linger on the palate of your grandson.

Today, Stevenson's prediction has come true. California wine has come into its own; there is no doubt about the success of California's great experiment with the wine grape.

Vineyard acreage in Napa dwindled to a few thousand after phylloxera had struck, and was never replanted to more than about ten thousand acres until the late 1960's. Now there are over twenty thousand acres planted to vines, and the few thousand suitable acres left in the county may be planted eventually as well. The rosy economic forecasts for the wine industry brought about by the "wine boom" have made vineyard prices in the valley soar to twelve thousand dollars an acre. Nonetheless, a number of large U.S. corporations and dozens of small producers continue to invest millions in the valley, confident that the future for fine table wine is assured. Recently their ranks were joined by the French corporation Moët-Hennessey, makers of Moët et Chandon Champagnes among others, which paid a tidy sum for eight hundred acres near the city of Napa. One of the reasons that the Napa Valley is becoming the most intensely planted wine district in the country is that unlike other areas in California it has been able to stave off the threats of urbanization which have gobbled up other fine wine districts. Recently a plan to put a freeway through the narrow valley was squelched, and the county's agricultural preserve plan keeps unincorporated land from being subdivided into housing tracts. There is even a movement afoot among some of the valley's wineries to investigate the possibilities of appellation control regulations for the valley. These active efforts to protect and promote the wine industry attract even more wineries to the valley, which will doubtless soon become an unbroken carpet of vines. Small plots of vines even appear in the front yards of many of the homes in the town, as often as a flower bed or tomato patch might appear elsewhere, and no doubt a local resident could practically absorb the necessary knowledge of viticulture and vinification from the atmosphere; wine-consciousness in the valley is all-pervasive.

There is a good deal of local argument in the Napa over virtues of mountain-grown grapes and valley-grown grapes. Mountain vineyard owners point out that the soil is often poor in the mountains, so that the yield is low, and thus, the smaller crop is of higher quality; mountain vineyards rarely experience frost, a great danger on the valley floor. It's cooler in the hills, an advantage when there's excessive heat in the valley, as it keeps the grapes from ripening too rapidly and losing some of their acid content. There is less fog in the mountains, which helps the grapes to ripen more evenly. Valley vineyardists claim this sort of thinking is based on the "challenge and response" theory advocated by European winemakers, who believe that the vine has to "struggle" to produce great wine. To their way of thinking, the best fruit grows in the best conditions; a vine, properly pruned, produces the finest grapes not when it is starved, but when vineyard conditions are optimal. They close their argument with the weighty assertion that, in any event, the greatest Cabernets from Napa Valley have always come from the valley floor.

Regardless of their differences of opinion, the winemakers of the Napa Valley are a cooperative lot, and exchange advice, information, and equipment readily. Winemakers here help each other out, like nineteenth-century farmers on the frontier. They borrow each other's equipment, buy, sell, and trade grapes or batches of wine, and help each other make wine. A winemaker may borrow the use of someone's fermentor, another may persuade a winery to sell him a particular lot of wine that would give his own the balance his needs. As one prominent Napa Valley winemaker puts it, "We're in competition with each other, not against each other."

The question of whether there is a characteristic style to Napa Valley wines is one which the great diversity of opinion on winemaking techniques makes it very difficult to answer. It is true, however, that the most adventurous, experimental wines in California are not made here. Other areas in California—notably the small wineries in the Santa Cruz mountains—make California's most dramatic and unusual wines. But no area surpasses the Napa Valley's ability to produce fine wines of polished sophistication; the whites are typically clean, fruity, and aromatic; the reds fat, full, and supple. While extraordinary wines from almost every variety grown in California have been grown and produced in the Napa Valley, its best efforts seem concentrated on Cabernet Sauvignon, long its classic wine, and its new star, Chardonnay; both are often big, full, and magnificent.

Suggested Samplings

Anyone wishing to sample some of the current high points of the region's wine production will certainly find some of them among the following types and producers. These are offered as a starting point, not a definitive list of the best, and readers are encouraged to go on and explore for themselves. Bear in mind that some of these wines are produced in small quantities and consequently may not be easy to find; many of them are readily available, however, at least in major U.S. cities.

RED:

Cabernet Sauvignon
Beaulieu Vineyard Private Reserve
Chappellet
Clos du Val
Freemark Abbey
Heitz Cellars
Inglenook Cask
Louis M. Martini
Mayacamas
Robert Mondavi
Stag's Leap Wine Cellars
Sterling Vineyards

Pinot Noir
Beaulieu Vineyard
Heitz Cellars

Zinfandel
Clos du Val
Louis M. Martini
Sutter Home

Gamay
Robert Mondavi

Barbera
Louis M. Martini

WHITE:

(Pinot) Chardonnay
Beaulieu Vineyard

Chateau Montelena
Freemark Abbey
Heitz Cellars
Mayacamas
Robert Mondavi
Spring Mountain
Stony Hill

White (Johannisberg) Riesling:
Freemark Abbey
Heitz Cellars
Joseph Phelps
Robert Mondavi

Sauvignon Blanc
Robert Mondavi (Fumé Blanc)
Sterling Vineyards (Blanc de Sauvignon)

Chenin Blanc
Chappellet
Charles Krug
Christian Brothers (Pineau de la Loire)

Gewürztraminer
Louis M. Martini

OTHER:
Sparkling Wine
Beaulieu Vineyard
Domaine Chandon
Hanns Kornell
Schramsberg

Rosés
Beaulieu Vineyard Beaurosé
Christian Brothers La Salle Rosé

These and other wines are discussed in the following pages, which cover some three dozen Napa wineries, starting with the northernmost ones near Calistoga and working down the valley in a roughly zigzag fashion. Some of the newest wineries are treated together.

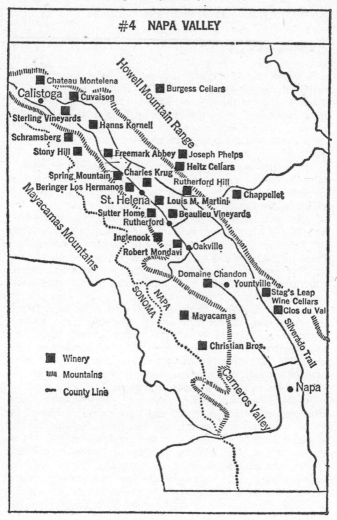

#4 NAPA VALLEY

Howell Mountain Range

Chateau Montelena
Burgess Cellars
Calistoga
Cuvaison
Sterling Vineyards
Hanns Kornell
Schramsberg
Stony Hill
Freemark Abbey
Joseph Phelps
Heitz Cellars
Charles Krug
Spring Mountain
Rutherford Hill
Beringer Los Hermanos
St. Helena
Louis M. Martini
Chappellet
Sutter Home
Beaulieu Vineyards
Rutherford
Inglenook
Robert Mondavi
Oakville
Mayacamas Mountains

Domaine Chandon
Yountville
Stag's Leap Wine Cellars
Clos du Val

SONOMA
NAPA
Mayacamas

Christian Bros.

Silverado Trail

Carneros Valley

Napa

■ Winery
mm Mountains
••• County Line

Principal Wineries

Schramsberg Vineyards

Schramsberg, first established in 1862, was one of California's pioneer wineries, and the first hillside vineyard in the Napa Valley. In the late nineteenth century, its wines had a great reputation and were regularly shipped to England and France. Twice fallen into decay, it has been restored under its present owners to a considerable measure of its former glory.

Near the town of Calistoga, Schramsberg occupies a hillside position on the forested slopes of Mount Diamond some five hundred feet above the valley floor. Its Victorian mansion, flanked by palms, and its ten thousand square feet of rock tunnels dug into the hillsides date from the 1870's and 1880's when Jacob Schram, a German immigrant from the Rhineland, used Chinese labor to transform Schramsberg from a wilderness plot granted him by the government to one of the most famed wineries of its day. Robert Louis Stevenson visited Schramsberg in 1880, and described it enthusiastically in his *Silverado Squatters.*

But after Schram's death in 1904, the vines went largely untended and the property was finally sold for a summer home at the start of Prohibition. After Repeal, there were two abortive attempts under two different owners, in 1940 and 1951, to revive the winery; the first, as an aging cellar, and the second, to make champagne—something Schram had never done. In 1960 the winery was closed.

In 1965, Jack L. Davies, a former metals industry executive, management consultant, and wine lover, purchased the estate with his wife and a college friend, moved into the house with his family, and as managing director, began to revive both the label and the reputation. Davies makes only bottle-fermented sparkling wine according to the *méthode champenoise*, and by utilizing the best modern equipment, enological advice, and quality grapes—in short, by taking no shortcuts—has produced what many wine lovers consider the finest sparkling wine in America.

Schramsberg's production is very small, under ten thousand cases a year at present. Davies buys most of his grapes from various vineyards in the valley, and in 1972 began supplementing his supply from Schramsberg's replanted vineyards of Chardonnay and Pinot noir. Davies has no plans for large-scale expansion; he believes the only reason for a small winery to exist is to offer something distinctive, and this requires specialization.

THE WINES:

There are three basic Schramsberg champagnes, all vintage-dated. The first is Schramsberg's principal wine, Blanc de Blancs, made primarily from Chardonnay with some Pinot blanc, and aged for two years (eventually it will be aged three years) on the yeast. I have had a number of vintages of this wine, and its tart, crisp, elegant character, light body, and lingering vinosity compare favorably with fine (though not the finest) French Champagne—a feat rarely equaled by American sparkling wines. Davies also selects the best lot of each vintage of Blanc de Blancs and ages it for an additional year on the yeast for more intense yeast flavor and nose; these bottles carry the additional label, "Reserve Cuvée."

Schramsberg's second wine is the Cuvée de Gamay, a medium-bodied, dry, and fruity wine with a lovely nose made from the free run juice of the Napa Gamay with a small amount of Pinot noir to give it an attractive salmon color. Schramsberg's third and most impressive wine is the Blanc de Noir. This pink-gold wine (shown off handsomely by its clear bottle) is made from about seventy percent of the juice of Pinot noir and thirty percent Chardonnay. Like the Reserve Cuvée, it is aged three years on the yeast (future vintages will be aged four). The several vintages I've tried have been beautifully made, although the '72, as one might expect from the vintage, was lighter than previous years. At its best, this wine has fine crisping bubbles that accentuate a deep, rich, lingering flavor and bring out a complex, yeasty nose.

Davies also offers a dessert champagne labeled Crémant (because it has only half the normal effervescence) Demi-Sec (half-sweet). Made from Flora (a Traminer-type grape developed by the University of California), it is very pleasant and fruity-sweet, with a touch of spice.

With the exception of the Crémant, there are no indications of sweetness—"Brut," "Extra Dry," etcetera—on the Schramsberg labels because they are all, according to Davies, "finished midway in the Brut scale."

Chateau Montelena

Chateau Montelena is another revived winery, this one at
the foot of Mt. St. Helena near Calistoga. The massive winery
with its castle-like turrets was built in 1882; in 1947 a
Chinese engineer bought the then defunct winery and added
Oriental water gardens and a five-acre lake. The Lee Paschich
family bought the imposing building in 1968 and began replanting the property's one hundred acres of vineyards. In
1972 Paschich brought in several more partners and an experienced California winemaker, Miljenko Grgich; by the
1973 season, the winery was in full operation.

THE WINES:

For a winery only a few years old, Chateau Montelena
has already gained an enviable reputation for the four wines
it offers under the Chateau Montelena label—Cabernet Sauvignon, Zinfandel, Chardonnay, and Johannisberg Riesling.
The winery supplements its own grapes with purchases from
the Alexander Valley in Sonoma. The wines, judging by the
samples of the '75 Johannisberg Riesling, the '73 Cabernet
Sauvignon, two vintages of Zinfandel, and four of the
Chardonnay that I have tasted, range from very fine, well-
made wines of their type to truly outstanding examples. This
latter praise belongs to the rich, ripe, fleshy '74 Zinfandel
and the beautifully balanced Chardonnays, with their expansive fruit-and-oak aroma and elegant body. The '73 is wonderfully stylish (as several well-publicized blind tastings have
confirmed), the '74 bigger and more impressive, and the
youthful '75 already shows considerable charm.

A second label, Silverado Cellars, is used for wines not
considered up to the Chateau Montelena standard.

Hanns Kornell Champagne Cellars

East from Schramsberg on the Napa Valley floor are the
cellars of Hanns Kornell, the latest in a succession of owners
since the 1880's of the Larkmead vineyard property. Hanns
J. Kornell's father and grandfather made wine and champagne
in Germany, and Kornell himself studied enology at Geisenheim, then worked at several European wineries until 1939,
when he fled Germany.

Kornell hitchhiked from New York to California and

worked at a succession of wineries; in the forties he made wine and champagne in Kentucky and Missouri, but returned to California in 1952 to lease a run-down winery in Sonoma and make his own champagnes. Six years later he was able to buy the Larkmead property, and by continuing his typical fourteen-hour workday, has now built up an inventory of some one and a half million bottles of aging champagne in his cellars. Kornell's expertise in making bottle-fermented champagne is widely appreciated, and he makes or finishes a number of champagnes for other wineries to sell under their own label.

THE WINES:

Although Kornell offers a line of eight still wines (Riesling, Cabernet, burgundy, etcetera) that he selects from other wineries to sell under his label, his principal and by far his best products are his champagnes, all non-vintage. His Brut champagne ranks with the better American sparkling wines —clean, crisp, lightly fruity, almost zesty in fact, and finely bubbled, although somewhat lacking in weight and character.

Kornell buys his grapes from a number of growers, and is partial to light fruity wines in his base wine; his Sehr Trocken (very dry) champagne, for example, uses White Riesling as a base wine. Aged seven (!) years on the yeast before disgorging, it has a complex and intriguing scent, but its light, leafy flavor is disappointing, and its severe dryness would probably strike most palates as excessively austere, perhaps bitter. It does, however, make an excellent aperitif wine.

Sterling Vineyards

Among the larger new wineries that have been bonded in recent years, Sterling is one of the most impressive. Peter Newton, an Englishman who came to the U.S. in 1951 and formed Sterling International, a large San Francisco paper company, had always been interested in fine wine. In 1964 he became interested in grape-growing, and began buying vineyard land near Calistoga (Region III). By the late sixties, Newton and his partners, Michael Stone and Martin Waterfield, began laying plans for a winery with an eventual seventy-five thousand cases a year production. Construction began in 1971 on what is now one of the most spectacular winery complexes in the Napa Valley. Looking something

like a Mediterranean monastery, the white buildings with
their bell towers sit astride a 250-foot-high pine-covered hill
in the middle of some four hundred acres of vineyards. Visitors have to park below and take an aerial tramway to the
winery, but there they are treated to a view that looks down
almost the entire length of the valley.

THE WINES:

The first Sterling wines date from the '69 vintage, and
from that time to the present they have been well-made,
complex, and distinctive; most are produced entirely from
grapes grown in the winery's own surrounding vineyards.
Sterling's talented young winemaker, Ric Forman, closely
follows classic Bordeaux techniques in making the Cabernet
and Merlot wines which comprise the bulk of the winery's
production. All the Sterling Cabernets are blended with a
good proportion of Merlot—up to thirty percent—and what
Merlot is left is made into a tremendously rich, heady,
superb wine, one that has stood up to the best Pomerols.

With the '73 vintage, Forman began a policy of selecting
outstanding lots of the Cabernet Sauvignon for a "Private
Reserve" Cabernet that receives additional aging in small
oak and is never filtered, only lightly fined. The '73 Private
Reserve had a deep, full, herbaceous nose, excellent balance,
austere tannin at this point, and fine, concentrated, lingering
flavor; it should make one of the most supple and memorable
of the '73 Napa Valley Cabernets. An inky-dark, marvelously
intense out-of-the-barrel sample of the '75 final blend, and
a fruitier, less massive, but impressive sample of the '76 final
blend, both tried in early 1977, indicated that Forman does
not intend to sacrifice style and finesse for mere weight and
power. The regular release Cabernets are made in much the
same elegant style, but don't have the same richness or concentration of flavor. So far, Sterling's other red, the Pinot
Noir, is not in the same league with the Cabernet and Merlot.

Forman also makes a lively Cabernet Rosé, and in 1976
he made a spicy, tart, characterful Cabernet Blanc—though
whether a white Cabernet Sauvignon is a worthwhile addition
to the ranks of California wines remains to be seen. Of the
generally fine whites Sterling offers, the most interesting is
the Sauvignon Blanc, surely one of the finest examples of
this varietal in California. The '75, which contains fifteen percent Sémillon, featured a lively, almost flowery, herbaceous

aroma with hints of oak and figs and a most attractive, lingering, spicy flavor set off by a fine, racy acidity.

A second line of ordinary to good inexpensive wines made from grapes purchased from local growers is offered under the Sterling Cellars label, which, confusingly, closely resembles the Sterling Vineyards label.

Cuvaison

Cuvaison was begun in 1970 by physicist Thomas Cottrell and sold in 1973 to the CT Corporation. Until its new Spanish-modern winery building on the Silverado Trail south of Calistoga was completed recently, a tiny wood-frame building housed the office, while most of the winery equipment stood out in the open. Cuvaison has forty acres of vineyards and buys additional grapes from growers. In 1974, veteran winemaker Philip Togni joined the winery.

THE WINES:

Under Cottrell, Cuvaison produced small quantities of a few varietals in a light, delicate style. The strong, heavy style that Togni favors, however, is already apparent in one of the three wines (Chardonnay, Cabernet Sauvignon, and Zinfandel) on which the winery will now concentrate: the '75 Chardonnay had a powerful, pungent aroma overlaid with oak and a rich, intense flavor, while a barrel sample of one wine that will eventually be blended to make up the '76 was even darker and heavier. The transition-period red wines seem less satisfactory: a Cabernet blend of the '73 and '74 vintages had a strange, earthy, cocoa-like note to the nose and a rather bitter-sweet finish; I found the '73 Zinfandel, despite its intensity, somewhat alcoholic and aggressive in flavor, although time may harmonize these elements and bring out subtleties. With its new owners and new winemaker, however, Cuvaison is a label to watch.

Stony Hill Vineyard

The proof of a vineyard's potential must lie in a taste of the best wine that can be made from grapes grown on it. To judge from the wines made from grapes grown in the Stony Hill vineyards, these thirty-eight acres are blessed with some of the best grape-growing conditions in California. Only white wine grapes—Chardonnay, White Riesling Sémillon, Gewürztraminer—are grown on the property some six hundred feet above the floor of the Napa Valley, between Spring and Diamond Mountains.

Stony Hill's potential as a vineyard, however, was discovered largely by accident. When Frederick McCrea, a former vice-president and manager of the San Francisco office of McCann-Erickson, and his wife Eleanor purchased the property in 1943, they had in mind nothing more than a summer home. Although it had been homesteaded years before, no grapes had been grown on the property until the McCreas experimented with several varieties and finally built a small winery to take in the first harvest in 1951. Since then, Stony Hill's reputation has grown enormously despite its very small production. It is not really surprising, however, since Fred McCrea was a gentleman winemaker with no interest in wine except to make the best. Mr. McCrea died January 1, 1977; the winery remains in family hands.

THE WINES:

Stony Hill's production is miniscule—about twenty-five hundred cases a year—about a thousand cases of top-notch Chardonnay and the rest divided between two merely very excellent wines, a Gewürztraminer and a White Riesling. Because the McCreas have never had any desire to expand Stony Hill, the entire output is sold each year in case lots to those on the winery's overcrowded mailing list. Stony Hill is carried in few retail outlets and on the wine lists of a few California restaurants. Its general unavailability gives it a certain cachet, but Stony Hill's reputation is based on more than scarcity. The '74 Chardonnay, for example, has the impressive balance of fruit and acid, fine, lingering flavor, light hint of oak, and great straightforward cleanness of character typical of this outstanding vineyard's best wine. More than most Chardonnays, Stony Hill develops marvelously in the bottle, and those fortunate enough to find some should give it several years to mature.

Freemark Abbey Winery

Freemark Abbey, like a great many new wineries in California, is a revived winery. The massive stone building right off Highway 29 a few miles north of St. Helena was built in

1890 by an Italian immigrant; in 1939 the winery was sold to a group of partners who combined parts of their names to coin "Freemark Abbey." (They were not monks.) In 1967 a group of seven partners, including several top growers in the valley (Charles Carpy, the managing partner, Frank Wood, and William Jaeger), leased the building, took over the winery, kept the name, and began making wine from some eight hundred acres of prime vineyard land that they control. Another partner is Bradford Webb, a biochemist and enologist well-known for his role as winemaker at the prestigious Hanzell winery in Sonoma. Currently the upper stories of the winery house a candle and gourmet shop and an antique store, among other enterprises, doing a brisk tourist trade. But in the hand-dug cellars below, Freemark Abbey concentrates on serious winemaking.

THE WINES:

In the ten years since the formation of its present partnership, Freemark Abbey has stayed with its original intention—to produce only a short list of top-quality varietal wines. Because of its small production (about twenty thousand cases a year) and its ability to draw on considerable winemaking talent and the best grapes produced by the extensive vineyards owned by its partners (as well as those from a few other top-notch vineyards), Freemark has been able to become one of the few California wineries that consistently produce both reds and whites of superlative quality. From 1968 on, a series of rich and stylish Chardonnays were produced; of the recent vintages, the ripe, round, generous '74 and the spicy, intense '75, set off with just the right amount of oak, should make grand bottles in just a few years. Both have enough polish and finesse to be enjoyed right now, however. The '76, sampled from the barrel, is big, flavorful, and very promising.

Two versions of the winery's other *grand vin*, Cabernet, are produced, both blended with small percentages of Merlot: the light but frequently elegant and complex regular release (the attractive, charming '73 stands out in particular); and the extraordinary Cabernet Bosché, one of the great Cabernets of the Napa Valley. The grapes for the latter come from an outstanding fifteen-acre Rutherford vineyard; in a great year, like 1970, they yield a wine of incredible richness and texture, with complex, lingering flavors and a heady, herbaceous aroma. The '71 and '72 vintages of both the regular release and the Bosché are thin and show the limitations of the vintage. The '73 Bosché is also, alas, quite light.

Freemark also offers a Pinot Noir. This wine has been quite light in certain years: The '73 was simply labeled "Red Table Wine" so as not to arouse unwarranted expectations. The '74, though somewhat light, has a moderately complex flavor and an attractive nose. The winery has understandably gained more attention for its rich, powerful, peppery-spicy Petite Sirahs.

Freemark offers one more wine, a Johannisberg Riesling. Through 1972 these were very un-Germanic in character— big, mouth-filling, bone-dry, even austere. In 1973, however, the grapes were infected with botrytis. This allowed the winery to produce a honey-scented, fabulously rich, golden, sweet wine, christened, for the occasion, "Edelwein." Depending on harvest conditions, Freemark's Rieslings can be expected to swing between the two styles.

Charles Krug Winery

The Charles Krug winery shares with the Louis M. Martini winery the distinction of being one of the largest family-owned premium wineries in the Napa Valley. Each makes a vast line of wines, from jug wines to occasional bottles that rank among California's greatest. But the Krug winery has a much longer history, although, like so many California wineries, a checkered one under several owners.

The Krug name dates from 1861, when Charles Krug, a Prussian immigrant, erected the original winery and set out his vines on the property. In 1874 a fire destroyed everything except the carriage house (now housing a cooperage), but Krug built another winery (still standing). By 1880 he made nearly three hundred thousand gallons a year of highly praised wines and even shipped some of them to Europe.

After phylloxera destroyed the vineyards of "The Wine King of Napa Valley," as Krug was called, the winery went into a decline; Charles Krug died in 1892 and his two daughters, with the help of his nephew, attempted to run the estate with dwindling success. It passed into other hands, and was closed with Prohibition. After Repeal, it was leased to another winery, and then in 1943 was sold to Cesare Mondavi and Sons. The Mondavi family still owns Krug, and is responsible for its rebirth and its present reputation.

Cesare Mondavi had shipped grapes in Lodi and Fresno, and had made bulk wine at the Acampo winery after Repeal, when at the urging of his sons Peter and Robert, he purchased a bulk winery in St. Helena, and then in 1943, the Krug ranch and a hundred acres of vineyard for seventy-five thousand dollars. The Mondavis worked hard to gain a reputation for the Krug wines, and in 1938 had been the first California vintners to pioneer in the cold fermentation techniques put forth by Dr. Cruess of the University of California.

Control of fermentation temperature is now a widely used vinification technique that helps insure quality in wine and especially the fragrance of white wines. The winery now boasts some of the most impressive large equipment in the valley, including giant glass-lined tanks to hold hundreds of thousands of gallons of wine after it has aged a precise time in wood and while it waits to be bottled—merely one example of their use of technology to insure control of quality. The winery is one of the largest producers in the valley, and now owns over a thousand acres of Napa vineyards, but only a fifth of its production is bottled under the Charles Krug label; the rest is sold under lesser brands—"CK," "Napa Vista," and "Mondavi Vineyards"—or sold in bulk to other wineries.

Cesare Mondavi died in 1959, and in 1966 Robert Mondavi left the Krug winery to start his own enterprise, which markets wines under his own name. Peter Mondavi manages the Charles Krug enterprise, but as this book goes to press, the Mondavi family is in litigation over control of the winery; it may be years before any final settlement is reached.

THE WINES:

While the CK and Mondavi Vineyards lines of jug wines offer competitive to good value compared with the jug wines of other California wineries, the Charles Krug line of some ten generics and sixteen varietals are comparable to the good-to-fine premium wines of the large Napa Valley wineries like Beaulieu, Louis M. Martini, and Inglenook. Most are varietally labeled, some non-vintaged, while some of the generics are vintage dated.

The Charles Krug whites are typically quite good, crisp, fragrant, and often show attractive spiciness. The non-vintage Chenin Blanc in some bottlings is absolutely first-rate, with a luscious balance of acidity and soft fruitness. The non-vintage Johannisberg Riesling deserves similar praise.

I find the reds less exciting although they are always well-made, reliable, and often very good. The vintage selection Cabernet can be quite fine, however, and the regular release Cabernet (notably the recent '73) is typically light, stylish, and attractive.

Spring Mountain Vineyards

Spring Mountain Vineyards is the creation of Michael Robbins, a former Los Angeles businessman who brought his winemaking ambitions to the Napa Valley in 1968, when he began his winery in the basement of a restored Victorian home north of St. Helena. By 1975 he had moved his operation closer to its namesake: He purchased the former Parrott estate on Spring Mountain, started replanting the once famed vineyards, and began building an elegant winery, complete with hand-dug tunnels. Robbins owns several choice vineyards in the valley—about one hundred and ten acres in all—and by careful blending and rigorous insistence on quality he has already gained a considerable reputation for his wines.

THE WINES:

Spring Mountain's current production of some ten thousand cases a year consists of three wines—a classically proportioned Cabernet Sauvignon, a superb, intense Sauvignon Blanc, and an elegant Chardonnay. Fine as the first two wines are, the Chardonnay at its best is that rarity, a beautiful wine: The '73 in particular offered an expansive floral-spicy aroma with the subtle vanillan hints of restrained oak aging and a long, harmonious flavor that left a delightful, faintly spicy, aftertaste. Barrel samples of some of the wines that will go to make up the final blend of the '76 Chardonnay promise richness and depth, racy acidity, and more of that almost woodland-floral Chardonnay aroma that distinguishes Spring Mountain's best white.

Beringer/Los Hermanos Vineyards

Beringer is the oldest continuous wine-grower in the valley; it has never missed a vintage since 1879 (it made sacramental wines during Prohibition). Jacob and Frederick Beringer came from the Rheingau, and Jacob, who had worked as a winemaker in Germany, worked at the Charles Krug winery from 1872 to 1878 under that early Napa Valley pioneer, while the brothers' own aging tunnels and winery were being completed nearby. Together the Beringers built the "Rhine House," a Gothic-looking architectural exercise in nostalgia, which today, because of its roadside location just north of St. Helena, is an enormously popular tourist attraction. The mansion is now largely devoted to tasting rooms and gathering groups for tours of its thousand-foot-long tunnels.

The winery was sold to the Nestlé corporation in 1970, along with some seven hundred acres of vineyards scattered around the valley. Nestlé invested a good deal of money for needed improvements, but in late 1973 had to divest itself of U.S. winemaking interests due to regulatory conflicts with its other divisions. Wine World Inc. of San Francisco are the new owners.

THE WINES:

Before the change of hands in 1970, Beringer's wines struck me as sound, cleanly made, and quite unexciting picnic fare. The wines produced under the new Beringer labels, however, seem to be improving, but are still uneven. The non-vintage Riesling and Fumé Blanc, for example, are quite undistinguished, barely out of the jug-wine class, and the non-vintage Traubengold, "a medium dry California Riesling," was coarse and greeny, with a bitter backbite. But I found the '73 Beringer Napa Valley Cabernet Sauvignon round, soft, and fruity, with hints of olives, when I sampled it in the spring of 1977, and the '74 Centennial Cask Selection Chardonnay was surprisingly characterful, well-balanced, and flavorful.

In the Los Hermanos line (a label Beringer uses for its inexpensive blends and jugs) the Chardonnay blend—at least the one I sampled in early 1977—was excellent, with a pleasant pungent-apple aroma and a full-bodied flavor, albeit a very slight bitterness to the finish; nonetheless, it was an extremely good wine for the price.

Louis M. Martini Winery

Just off the highway a few miles south of St. Helena are the imposing concrete hangars that house the Louis M. Martini winery. The building, though partly covered with ivy, and the setting, next to a railroad track, are unromantic, but the Martini reputation generates its own aura, for Louis M. Martini is one of the most prestigious of the large premium California wineries still in family hands.

Louis M. Martini was born in 1887 on the Italian Riviera, and came to America at the turn of the century to join his father selling fish in San Francisco. In 1906 his father started a winery and sent Louis back to Italy for eight months to learn winemaking. Louis later worked for a variety of California wineries and finally built one at Kingsburg in the San Joaquin Valley to make sweet wines and brandy.

At Repeal, Martini established the present winery in St. Helena and by the 1940's had established the reputation of the winery. In 1960 (at seventy-three) he stepped down and his son, Louis P. Martini, now runs the winery. The elder Martini died in 1974. The Martinis own almost nine hundred acres of prime vineyard land in Napa and Sonoma, in various locations and microclimates—in St. Helena along the Mayacamas foothills, on the Russian River in Sonoma, in the Carneros district south of Napa, a thousand feet up the Mayacamas range, and elsewhere in the area—all planted to a variety of grapes. The wines from these vineyards are often blended in each vintage to produce the thirty-odd wines Martini offers.

THE WINES:

Louis M. Martini produces about a dozen vintage-dated varietals, a number of generic and dessert wines, as well as "special selection" and "private reserve" wines. The "special selection" wines are just that, special lots of especially promising wine, often a cask from a single vineyard, sometimes more, that is handled apart from the rest; these are only made in outstanding years. "Private Reserve" wines are simply small amounts of the regular release wines which have been set apart at the winery for extra bottle age.

Martini's reputation is built on its reds, which are made in a remarkable style that allows them to be attractive when released for sale, yet leaves them sufficient stuffing to develop and improve with several years further aging. Some three-quarters of the winery's current 270,000-cases-a-year production is devoted to reds, all of which spend several years in large redwood and oak cooperage to give them round, soft appeal without imparting a distinct oaky overtone.

The fruity Barbera—one of the state's finest examples of this varietal—can be rather forceful and rough when young, but ages particularly well; my last '64 was magnificent drinking a year ago and had just reached maturity. The Martini Zinfandel, considered something of a benchmark for the grape, is vinified in a moderately light style to emphasize its spicy fruitiness and is at its best some four to six years after the vintage. The Pinot Noir can be very good and quite satisfying, but as with so many California examples of this varietal, rarely superb. The newly introduced Gamay Beaujolais actually contains some forty percent Pinot Noir; the '74 is delightful—round, full, fruity, a little heavier than many Gamays.

The regular release Cabernet Sauvignon is made in a light style for early drinkability, and although always well-balanced, can be a bit short on flavor and complexity except in the best vintages, such as '70. The "special selection" Cabernet Sauvignon is a different sort of creature; it can have the kind of concentration and balance that unfolds into magnificent drinking with a decade or more of aging. The "special selection" wines, however, rarely appear on the retail market, as there is usually only enough to sell at the winery.

I find the whites in general less successful than the reds, though the Gewürztraminer can be very nice, and the Folle Blanche consistently crisp, acid, and refreshing. The Chardonnay is improving markedly.

Sutter Home Winery

Sutter Home Winery, a small operation with a giant wine barrel facade, sits across the highway from the massive concrete hangars of Louis M. Martini near St. Helena. Wine enthusiasts might mistakenly assume that it caters strictly to locals who come to fill up their gallon jugs with country red from a redwood tank, and pass it by on their way to more obvious points of wine interest.

Parts of the winery were built in 1874, but it acquired its present name from John Sutter, who started his own winery in 1890 and moved to the present winery in 1906. The Trinchero family has owned Sutter Home since the mid-1940's. Sutter Home for years bought grapes from a variety of growers and like almost every winery in the days before the wine boom, turned out a line of wines of every description: It used to offer forty-seven different wines and even made vinegar.

In the mid-sixties when Napa Valley grape prices began soaring, the Trincheros began looking elsewhere for other sources of quality grapes. They found neglected but promising vineyards in Amador County in the foothills of the Sierras northeast of Sacramento. Some of the vineyards dated back into the nineteenth century, and due to the soil, climate, and advanced age of the vines—in some cases, apparently, over eighty years—the yield was extremely small. Sutter Home contracted with the Deaver vineyard for their '68 and succeeding crop, and the enormous success of the '68 and succeeding Zinfandels have encouraged the Trincheros to specialize in Zinfandels from such vineyards.

THE WINES:

Sutter Home now produces around fifteen thousand cases of its first-rate Zinfandel, and small amounts of a White Zinfandel and a popular Moscato Amabile. This winery was one of the first to make big, heavy, tannic Zinfandels—in other words, to treat Zinfandel as a serious grape—and their initial effort in this style, the 1968 Deaver Vineyard Lot No. 2 Zinfandel, was a superb, deep, rich, memorable wine, with plenty of tannin and an impressive finish. The '72 from this vineyard was light in body and not in the same league as examples from better years, but still offered an intriguing nose that evolved into an attractive earth-and-fruit mélange after several hours. It may develop more, but is probably best enjoyed now, while looking forward to the '73 and '74.

Heitz Wine Cellars

Although Heitz Cellars was founded a little over fifteen years ago, it has already gained a reputation for producing some of the finest Cabernet Sauvignons and Chardonnays in the country. A small, family-run operation, it produces a surprisingly extensive list of wines, partly because of the way in which its operations began.

Joe Heitz, the founder and winemaker, grew up on a farm in Illinois and had wanted to be a veterinarian. Stationed in Fresno in World War II, he worked on the base during the day, and got a part-time job at a winery at night. When he decided on a career in wine, he studied enology at the University of California at Davis, and later went on to teach viticulture and enology at Fresno. He has worked for the largest

California wineries, among them E & J Gallo and Italian Swiss Colony, and smaller premium wineries; he was assistant winemaker for seven years at Beaulieu Vineyards under its eminent winemaster André Tchelistcheff.

Joe Heitz has attained his present preeminent position through little else than hard work and his extraordinary skills as a winemaker; today he enjoys, in fact, a reputation among many as the best winemaker in Napa Valley.

After years of working at other wineries, Heitz struck out on his own, and in 1961 he purchased a small roadside winery and plot of grapes just south of St. Helena, which had produced a single wine, a Grignolino, sold under the "Only One" brand. Heitz and his wife Alice worked hard to develop the business, and bought grapes from growers to make wine, as well as wine in the cask from other wineries to age, blend, and bottle in their own cellars. Because of his skill as a winemaker, Heitz gained a great reputation for bringing out the full potential of wines that he selected, matured, and bottled under his own label. He soon began looking for larger quarters to expand his production, and after much searching bought Spring Valley Farm in 1964, which had become a cattle ranch after the winemaking Rossi family sold it in the 1920's. The property consists of a hundred and sixty acres, and Heitz is in the process of replanting the original ninety acres of vineyard. There are also now ten acres of vines attached to the highway winery in which Heitz established his cellars. His operation has grown considerably, to the point where he now produces up to twenty thousand cases of wine annually.

His winery began as and still is largely a cellar operation in which he buys grapes, or wine in bulk to make, age, and bottle himself. Heitz obtains grapes from some of the best vineyards in Napa and elsewhere, and often identifies them on his label.

THE WINES:

Heitz Cellars offers a long line of wines for a small winery—chablis, burgundy, champagne, a number of non-vintage varietals, as well as the "top varietals," some from specific vineyards. Heitz's less ambitious wines are sometimes very good for their price and often exhibit character not expected and not usually found in inexpensive table wines. His Barbera, burgundy, and Grignolino are fruity, light, very enjoyable table wines, and his chablis is better than most California wines of this type, though unremarkable.

Heitz may someday limit his production to three or four wines—the ones that his fame rests upon: Cabernet Sauvignon, Chardonnay, Johannisberg Riesling, and Pinot Noir. His Riesling is often very good, in the typical "big" California style of this varietal. The vintages I have sampled from '68 to '76 have had full flavor and good balance, with a strong flowery varietal aroma, and attractive tart fruitiness. His Pinot Noir can be very fine; I particularly remember the '68 vintage with its complex, lingering flavors, and an exotic spicy nose. But as Heitz purposely makes his Pinot Noir to be drunk young, in order to emphasize its lively delicious suppleness, it does not last well. That particular vintage is now over the hill.

His Chardonnays and Cabernet Sauvignons, however, are absolutely first-rate wines. The Chardonnays typically carry a lot number indicating origin. The Z-lot Chardonnays, for example, come from grapes grown in the Zinfandel Associates vineyard near his Spring Valley winery. The 1968 Lot Z-82 Chardonnay, sampled on a number of occasions, stands out in my mind as one of the greatest white wines I've ever tasted. Golden, round, unified, almost oily on the tongue, and perfectly balanced in all respects, it combined great finesse, richness, and power with a marvelous deep nose and a complex, lingering finish. That overwhelming wine has topped the finest French White Burgundies at my table many times. Subsequent vintages of the Z-lot Chardonnays, while less opulent, have all been outstanding, ranking with the state's best in most vintages. Alas, due to Pierce's disease, the vineyard supplying the grapes for this wine recently had to be pulled out; the '76 vintage will be the last of the Z-lot Chardonnays. But there will certainly be future Heitz Chardonnays; Heitz has already planted twelve of his own acres to the grape.

The Cabernet Sauvignons come in two versions—a regular release and one from a special twelve-acre Oakville vineyard, "Martha's Vineyard." In 1968, when a dozen or more California wineries turned out classic Cabernets, Heitz's regular release was near or at the top of the heap. On a recent tasting, this dark ruby wine had a most intriguingly complex, subtle, yet deep varietal nose overlaid with a mélange of perfume-earth-cinnamon-spice nuances. With a deep, rich flavor that spread on the palate, the wine left an impression of great harmony and is probably at its peak now. The '72, the latest vintage available, is a light but lovely wine with a most attractive aroma; it will doubtless mature quickly.

Overshadowing the superb regular release Cabernet Sauvignon is the "Martha's Vineyard" Cabernet. Heitz makes only about a thousand cases of this unique wine each year, and the praise which has been heaped upon it is extraordinary. The wine, however, lives up to its billing, and the '68, '69, and '70 have frequently been ranked above the best of Bordeaux in blind tastings. With their deep, rich, minty-spicy, bay-leaf aroma and enormous mouth-filling concentration of fruit and flavor, they are unmistakably great, but too rich, ripe, and individual to be easily mistaken for Bordeaux. The only vintage of this grand Cabernet that appears anywhere near maturity is the "light" '67. (Heitz did not make a '71 Cabernet under the "Martha's Vineyard" label as he did not feel the resulting wine was up to standard.) The '72, tasted in the spring of 1977, is by no means a lightweight; it has an abundance and depth of flavor similar to the '70, marking it as one of this difficult vintage's few successes.

A number of wineries now produce big, dramatic wines, and while Heitz's can certainly be that, too, at their best they possess in addition those elusive hallmarks of greatness so difficult to achieve: style, complexity, and finesse.

Inglenook Vineyards

The history of Inglenook closely follows the history of the California wine industry; founded in the nineteenth century, it has now become one of the state's larger premium wineries. Inglenook is one of the oldest labels in the valley and like Beaulieu, has enjoyed a great reputation over the years, especially for its Cabernet Sauvignon. Inglenook was the creation of Captain Gustave Niebaum, a native of Finland, who made a fortune in his early twenties in the Alaska fur trade and became interested in wine during a number of trips to Europe. In 1879 he purchased a vineyard in Rutherford called "Inglenook," retained the name, and set about building a showcase winery. Niebaum was in a sense a "gentleman winemaker" as he was only interested in producing the finest wines possible. He studied all aspects of viticulture and winemaking and made further trips to Europe to collect cuttings and study technique. By 1887 he completed the still-standing stone winery building and began building the Inglenook reputation. Niebaum was a white-glove inspector of his equipment, and only his finest wines were sold under the Inglenook label. By 1889 his wines were winning honors abroad, and some of the nineteenth-century vintages made under his reign are still alive today. The Captain died in 1908, and the husband of his widow's niece, John Daniel, ran the winery until Prohibition closed it down.

After Repeal, John Daniel, Jr., took charge of it until 1964, when he sold the winery to United Vintners, which was acquired by Heublein, Inc., in 1969. Under his direction, the winery continued its high standards; Daniel was one of the first California winemakers to use varietal labeling, and pioneered a number of new varietal wines. He also refused to bottle any of the '45 or '47 vintages of Cabernet Sauvignon under the Inglenook label because they were not up to standard. Some of the Inglenooks from the thirties to the fifties were some of the finest Cabernet Sauvignons to be produced in California; it was something of a shock, therefore, when Daniel sold Inglenook to United Vintners.

Inglenook did not take the rapid nosedive in quality that some feared would be the result of being run by a conglomerate, but what did occur was that the Inglenook line of wines, originally a dozen vintage-dated varietals, was expanded to include jug wines, north coast wines, a number of new dessert wines, and even champagne; in one year alone, 1970, it quintupled its production. Inglenook has grown from a medium-sized winery to a very large one, and the label, like that of many wineries, now stands for wines in a range of quality from fine to ordinary.

THE WINES:

Inglenook now has three distinct product lines: the "Vintage" line, made from north coast county grapes; the "Navalle" line of everyday table and jug wines made primarily from Central Valley grapes; and the "Estate Bottled" line of vintage-dated varietals from the Napa Valley. This last group is produced and bottled at the Napa winery; annual production is about two hundred thousand cases, a tenth of the Navalle production, which is bottled at United Vintners' Sonoma winery. The "Vintage" and "Navalle" wines are

average in quality, comparable to similar wines from many
of California's large and giant producers. The "Estate Bottled"
line, however, is competitive with the valley's large premium
producers.

Like most of the big Napa Valley wineries, Inglenook's
whites were not particularly fragrant and refreshing until
technological advances in winemaking, especially cold fermentation, became widespread in the sixties. Now many of
the Inglenook whites are of good quality, though often
uneven. A '75 Gewürztraminer was too varietally perfumey
for my taste, but certainly well-made. The '75 Pinot Chardonnay was excellent, featuring a pungent nose laced with
oak and fine, full flavors that need a year or so to harmonize.

Inglenook pioneered a red Italian grape, Charbono, as a
varietal, and it has been consistently popular—a hearty, tart,
full-bodied red much like Barbera that can gain a good deal
with bottle age. The '73 was fruity, racy, and rather simple.

It is with the Cabernet, and deservedly, that Inglenook
made its reputation. Of the vintages of Inglenook Cabernet
I've tried from 1933 to the present, the 1941 stands out in
my memory as an extraordinarily impressive, austere, angular, straightforward, scented Cabernet—and it is still going
strong after more than thirty years. The greatest of the Cabernets produced under J. Daniel, Jr., were sometimes aged
as long as five years in wood, starting with large casks and
then racking the wine into progressively smaller ones. Different lots were often set aside in the German manner as "cask
bottlings," and sold separately. There were sometimes several
different cask bottlings, often with a small amount of Merlot
added, as well as a regular release, and this admirable
practice is being continued. Recent cask bottlings of the
Cabernet, if not as impressive as past bottlings, have been
excellent Cabernets nonetheless. The '70 merited the praise
it received, but the current '72 cask bottling, while well-
made, is, like most '72 Napa Cabernets, very light, and
lacks intensity of flavor.

Beaulieu Vineyard

Among the larger wineries in the Napa Valley, Beaulieu
has for decades enjoyed a reputation for quality, largely due
to its great success with Cabernet Sauvignon. The plain block
buildings that house the winery are right across the highway

at Rutherford from Inglenook, its long-time competitor until they were both bought by Heublein, Inc.

Beaulieu was founded in 1900 by a Frenchman, Georges de Latour, who came to the U.S. in 1883, tried gold mining, and then, for a number of years, ran a cream of tartar business in Sonoma before purchasing an orchard near the already famous Inglenook in 1899. His wife named it Beaulieu—"beautiful place." (Since most Americans, including valley locals, mangle the pronunciation so that it comes out something like "bow-loo," the winery has for years featured its initials on its labels, and now everyone commonly refers to it as "BV.")

After making a trip to France to obtain cuttings, de Latour acquired nearby vineyards and eventually acquired the present winery buildings in 1915. Beaulieu, unlike Inglenook, stayed in business during Prohibition by making sacramental wines—something it does to this day. In 1937 Beaulieu's enologist retired and the de Latours went to France to find a successor. The man they persuaded to come to California was André Tchelistcheff, whose influence on the California wine industry in succeeding years has been as considerable as any one's. Tchelistcheff, born in 1901, left Russia with his parents in 1917 for France and later studied enology in Czechoslovakia. He came to the Napa Valley in time for the 1938 harvest and oversaw thirty-five succeeding vintages at Beaulieu until his recent retirement. Although Tchelistcheff was an advocate of specialization for wineries, BV, like every other large winery in the decades after Repeal, produced and still produces a long line of wines (about two dozen), including varietals, generics, five dessert wines, and four champagnes. Tchelistcheff believed in the potential of Cabernet Sauvignon in Napa, and persuaded de Latour to let him begin making a "private reserve" Cabernet Sauvignon which would be given special handling and additional aging. De Latour died in 1940, and the first private reserve Cabernet was released a year later. It has since become the best-known American fine wine, and certain vintages have been widely recognized as unquestionably great wines.

After George de Latour's death, the winery was run by his widow, and after her death, his daughter, Madame de Pins, and the de Pins' daughter, Mrs. Dagmar Sullivan. By the late 1960's Beaulieu had seven hundred and fifty acres of vineyards in the valley; three large blocks around Rutherford, one further toward the eastern edge of the valley, and a large tract in Carneros planted in 1963 to Pinot noir and Chardonnay. In 1969 the family sold the Beaulieu winery and vineyards to Heublein, although they retained the family estate and de Latour's original Cabernet vineyard. In 1970 André Tchelistcheff stepped down from his post as winemaster.

The impact of ownership by a large corporation has not so far been as obvious at Beaulieu as it was at Inglenook. It appears that Heublein intends to keep BV much the same as it has been, and its growth should stabilize when it reaches 250,000-cases-a-year production.

THE WINES:

BV's whites vary from unremarkable to very fine. The Johannisberg Riesling, while not distinguished, is consistently fruity and tart, with attractive varietal character; the Chardonnay can be excellent—in a good vintage, like '75, this partially fermented-in-oak white has a full, pungent varietal aroma with oak nuances, a rich, fat taste, and crisp acidity. The Brut champagne, to judge by the '71, is clean and assertive, with crisp bubbles and a dry finish.

The reds—two-thirds of the production here—are on the whole very good, although I find BV's two new "light-style" reds, the "Beau Tour" Cabernet Sauvignon and the "Beau Velours" Pinot Noir, simple and rather characterless. Beaulieu does make a good burgundy, however, an appealing rosé called "Beaurosé", and from time to time has also been very successful with that difficult grape, Pinot noir. The '68 "Beaumont" Pinot Noir was surely one of the most memorable California Pinot Noirs of recent years, but now, alas, is long past its prime.

The regular release Cabernet Sauvignon is typically well-balanced, characterful but light, and at its best within a decade after the vintage. In a strong vintage such as '74, it has good, full body and texture and ripe, round, rich Cabernet flavors.

The Private Reserve Cabernet Sauvignon seems to be keeping up to the standards it has set over the last three decades. In a fine vintage it is outstanding, and is grand drinking at maturity. When I enjoyed the marvelously rich and opulent '54 and the very harmonious '65 in the spring of 1977, both were still developing in the bottle, and the '70, the finest

Private Reserve of recent years, had an enormous depth of
ripe, round flavor and a nobly sweet lingering finish, that
promise an equally long life. This wine, far from mature,
is on par with the finest Napa Cabernets produced in that
unusually good vintage. After the cool growing season of
'71 and the rainy harvest of '72 (the latter yielded the most
anemic Private Reserve in years), the '73 vintage (sampled
just prior to its release) resulted in a lovely, charming, very
stylish Private Reserve, with the characteristic ripe, almost
buttery texture the best of BV's Cabernets have, and hints of
blackberries in the aroma.

Robert Mondavi Winery

One of the more encouraging developments among the
large wineries has been the establishment of wineries concentrating on volume production of fine vintage-dated varietals.
One such winery was founded in 1966 by Robert Mondavi.
The Mondavi family is a prominent one in the Napa Valley;
since purchasing it in 1943, they have run the Charles Krug
winery and made it into one of the larger, prestigious premium wineries of California. After more than twenty years
at Krug, Robert left his post as general manager to start his
own winery and put his own ideas about winemaking into
practice.

Inside a striking new winery building in Oakville, done in
"mission modern" style, Robert and his son Michael preside
over one of the most impressive arrays of modern winemaking equipment in the valley, including revolving fermentors,
continuous centrifuges, and the like, together with an equally
impressive array of American, Limousin, Nevers, German,
and Yugoslavian cooperage. Since 1968, the Rainier Brewing Co. of Seattle has owned a half interest, giving the
winery needed capital, but leaving the operation in Mondavi's
hands. At first the winery bought all its grapes from other
growers, but now has some eight hundred acres of vineyards,
several hundred of which lie directly behind the winery.

Mondavi's high aims and restless experimentation with
techniques, equipment, and methods from vineyard to bottle
have shown in the remarkable reputation his wines already
have. Best of all from a wine consumer's standpoint is that
the quality of his wines has not diminished as his production
has increased. The winery now produces about two hundred

and fifty thousand cases a year, and will continue to grow at a pace consistent with Mondavi's quality standards.

THE WINES:

The Robert Mondavi Winery produces some dozen vintage-dated varietal wines, all of which are usually a noticeable step above the typical Napa Valley wines put out by the larger wineries—no small accomplishment. Many formerly carried label notations such as "unfined" or "unfiltered" to indicate special handling and, by implication, a superior lot of wine. Now the term "Reserve" will tip off the wine lover that the wine behind the label is considered a cut above the regular release, though "unfiltered" and "unfined" may still be used from time to time.

The whites are especially fine here: Chardonnay, Chenin Blanc, Johannisberg Riesling, and Fumé Blanc (a dry Sauvignon Blanc) are all very good to very, very fine, varying in this range, as all fine wines do, with the vintage. The whites are all exceptionally clean, and very fragrant. Mondavi believes in aging his wines in the appropriate oak cooperage to give them added complexity—what he calls "the kiss of oak," although the Chardonnay is the only one which exhibits a very noticeable wood character.

At first Mondavi had better success with his whites than his reds, his excellent "unfined" '66 Cabernet Sauvignon notwithstanding. But his '69 Cabernet became something of a sensation. I was utterly charmed by its lovely nose, light, supple body, and marvelous olivey finish. While not the big, heavy, dark Cabernet some vintners made in this vintage, it was not the clumsy, imbalanced wine in its youth that most of those are. In early 1977, it appeared to be rapidly approaching its peak. Excluding the weak '72, the Mondavi Cabernets since then have all been very good to outstanding; the '73 is particularly well-built, stylish, and appealing, and should make a delicious bottle by, say, 1980. Mondavi considers the '74 the best Cabernet he has made, and its impressive depth of fruit, full, young, olivey aroma, and excellent structure of acid, tannin, and alcohol all promise to develop into a superbly balanced wine by the early eighties.

Fine as the regular release Cabernets have been, the "reserve" '73 and '74, which had not yet been bottled when I tasted them in early 1977, are noticeably richer and more concentrated in flavor—the '74, in fact, had positively massive dimensions and a deep, low, spreading aroma. The '75 and '76 reserves, tasted out of the barrel, were simply too inky and uncompromisingly tannic to assess adequately, but the '76 in particular seemed to have everything in abundance.

The winery's other reds include a sappy, grapey Gamay, a refreshing, simple Gamay Rosé, and a Pinot Noir. Of the recent Pinot Noir releases, only the '71 had finesse and real Pinot Noir flavor; it's probably at its best now. The somewhat warm, "Rhône-ish" '74 lacked classic balance and character.

In 1975, Mondavi added two good everyday blends to his list: Red Table Wine and White Table Wine.

Burgess Cellars

Burgess Cellars came into existence in 1970, when Tom Burgess purchased and renamed the original Souverain Cellars winery high up on Howell Mountain overlooking the upper Napa Valley from the east. Souverain was the creation of J. Leland Stewart, one of the pioneers of the small, fine winery movement in the state, who established his winery in 1943 and gained a considerable reputation for the label. In 1970 Stewart sold the Souverain label (see *Souverain Cellars* in Chapter 7) to an investment group which was joined by the Pillsbury Corporation, and his Howell Mountain winery to Burgess. Burgess has kept to the concept of a small, fine winery. He supplements the production of the original twenty-acre vineyard, as Stewart did before him, with grapes purchased from local growers.

THE WINES:

The wines I have had from the '72 vintage (the first to appear under the Burgess Cellars label) to the presently available '74 vintage have all been well-made, and most have exhibited good to excellent varietal character. Burgess bottles a number of varietals, including sturdy Zinfandels and Cabernets. I have been most impressed, however, with the Chardonnay, particularly the '74 from Winery Lake Vineyards. When I sampled it in early 1977, it had a very strong, deep vanilla-oaky scent and strong oak flavor. But its excellent acidity and varietal intensity hold out the promise that with several years bottle age more fruitiness will emerge and round out the substantial but raw, imbalanced impression the oak now gives to the palate.

Joseph Phelps Vineyards

This architecturally dramatic modern winery sits on a knoll surrounded by its own hundred and twenty acres of vineyards in Spring Valley east of St. Helena. Only a few years old— it was established in 1973—it has already produced some remarkable wines and clearly seems destined to join the ranks of the state's top producers. Joseph Phelps heads his own construction firm in Colorado, and became involved in building several California wineries in the late sixties. That experience, combined with his interest in farming and appreciation of fine wine, inspired Phelps to take up a new career. Walter Schug, a German born and trained winemaker with considerable California experience, joined the enterprise in 1973; by 1978 he expects to be about halfway toward the winery's eventual annual production goal of thirty-five thousand cases.

THE WINES:

Phelps already produces eight varietals and may expand this list in the future. About half its production will come from its own vineyards; additional grapes will be purchased from local growers to fill the winery's needs. All the '76 whites I sampled from the barrel in early 1977 were stylish and polished, but of the Phelps' whites I've had so far (Fumé Blanc, Gewürztraminer, Chardonnay, and Riesling), the most impressive is the Johannisberg Riesling. Schug joins a very short list of winemakers who have managed to set new standards for White Riesling in California in the past few years, producing wines that remind one of the best of the Rhine and Moselle. The '75 is remarkable for its lightness (11.8 percent alcohol) and its lovely, almost citrusy balance of rich, lingering fruitiness and lively acidity. In the same vintage, Schug also produced a Selected Late Harvest Riesling with over ten percent residual sugar from botrytized grapes. This luscious dessert wine is all honey and spice, but its high total acidity (.96) keeps its sweetness from cloying. Schug managed to top this achievement by producing in 1976 an even richer and sweeter Selected Late Harvest Riesling—this one with over twenty-two percent residual sugar and 1.2 percent total acidity, the equivalent of a German Trocken-

beerenauslese! This, tasted out of the barrel, was simply
stunning.

To date, the winery's most exciting red is its Syrah. Most
of what is called Petite Sirah in California now turns out
not to be derived from the true Syrah grape, but from the
Durif, a common Rhône grape. Phelps' Syrah comes from a
small block of true Syrah grapes planted some years ago
in the valley; in future years these will be supplemented by
grapes from its own twenty-acre plot of Syrah vines. The '74,
to be released in late 1977, has the pepper and spice of the
best Petite Sirahs but is less powerful and tannic, with a
softer texture and a more delicate, faintly cinnamony finish.

Chappellet Winery

The Chappellet Winery overlooks Lake Henessey in the
Howell Mountain Range that borders the east of the Napa
Valley, and looks very much the part of the ambitious
project it is. In a natural amphitheater on the top of Pritchard
Hill, a hundred acres of vines at an average elevation of
fourteen hundred feet sweep up in a giant basin, the upper
edges of which are terraced. At the lower edge of the basin,
a huge triangular pyramidal building of rusted steel houses
the winery, which, in spite of its stark geometry, looks surprisingly natural in its setting.

A successful vending-machine entrepreneur, owner Donn
Chappellet gave up his business in the mid-sixties, and has
spent considerable time and money since on his vineyards and
winery. Chappellet expects to expand to a maximum of
twenty-five thousand cases a year; its current annual production is about fifteen thousand cases. The winery is virtually
an estate operation, as its half-dozen varietals are produced
from grapes from its own Pritchard Hill vineyards and some
additional grapes purchased from Pritchard Hill growers.
Chappellet is a strong believer in the superiority of mountain
grapes and the artful use of oak aging for producing distinctive wines. His Cabernet has gained an enviable reputation,
and has put the Chappellet label in the first rank of California
producers.

THE WINES:

Chappellet offers four whites—Johannisberg Riesling,
Chenin Blanc, Chardonnay, and a white blend, Pritchard Hill,

composed primarily of the press wines from the first three. The Riesling and the Chenin Blanc are both bone-dry, and consequently rather austere, even steely to some palates. About a quarter of the Chenin Blanc is aged in wood to add even more definition to the final blend. The '75 I sampled was particularly lively, with a fine scent and an intense, tangy flavor. A barrel sample of the '76 Chardonnay, tasted in early 1977, exhibited excellent balance and the almost pineapple-ish fruitiness I associate with the early stages of fine young examples of this varietal. The Pritchard Hill blend also spends some time in oak, which adds considerable interest to it. The attractive '76 will probably be released in late 1977.

Cabernet Sauvignon has been Chappellet's finest wine to date, and no small part of his success has been due to the microclimate of his mountain vineyard, which has enabled him to harvest outstanding grapes even in problematic vintages like '71 and '75. All of the Chappellet Cabernets have up to ten percent Merlot blended in; the Merlot is grown primarily for this purpose, but excess production is bottled on its own. Chappellet likes to make as big and long-lived a Cabernet as he can without sacrificing style and balance. The marvelously rich '69, certainly his biggest Cabernet to date, was nowhere near its maturity when I had it again in 1976; the powerful olive-and-blackberry aroma, austere, concentrated flavor, and elegant balance ensure that the future development of the '71, which has already won laurels in blind tastings with the best of Bordeaux, will be outstanding. The '73, just released, is much in the same style as the '71, but more charm and lovely spreading flavor are apparent in it at present. Still, it will need several more years at the minimum to show its real potential. Of the Cabernets still in the barrel, I was particularly struck by the intensity, richness, and texture of the '75.

Stag's Leap Wine Cellars

In recent years, a number of small, fine wineries have gained considerable reputations in a remarkably short period of time, but none has gone so far so quickly as Stag's Leap Wine Cellars, a small winery founded in 1970 by Warren and Barbara Winiarski. Mr. Winiarski taught political science at the University of Chicago before giving up the academic life to work for several Napa Valley winemakers. After serving his vinous apprenticeship, he began an elaborate search for outstanding vineyard land and eventually built his winery and planted his vineyard near the rocky promontory known as Stag's Leap Ridge off the Silverado Trail. Winiarski believes that meticulous attention to minute details is what spells the difference between fine wine and great wine, and from the careful arrangement of the vineyard to the efficient layout of his tiny, immaculate winery, no detail that might contribute to the quality of the wine was overlooked. In 1973, he produced a Cabernet Sauvignon from his three-year old vines that took first place over several first growths of Bordeaux in a well-publicized 1976 Paris tasting, an event that gave Winiarski's winery international attention.

THE WINES:

The '73 Cabernet Sauvignon—as one might expect, now long gone from retail shelves—was outstanding for its superb, polished, classic Claret style and balance. The '74, tasted in early 1977, is bigger and deeper, but the style and flavor structure are very similar. This concentrated wine needs years before it will show its best form. The inky and intense '75—tasted from the barrel—had a fine structure, and the '76, although rough and tannic in early 1977, holds out the promise of great richness and depth. Winiarski aims at a continuity of style in his Cabernets, and to that end, may or may not add small percentages of Merlot, depending on the vintage. He produced a separate bottling of an outstanding rich and velvety Merlot in 1974.

The fifteen-thousand-case annual production Stag's Leap Wine Cellars hopes to attain in a few years includes a fruity, characterful Gamay that is given some oak aging (the '76, tasted from the barrel, was particularly striking) as well as a Johannisberg Riesling; the grapes for both have been and will continue to be purchased from local vineyards. A second label, Hawkcrest, will be used for wines not up to the Stag's Leap Wine Cellars label.

Clos du Val

The Clos du Val Wine Company, Ltd.—its full name—was established in 1972 by Bernard Portet, a Frenchman who became enamored of California after visiting in 1968. He formed a partnership with John Goelet, an American investor residing in France, and returned in 1970 to buy land in the Stag's Leap area for a vineyard and winery. One hundred and twenty acres were planted, the majority with Cabernet Sauvignon, the rest with Merlot and Zinfandel. Clos du Val will specialize in two reds, Cabernet Sauvignon and Zinfandel, and while waiting for its own vineyards to come into bearing, has been buying grapes from nearby vineyards with grape-growing conditions similar to its own. Eventually it hopes to become an estate operation producing some eighteen thousand cases a year, about four-fifths of which will be Cabernet. Currently it is about halfway to that production goal.

Mr. Portet brought excellent wine credentials and an impressive wine heritage with him to California: His father, until his recent retirement, was the *régisseur*, or manager, of Chateau Lafite and Mr. Portet himself studied enology at Montpellier.

THE WINES:

Because of Mr. Portet's background, some wine lovers are convinced that he has been able to coax a Pauillac character out of Napa Valley Cabernet Sauvignon. Others are less sure of that, but there is no denying that the Cabernets he has produced thus far are remarkable for their elegance and excellent balance. His first, a '72, was one of the outstanding wines from that generally poor vintage; when I resampled it in early '77, its classic Cabernet nose had begun to develop considerable complexity and its fine, lovely flavor spread and lingered on the palate. Portet believes his best vintage to date is the '74, and when I tasted it in the spring of 1977 it was not hard to see why. Its deep, opaque color stained the glass and a swirl released a marvelous, intense aroma of fine young Cabernet, hinting of currants, blackberries, and just the right amount of oak. The taste was rich and full-textured, but not inky with tannin. Although it will certainly not be near maturity until 1980, Portet has deliberately aimed at a softer, more elegant style for his Cabernet than many California winemakers adopt, and to achieve this has been blending in ten to twenty percent Merlot. The '76, to judge by a taste from the barrel, will probably not be quite as deep and round as the '74.

When it comes to Zinfandel, however, Portet is more willing to let the vintage dictate the wine's character. The '73 was full and rich, with a well-knit texture and fine, spicy flavor, one of the best produced in the state that year, but the '74 is a massive mouthful, just under fourteen percent alcohol and full of tannin; with its purply-ruby color, heady aroma with hints of briars, berries, and oak, and its solid structure, it ought to be magnificent—in, say, 1985.

A second label, Gran Val, will be used for wines not up to the Clos du Val standard.

Mayacamas Vineyards

Mayacamas has the highest vineyard in the Napa Valley, some twenty-four hundred feet off the valley floor, nestled in the collapsed cone of an extinct volcano, Mt. Veeder, in the middle of the rugged Mayacamas range. From the turnoff at the main highway in the valley to the winery is nine tortuous miles through the mountains, giving Mayacamas a splendid isolation from the world of the large wineries in the valley below, in size and in spirit.

"Mayacamas" is a Spanish adaptation of an Indian word meaning "the howl of the mountain lion," and the road to the winery twists and climbs around peaks and canyons as wild and forested as they ever were, populated with deer and doubtless still a few predators as well. While the valley floor is as civilized and tame as only long-tended agricultural land can be, inviting bicycle tours and picnics in its meadows, the rugged mountain country here is primitive, wild, and almost jungly, especially during spring rains.

The old cellar at Mayacamas, whose lower door looks out over the vineyards cupped in the surrounding hills, was built in 1889, when John Henry Fisher, an immigrant sword engraver from Stuttgart who became a successful pickle merchant in San Francisco, purchased the property. He converted the former sheep ranch into a winery, Mt. Veeder Vineyards, and planted it to Zinfandel and other grapes. Fisher produced red and white wines in bulk, and even ran a small distillery. The 1906 earthquake, however, destroyed his pickle factory, and he was forced to turn the vineyard over to a creditor. It fell into various hands, and finally fell into disuse.

In 1941, it came to life again as a winery, when the property was purchased by Jack and Mary Taylor. Taylor, an Englishman, former president of the Shell Development Corporation and wine lover, terraced and replanted the old vineyards—mostly to Chardonnay—converted the distillery into a house, and renamed the vineyard "Mayacamas."

The Taylors managed to create a viable business, made and sold local wines under the Lokoya label (named for a nearby canyon), and made superb Chardonnays in small lots for their loyal customers. In 1958, the Taylors formed a corporation to raise capital to expand their very small enterprise and, in 1961, retired from the actual operation, leaving it in the hands of their staff. In 1968, they sold it to Robert Travers.

A San Francisco stockbroker for eight years, Travers had no background in wine before taking it up in 1967. In fact, he first became interested in wine in the early sixties, when he began reading about and drinking it as a hobby. He became fascinated with wines, toured Europe, and worked for Joe Heitz in 1967-68. After looking over scores of properties, he took the plunge and purchased Mayacamas.

THE WINES:

Travers' ambition has been to make Mayacamas as well-known for its Cabernet as it had been for its Chardonnay. For that reason, he pared down the list of wines originally made under the Mayacamas label to Cabernet Sauvignon, Chardonnay, and Zinfandel—the last offered only when "an interesting one can be made." By that, Travers means a substantial "late harvest" style Zinfandel, usually from Amador county grapes. His '74 Late Harvest Zinfandel is a good example: Deep, rich ruby in color, it had an almost cherry-like fruitiness to its powerful, heady aroma when I tried it in early 1977 and a full fruity character and cherry-like flavor. Although not particularly tannic, its excellent acidity and sixteen percent alcohol augur well for its future development. Despite its power and strength, it was remarkably smooth and showed none of the hot, coarse character too often typical of high-alcohol big-style Zinfandels.

But most of the Mayacamas' tiny four-thousand case-per-year production centers on the two wines it makes from its own grapes. Since thirty of the winery's forty-four acres of vineyard are planted to Chardonnay and only fourteen to Cabernet, Travers occasionally buys additional Cabernet (and sometimes Merlot) to supplement the low yield (sometimes as little as a half ton an acre) of these mountain vineyards.

The Chardonnay is one of California's finest. Since Travers began overseeing the winery, Mayacamas' only white has been given a lot more oak aging than before—although Travers thinks the '72, widely praised for its richness, picked up more oak character than he cares for. The '75, which was to be bottled a month after I tasted it, had a beautiful young Chardonnay nose only lightly laced with vanillan hints of oak, mouth-filling dimensions and lingering vinosity, and a smooth, lovely flavor already; a few years of bottle age will give it additional harmony and subtlety.

With his recent Cabernets, Travers has fulfilled his goal of making wine lovers think of Cabernet as well as Chardonnay when they hear the name Mayacamas. From the '68 vintage on, the Cabernets went from strength to strength; the '70, a huge, purple-red wine with a tremendous almost overwhelming Cabernet aroma, had such sheer mouth-filling depth of flavor the last time I tasted it that I felt its style could only be described as swashbuckling. Although loaded with tannin and years from maturity, considerable complexity was already evident. Given the less than ideal growing seasons of '71 and '72, these Cabernets were much less awesome, but the '73 vintage allowed Travers to make what may be his most beautifully balanced Cabernet to date. Bottled eight months when I tasted it, it was already beginning to show finesse as well as power and exhibited an expansive aroma with notes of earth and oak, heavy but not overwhelming tannin, and a most appealing fruitiness. The '74, sampled out of the barrel, was opaque and inky-dark, with an aggressive, raw grapey aroma, but showed a solid, ripe structure and fine balance under its heavy tannin.

The Christian Brothers

The Christian Brothers—actually the Mont La Salle Vineyards—is the largest church-owned producer of wine in the world. It is also the largest producer of Napa grapes and wine and California brandy and premium dessert wines; if you count altar wines, the Brothers make about fifty different products. The Christian Brothers is a Roman-Catholic teaching order founded in 1680, with headquarters in Rome; the order has been in this country since the mid-nineteenth century and operates about a hundred and ninety schools and institutions in the country. Though not priests, the Brothers take monkish vows and wear clerical garb. Sales of The

Christian Brothers wines help support a number of schools and the novitiate at the Mont La Salle vineyards. In 1931, the order purchased the mountain vineyard and its 1903 winery some eight miles northwest from the town of Napa, built its mission-style novitiate, and now has almost two hundred acres of vineyards planted there. The Christian Brothers have been making wine in California since 1882 and have five wineries—three in the Napa Valley and two in the San Joaquin Valley, the latter principally for the production of brandy and premium dessert wines. They have about fifteen hundred acres of vineyard in Napa County, and about a thousand in the San Joaquin Valley. Current production is around two million cases per year.

The Mont La Salle winery is principally used for bottling and bottle aging. There are two other wineries located in St. Helena, both just off the highway; one is a relatively new crushing, fermenting, bottling, and storage facility; and the other, the imposing Greystone Cellars across the road from Charles Krug. Greystone, at one time (in the 1880's) the world's largest winery building, was purchased by the Christian Brothers in 1950 and is now used principally for the wood aging of wines and tours.

Of the Brothers who oversee the winery operations, the best-known is Brother Timothy, who is vice-president and cellarmaster. Since 1936, when he came to Mont La Salle, Brother Timothy has been one of the principal figures in its growth from a debt-ridden altar wine business to a giant of the industry, exporting wine and brandy to forty-five countries.

THE WINES:

Christian Brothers does not vintage any of their several varietal and generic wines, on the grounds that they aim to produce, through blending, wines of consistent style and quality that are ready to be consumed soon after bottling. This marketing philosophy has made their label something of a watchword for reliability rather than excitement.

Their wines are typically light, smooth, and round, with good acidity, and while not particularly complex, the reds especially exhibit attractive nuances from long aging in large wood cooperage. They are always sound, well-made, very clean in flavor, and often good values. The top varietals are quite good. In fact, while I would not call their Cabernet

Sauvignon a fine wine (it lacks complexity), it is very, very good, and in the recent batches I have sampled, it is an immensely drinkable light wine with a fine finish. The Cabernets are generally a blend of the past four or five vintages, occasionally up to a dozen different vintages, and like the other reds are aged four to five years before being marketed. The Pinot St. George is a robust, slightly spicy good wine. The other reds are similar in style.

The whites vary from clean, dull, and ordinary to clean, crisp, and flavorful. The Sauvignon Blanc is very good but a bit sweet. The Chardonnay is a very good wine indeed, with good varietal character. The Pineau de la Loire (Chenin Blanc) is also very well made, fruity, not too dry, and very drinkable. The La Salle Rosé is very sprightly and pleasant, almost strawberry-like in flavor.

In addition, there are "Brother Timothy Special Selections" of several red varietals—Cabernet Sauvignon, Zinfandel, Pinot Noir, and Gamay Noir (Gamay)—which consist of special lots of wine set aside for additional bottle age before release. I found that several special selection Pinot Noirs and Gamay Noirs I sampled had unattractive, dank, vegetable-raisin scents and flavors; on the other hand, some of the Cabernet and Zinfandel special selection bottlings I tried were fine drinking, mature and silky on the palate, with lovely spreading flavors. There seems to be quite a bit of bottle to bottle variation in these special selection wines, which may account for the occasional tired, unhappy specimen that turns up.

Different lots of the Christian Brothers wines are sometimes supplied with cuvée numbers, but a much more important number to look for is the stamped code which appears on the back label of each bottle of varietal wine. The first two numbers stand for the month, the third stands for the year, and the last two indicate the day of bottling. While the Christian Brothers wines, as marketed, are ready to be drunk, the code enables one to determine if the whites one buys are tired veterans of the shelf or reasonably fresh, as well as how much bottle age the reds have had.

The dessert wines of the Christian Brothers—Meloso Cream Sherry and Tinta Madeira Port, for example—are well-made, but undistinguished for these types of wines. Their XO rare reserve brandy is another matter. A fifty percent pot-still brandy aged ten years in wood, it possesses a most attractive vanillan nose and very smooth body and flavor.

Domaine Chandon

If there is one new winery whose establishment implies international recognition of California's viticultural achievement, it is Domaine Chandon. A subsidiary of Moët-Hennessey, the French firm that produces Moët & Chandon Champagnes, Domaine Chandon was founded in 1973 to produce fine sparkling wines in the New World. After a careful search, the Napa Valley was chosen and some eight hundred and fifty acres of vineyard land were purchased, primarily in the cool Carneros district. Until its impressive new sparkling wine cellars in Yountville are fully operational and its vineyards fully bearing, the winery has been using the facilities of Trefethen Vineyards in Napa and purchasing much of its grape needs from them. Domaine Chandon expects to reach about one hundred thousand cases per year production in the early 1980's.

THE WINES:

Domaine Chandon will specialize entirely in non-vintage sparkling wines. As one might expect, it does not call its products "champagnes," taking the position that Champagne is the product of the Champagne district in France. The wines are produced under the direction of the *chef de caves* of Moët & Chandon, according to the classic *méthode champenoise,* however. After experimenting with various cuvées, the winery released its first products, Chandon Napa Valley Brut and Chandon Cuvée de Pinot Noir, in late 1976. The first, made from about two-thirds Pinot Noir and one-third Chardonnay, had a lovely pale gold color lightly tinged with pink, fine, long-lasting bubbles, light, clean, fruity-yeasty aromas, and a most attractive fruity-soft flavor that left an impression of creaminess on the palate. Altogether it was a superb sparkling wine, and I gave it the edge over the somewhat simpler and fruitier Cuvée de Pinot Noir, a pale bronze-pink wine made entirely from Pinot Noir, which was nevertheless full of Pinot fruitiness and character, set off by fine acidity and crisping bubbles. The style of these wines will vary somewhat from lot to lot until the winery is able to build up its reserves to ensure continuity of style. (I tasted these in early 1977.) Although much fruitier than French Champagnes, they are no less attractive for that, and their evident polish and sophistication easily put them on a par with the very finest American sparkling wines. Domaine Chandon's first efforts have made it evident that truly fine California sparkling wines can be produced in large volume.

Other Wineries

The number of new wineries that have begun operations recently in the Napa Valley continues to grow, and the following notes discuss only some of them.

Chateau Chevalier, a handsome stone Victorian winery built in 1891, was purchased along with a hundred acres of vineyards in 1969 by the Gregory Bissonette family and will be marketing wines from their replanted vineyards in the late seventies.

Diamond Creek Vineyards is a small twenty-acre plot of Cabernet Sauvignon on the slopes of Diamond Mountain in the northwest corner of the Napa Valley, and its owner, Al Brounstein, plans to confine its production to Cabernet.

At Rutherford, Charles Wagner, a long-time grower, has opened up a new winery, Caymus Vineyards, to make wines from his seventy acres of Cabernet, Pinot noir, and White Riesling. He already has a second label as well, Liberty School.

In 1976, a group of partners (some of whom are partners in Freemark Abbey) purchased the former Souverain of Rutherford winery and renamed it Rutherford Hill. Wines under the new label should be on the market sometime in 1977.

New names continue to be added to the valley's roster of wineries, it seems, every few months. Franciscan Vineyards, Silveroak Cellars, Carneros Creek Vineyards, Stonegate Winery, Trefethen Vineyards, Villa Mt. Eden, Mt. Veeder Vineyards, Veedercrest Vineyards, Raymond Vineyards, Yverdon Winery, and Stag's Leap Winery (not to be confused with Stag's Leap Wine Cellars) have all been bonded recently and are in various stages of planting, building, and winemaking. Even some small local enterprises that have been around for decades, like Nichelini Vineyards in the Chiles Valley district and the J. Mathews winery in the town of Napa, have begun sending their wines out of state. Others are certain to follow.

Chapter 7
Sonoma and North

In the 1920's the county of Sonoma produced the most wine of any area in California, but it is now far down in production compared to other areas. Its vineyard acreage has dwindled from around sixty thousand acres to a fifth that figure, but has in recent years rebounded to over twenty thousand. In the past, much of Sonoma's production was bulk wine, and most of its grapes went into generic wines. The smaller number of wineries in Sonoma, compared with Napa, has contributed to the fact that its wine tradition and history are more erratic and spotty than Napa's, and obscured by long periods of near stagnation. The large number of new wineries that began in the late 1960's, however, ensures Sonoma not only increased production in the future, but a stronger continuity of winemaking traditions.

The new plantings, for one thing, consist almost entirely of fine wine grapes. Most of the new enterprises are aiming their production at vintage-dated varietal wines, and when their new wineries reach full production, the historic appellation "Sonoma," as well as sub-appellations like Dry Creek and Alexander Valley, are certain to become well-known.

The potential for the production of fine wines in Sonoma has been proved in the past, and several new areas not thought suitable for fine wine grapes have been opened up in the past few years. In this respect, Sonoma is fortunate in having some of the most varied grape-growing conditions in California. Bordered on the west by the Pacific, its narrow valleys are shielded by coastal mountains. The eastern border of the county shares the Mayacamas Mountains with the Napa Valley. From the central city of Santa Rosa south the district is a relatively flat plain, but farther north the Russian River and Alexander Valley regions are characerized by hills, timberlands, and pastures, crisscrossed with rivers and creeks. As might be expected, both the climate and soils are diverse. The lower part of Sonoma, around the town that gives the county its name, is known as the Valley of the Moon, and like the Napa Valley, its climate varies from Region I in the south to Region III further north. The Russian River Valley and to the north the Alexander Valley and lower Mendocino County repeat this diversity: their climatic conditions also range from Region I to III, but without following any obvious pattern—in fact Sonoma county is something of a patchwork of microclimates, some of which can suffer yearly temperature ranges of almost one hundred degrees. Their soils, too, vary considerably, from rich river soil to soils so hard vine roots can hardly penetrate. Couple this geographic and climatic diversity with a wide variety of grape-growing and winemaking attitudes and practices, and one can understand why the area expects to become one of California's most important districts in the near future.

But Sonoma not only has a significant future, it has a significant past. There are two Sonoma wineries in particular whose influence on the state's wine industry has been historically important, if not pivotal. Both of these wineries are located close to the town of Sonoma in the southeast corner of the county, and, under new ownership, have been revived, and are still in production today. The first is Buena Vista, the winery of Colonel Haraszthy, often called the father of California viticulture, and the second is Hanzell, founded by J. D. Zellerbach in the 1950's with the aim of creating great wine in California. The story of each of these influential enterprises and their impact on California wine is worth tracing.

As with all important historical figures whose lives are partly hidden in legends, Colonel Agoston Haraszthy has come in for his share of debunking, and today he is not thought to have been as influential a wine pioneer as he was once regarded. If he did nothing else, however, he certainly drew considerable attention to California and its potential as a wine-producing region, in part because he was one of the more colorful figures in a colorful age.

Count Haraszthy came from Hungarian wine-growing nobility (or so he said), gained his title of Colonel while a member of the Royal Hungarian bodyguard and became secretary to the Viceroy of Hungary. He apparently sided with the rebels in the unsuccessful Hapsburg Revolution of the 1840's and fled his homeland under sentence of death in disguise and, according to legend, with a satchel of vineyard cuttings.

Haraszthy sailed for America and, joined by his family, be-

gan searching for vineyard land. He experimented with plantings in Wisconsin, but eventually found its climate too harsh.
Before the discovery of this disappointing fact, he founded
the town of Haraszthy (now known as Sauk City), planted
the first hops in the state, ran a steamboat concern, and
wrote two volumes of his impressions of America. At the
same time, true to the cause of revolution in Hungary, he
collected money and ammunition which he sent to the Hungarian rebels.

Moving west in 1849, still with the intention of founding a
vineyard, he became San Diego's first sheriff, and tried setting
out his vines again. He soon found the climate too mild for
ideal grape-growing conditions, and moved to San Francisco
to try his plantings there. But new problems beset him and
his vines: frequent fogs apparently caused difficulties with
ripening, and Haraszthy faced court actions over accusations
that he had been less than scrupulous in his new position
there as official melter and refiner of gold at the U.S. Mint.

But Haraszthy survived these setbacks; he won his case
(although court costs amounted to twenty-five thousand dollars), and he took his vines to Sonoma. There he purchased
the first few hundred of the six thousand acres he eventually
owned from the last of the Spanish dons, General Mariano
Guadalupe Vallejo, who had once been the Mexican Com-
mandant of Northern California. Vallejo had been a pioneer
wine-grower of some distinction; his estate produced a wine
of great repute with the romantic name *Lachryma Montis*
(Tears of the Mountain). Haraszthy soon became a successful winemaking rival, but a friendly one; in 1863, Haraszthy's
two sons married the General's two daughters in a double
wedding.

Haraszthy's effect on the growth of California winemaking
during this period appears to have been substantial; he
seems to have been largely responsible for bringing good
winemakers to Northern California (among these Charles
Krug, who established his winery in 1861); he was the first
Californian to demonstrate that superior wines came from
non-irrigated grapes; and he was the first to use native redwood casks. He established the Buena Vista Winery and
Vineyards in 1857, relying on Chinese coolie labor to build
extensive aging tunnels and a Pompeiian villa for a home.
By 1859, Buena Vista produced four thousand gallons of
wine which sold for $1.50 to $2.00 a gallon—a high price in
those times.

Haraszthy's winemaking success in Sonoma prompted his famous 1858 "Report on Grapes and Wines of California" in which he propounded his thesis to a dubious world that California could produce "as noble a wine as any country on the face of the globe." But in 1861 Haraszthy went further, performing a service to California viticulture that helped to bring about his prophecy; appointed by the Governor to report on European viticulture and how it could be adapted to California, he traveled to all the major wine regions in Europe and collected some one hundred thousand cuttings from over three hundred grapes varieties, and brought them back to California. Unfortunately, the California legislature was, by the time of his return, of a different political complexion, and Haraszthy was never reimbursed for the expenses (some twelve thousand dollars) of his trip. Undaunted, he had some of the cuttings planted in his own vineyards, sold most of them to other growers, and distributed the remainder throughout the state.

Haraszthy was not dismayed by the lack of cooperation and interest shown by the short-sighted state government; he was at the height of his fame and success. Buena Vista was the world's largest vineyard, and its wine company had offices across the country and as far away as London.

The mid-1860's, however, brought a number of disasters to Haraszthy's estate: the first wave of the worldwide blight of the root louse, phylloxera, attacked the Colonel's vineyards, heavy losses on the stock exchange dwindled his capital, new taxes ate up the rest, the winery was nearly destroyed in a fire, and the final blow, loss of credit, forced the Colonel to move on. Haraszthy left California for good, and began distilling spirits from sugar under a government contract in Nicaragua. Appropriately enough for a pioneer figure, his career ended as well as began in legend. Haraszthy vanished mysteriously in July of 1869; he seems to have placed too much trust in the strength of a tree limb overhanging a stream inhabited by alligators.

Buena Vista Vineyards fell on even worse days after the Colonel's departure, finally literally falling into ruin in the San Francisco earthquake of 1906, which collapsed even the limestone aging tunnels containing thousands of the Colonel's wines. Unlike Vignes' El Aliso Vineyard in Los Angeles, Buena Vista has not been paved over, and was successfully revived as a winery in 1943.

Hanzell's influence on Caifornia winemaking came about

in a much different fashion and in a far less dramatic way, yet its influence has been widespread and profound. It showed that the goal of creating great wines in California was not an impossible one for a small winery dedicated to quality to achieve. In addition, the methods used at Hanzell to achieve that goal have been copied and adopted all over California.

James D. Zellerbach, Chairman of the Board of Crown Zellerbach Paper Company, and United States Ambassador to Italy (where he had served as Chief of the Marshall Plan from 1948 to 1950), decided upon his retirement to create a model winery in California that would produce Chardonnay and Pinot Noir wines as great as any in the world. The Ambassador—as he is referred to at Hanzell—seems an unlikely successor to the tradition of Haraszthy but his attitude was identical: that great wine can be made in California, so long as one has vision, boldness, and considerable resources. Zellerbach may have been an amateur, but he was an amateur in the grand manner, and took his "hobby" as seriously as any professional winemaker.

The Ambassador liked Burgundy. Not just any Burgundy, but Montrachet and Romanée-Conti. He wanted no slavish imitation of two of France's glories, but a California Chardonnay and Pinot Noir that would challenge France's claim to have made the finest wine possible from those noble grapes.

Zellerbach faced this challenge in a daring and impatient manner; perhaps the Burgundians had found the best vineyards and the best methods for their grapes after centuries of trial and error, but the Ambassador did not have centuries —and wasn't interested in failures. Since obviously nothing could be left to chance, he would have to use whatever equipment, methods, talent, and skills that were available that could possibly aid in the quest for great wines. If available equipment and methods were inadequate, then better equipment would have to be invented and better methods devised. In such a grand scheme, there could be no room for accidents and mysteries. What wasn't known about wines would simply have to be discovered. In short, Zellerbach's scheme was simple: given enough scientific talent, the best methods, the finest equipment—and hang the expense—the dream could be realized.

Such boldness has its risks, but the Ambassador was out to minimize them. He began by having viticultural sages from the University of California at Davis seek out an ideal location for Chardonnay and Pinot noir. The plot of land the Ambassador finally chose in 1951 was a rocky hillside in Sonoma overlooking the Valley of the Moon from the Mayacamas range. Naturally, its soil, underlying lava rock, exposure, and elevation (seven hundred feet) were all carefully considered for drainage, protection from frosts, ripening, and possible contribution to taste. The Ambassador named the auspicious property "Hanzell," a contraction of his wife's name, Hanna, and Zellerbach.

The Ambassador did not do things by halves, and had the winery built in 1956, as a modern echo of Burgundy's Clos de Vougeot. The architecture is not accidental; Hanzell was intended from the beginning to be traditional in quality but thoroughly modern in methods, as proud as any château, but completely Californian.

Although Hanzell looks as if it sprang as a full-blown conception from the Ambassador's imagination, it only did so in appearance. Zellerbach invested large sums in lengthy experimentation with various methods and designs, and to oversee the winery and the research, he hired a University of California graduate in biochemistry, Bradford Webb. In the winery's impressively equipped laboratory a good deal of research was carried on to determine the contribution of bacteria to the flavor of Burgundies. Webb actually produced the first commercial culture of malo-lactic bacteria in the course of studying the complicated process by which some wines undergo a conversion of malic acid to lactic acid after fermentation, resulting in a decrease in acid and a gain in subtle flavor complexities. Every winemaking method was studied or experimented with before adoption, and all the elaborate equipment was specially built and scaled to the winery's goal of one thousand cases of wine per year from its own vineyards.

Hanzell's innovations began in its vineyards, where the vines in its sixteen (later expanded to twenty) terraced acres were rigorously pruned to limit their yield to one to one and one-quarter tons per acre. Zellerbach insisted on selected picking of only perfectly ripened bunches of grapes, and each bunch had to be inspected for imperfect berries before going into the especially designed crusher. Sensible as this sort of harvesting might sound, it is not emulated because of its great expense, and the consequent difficulty of using it on a larger scale.

Cold fermentation was one of the innovations adopted at Hanzell, as was the use of inert gas "caps" to minimize the wine's contact with the air during transfer, storage, and bottling. For example, after aging in oak, the wine may be kept in a large closed storage tank awaiting bottling, under a cap of nitrogen, which, unlike air, will not interact with the wine. At Hanzell, the bottles themselves are first purged with nitrogen before being filled with wine, and then are corked, so that there is actually a small amount of nitrogen between the cork and the wine.

The guiding notion behind all this effort was to eliminate, as far as possible, all unknown and accidental factors from the winemaking process that might adversely affect the quality of the wine. At Hanzell, the goal was great wine, and its outstanding success in using science and technology to that end is an effective rebuttal to those who maintain great wine can only be made with pre-industrial methods.

Apart from showing the value of modern science and technology in making fine wines, Hanzell's most copied innovation is a traditional technique, that of aging young wines in small oak barrels.

Zellerbach's insistence on importing oak barrels from Burgundy in which to age his wines was thought by many merely another example of the Ambassador indulging his whimsy, since he could just as easily have used American oak barrels. But what appeared to be inconsequential turned out to be momentous. For years it had been widely supposed that the greater complexity of French White Burgundy compared with California Chardonnay had to do with the superiority of French soil or French conditions; but those who tasted the first vintage of Hanzell Chardonnay made the astonishing discovery that it tasted like a French wine!

What accounted for this added nuance the wine possessed was the Limousin oak that the Ambassador had insisted upon, and it was soon discovered that French oak—Limousin and Nevers are used in Burgundy and Bordeaux respectively—imparts a certain subtle flavor to wines that American oak, perhaps because the wood is cut and dried in a different manner, perhaps because it is a different species, does not. Now, of course, one finds imported oak, principally French, in nearly every other cellar in California, and today a number of California wines—Chardonnays, in particular—equal or surpass their Old World counterparts in quality and in fact can be extremely difficult to distinguish from them.

Thus, after five years of design and experimentation, Han-

zell's first vintage in 1956 was a triumph, and thereafter an
outstanding series of Chardonnays were produced that showed
the Ambassador's dream to create great wines was a realistic
goal. California winemakers and wine lovers watched developments at Hanzell closely, and all alike applauded the wines;
then suddenly, the Ambassador died just before the 1963
harvest. The winery was closed; its wines and entire inventory of French oak sold off. It is said that soon after, in
the winery's office, a wooden figure of St. Vincent, the patron
saint of winemakers, developed a long crack.

The dream was over. Or so it seemed, until 1965, when
the winery was purchased from the estate, and perhaps the
greatest testament to the Ambassador's vision is the fact that
in its production, methods, and wines, it has remained virtually unchanged to this day.

Both Buena Vista and Hanzell were built to prove what
California could do with her wines, and each signaled the end
of one era and the beginning of another. Each was succeeded
by other wineries which equaled or surpassed it, but their
profound impact on California's wine history remains.

The Valley of the Moon today, however, hardly looks to
the casual visitor like a place where events of any magnitude,
political or viticultural, occur. These days the Valley of the
Moon is quiet and rural, and has only a handful of wineries,
only two of which have sizable productions.

The town of Sonoma itself still has an air of old California; a surprising number of historic adobe buildings still front
the town plaza near where the Bear Flag party raised their
flag to proclaim their independence from Mexico in 1846.
The countryside seems as wild and undeveloped as it must
have been in the days of Vallejo and Haraszthy, or for that
matter when Jack London lived and wrote there. The Indians
called Sonoma Valley the Valley of the Moon after the way
the rising moon seems to play among the peaks of the Mayacamas Mountains. All summer long and into the fall the
softly rounded foothills of the Mayacamas range are dry-
brown, covered with wheat-colored grasses swept by the wind
into giant cowlicks, dotted with dark scrubby oaks, and so
evocative of the Old West that one almost expects to see a
stagecoach thunder over them.

Farther north the Russian River Valley district has some
of the largest, some of the smallest, and some of the newest

wineries in California. It too is an area steeped in history, and its early wineries seemed to swing from dizzying success to utter ruin with equal rapidity. My personal favorite for romantic zaniness among its early wineries is the now defunct Fountaingrove, which was begun by a mystical cult, complete with a sage and his books of elaborate revelations. The members of the cult formed yet another utopian community, The Brotherhood of the New Life. After the mysticism waned, the vines the cult had planted still flourished, and its proprietor for many years was a former disciple, a Japanese nobleman raised in Scotland, given to a burr in his speech and kilts for dress. If the wine was as rich as its history, it must have been impressive indeed.

The last wine district farther north is in Mendocino County, where the new wineries, as everywhere in California, proclaim that the conditions for growing grapes are the best in the state.

In all these areas today one still finds a fair number of "country wineries." This group needs a short explanation: these are small wineries that for years have been making simple honest jug wines for local customers. They are almost always family operations, and often the families are Italian in heritage. A good many of these are not mentioned in this book, just as a good many very large bulk wine producers are not mentioned either, because very few people, ever encounter their wines. Some of these "country" wineries, however, have begun to take varietal production seriously, and some now produce very good to fine wine.

Suggested Samplings

Anyone wishing to sample some of the current high points of the region's wine production will certainly find some of them among the following types and producers. These are offered as a starting point, not a definitive list of the best, and readers are encouraged to go on and explore for themselves. Bear in mind that some of these wines are produced in small quantities and consequently may not be easy to find; many of them are readily available, however, at least in major U.S. cities.

RED:

> ### Cabernet Sauvignon
> Buena Vista
> Fetzer Vineyards
> Parducci
> J. Pedroncelli
> Sebastiani
> Simi
>
> ### Pinot Noir
> Geyser Peak
> Hanzell
> ZD
>
> ### Zinfandel
> Buena Vista
> Fetzer
> Joseph Swan
> Kenwood
> Sonoma Vineyards
>
> ### Barbera
> Sebastiani

WHITE:

> ### (Pinot) Chardonnay
> Chateau St. Jean
> Hanzell
> Simi
>
> ### Chenin Blanc
> Dry Creek
>
> ### White (Johannisberg) Riesling
> Chateau St. Jean
> Sonoma Vineyards
>
> ### Gewürztraminer
> Simi
>
> ### French Colombard
> Parducci

OTHER:
> *Sparkling Wine*
>> Chateau St. Jean
>> Korbel

> *Rosés*
>> Simi (Rosé of Cabernet)

These and other wines of the region are discussed in the following pages. In looking at the wineries in these areas, I will start first with the ones grouped around the town of Sonoma, and then work north through the Russian River Valley to Mendocino.

Principal Wineries

Buena Vista Winery

Buena Vista's history is one of the longest in California— it was founded in 1857 by California's most influential wine pioneer, Count Haraszthy. After the 1906 earthquake, however, Buena Vista underwent a number of unfortunate vicissitudes; at one time it was even a women's prison farm. In 1941 Frank Bartholomew, now board chairman of United Press International, purchased a tract of Sonoma land and two abandoned winery buildings in a eucalyptus grove that turned out to be what was left of the once great Buena Vista. By 1943 Bartholomew had revived the winery, and over the next several decades restored Buena Vista to prominence, gaining attention for such wines as Zinfandel, which, the legend goes, the Count brought to California from an unknown European origin. In 1968 Bartholomew sold the winery to Young's Markets of Los Angeles, which has purchased some seven hundred acres of vineyard land in Sonoma and Napa and built a new winery in the nearby Carneros district of Napa (the old one will continue to be used as an aging facility). Planted to top varietals, the vineyards are now coming into bearing, and the expected quality of the grapes should result in improved quality in future Buena Vista wines. In recent years, Buena Vista's annual production has been around twenty thousand cases, but if all goes well, it is expected to reach two hundred thousand cases per year in a decade.

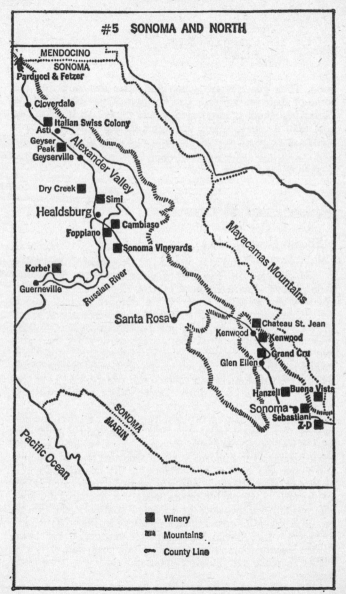

#5 SONOMA AND NORTH

MENDOCINO
SONOMA
Parducci & Fetzer
Cloverdale
Italian Swiss Colony
Asti
Geyser Peak
Geyserville
Alexander Valley
Dry Creek
Simi
Healdsburg
Cambiaso
Foppiano
Sonoma Vineyards
Korbel
Guerneville
Russian River
Santa Rosa
Mayacamas Mountains
Chateau St. Jean
Kenwood
Kenwood
Grand Cru
Glen Ellen
Hanzell
Buena Vista
Sonoma
Sebastiani
Z-D
SONOMA
MARIN
Pacific Ocean

Winery
Mountains
County Line

THE WINES:

As is often the case with many of the older California wineries, Buena Vista's reds are better than their whites. All the ones I have tried have been well-made, usually of standard quality, with some quite undistinguished and some quite good. Their generics are sound and offer few surprises, but some of their red varietals can be interesting—especially the Zinfandel, which is less sprightly and berry-like in character here than is usual in, say, the Napa, though it is not a huge intense wine like those of the new smaller wineries. The '73 was typical: robust with good character and dusty-earth and fruit nuances in nose and flavor. Since the winery is undergoing considerable change and expansion, the label bears watching.

Sebastiani Vineyards

Sebastiani is one of the largest family-owned wineries in California, and was founded in 1904 by Samuele Sebastiani, a native of Tuscany who began his career in California as a laborer and stonemason. He made his first wine, a Zinfandel, in 1895, and began his winery by purchasing some of the former holdings of General Vallejo. In 1906 he bought a failing winery, later built a larger one around it, and built his bulk wine business into one of the largest North Coast wineries. It still occupies a corner of the quiet little town of Sonoma. Before his death in 1944, Sebastiani had become one of Sonoma's leading citizens, and the name Sebastiani appears on a number of local businesses and other enterprises, from theaters to bus depots.

August Sebastiani took over from his father in the midthirties, after the Prohibition lull during which production was limited to altar wines and "tonics," and twenty years later began shifting the winery toward premium varietals. Now Sebastiani's two sons, Sam and Don, have joined him at the winery, and in recent years the Sebastiani enterprise has not only staked out a good share of the premium varietal jug market—expanding the winery's annual production to 1.5 million cases a year in the process—but has also consolidated its list of offerings and added a number of new fine wines. The winery now owns or controls some four hundred acres of vineyards, but continues to buy most of the grapes it needs.

THE WINES:

Sebastiani now offers wines in three broad categories. In the first are the "mountain" wines: non-vintage generics and varietals offered in jugs (as well as bottles) that are competitive in quality with similar offerings from the big California producers.

The second category is a line of some ten varietals and generics, both vintage and non-vintage, that carry North Coast or Sonoma appellations. I find the whites in this group well-made but undistinguished; the Green Hungarian and Gewürztraminer, for example, are fruity, simple picnic fare. The reds vary from hearty to very fine, and include several substantial specimens upon which Sebastiani's wine reputation in the past principally rested. The Sebastianis do not believe in being slavish to bottling only one hundred percent varietals and advocate long aging in redwood to soften reds, with only a few months additional aging in small oak cooperage to enhance flavor. The reds that result from this basically Italian-style production method are typically light to medium-bodied, and have a round, sometimes soft texture, a core of warm flavor, and a faint, not unattractive bitter-sweet note in the finish. Although such wines are not tremendously complex, they can be very fine and very satisfying. Sebastiani also has an admirable policy of not releasing its best reds until they've acquired several years' maturity in the bottle, making this winery virtually the only California winery with wide distribution to offer such well-aged wines. In 1977, the winery was still selling reds from the '67, '68, '69, '70, and '71 vintages. Their Barbera, one of the top examples of this varietal in the state, was outstanding in '70, with a big, tarry-rich nose; what had doubtless been a rather fiercely flavored medium-bodied wine had mellowed by early 1977 to an intense, round, immensely satisfying wine with a touch of warmth in the finish and a fine future ahead of it. The '68 Cabernet Sauvignon, another aged Sebastiani red still available in '77, was marvelous drinking: medium-bodied, round, with a hint of warmth in the flavor and the cedary bouquet only bottle age can give this varietal.

"Proprietor's Reserve" wines, the third category, currently include the light, fruity, almost cranberry-scented Gamay Beaujolais Nouveau (bottled in November of each vintage year), an attractive, full-bodied lot of '71 Pinot Noir, and Sebastiani's best white by far, Pinot Noir Blanc, called

"Eye of the Swan" on the label. Although the '75 vintage of this bronze-colored, powerful white struck me as an aggressively flavored, even greeny wine, the '76 has excellent balance, a lovely Pinot Noir fruitiness in the nose, refreshing acidity, and a fine, bone-dry finish.

Hanzell Vineyards

Hanzell, a tiny twenty-acre vineyard and winery estate in the hills above the town of Sonoma, was built by the late James D. Zellerbach in 1956 to produce great Chardonnay and Pinot Noir. From the use of special picking methods to specially made bottles, no detail of production that might contribute to the wines' quality was overlooked, and by the time of Zellerbach's death in 1963, Hanzell had indeed produced great Chardonnay, and its Pinot Noir, produced only since 1965, may yet come to match the Chardonnay in quality. Hanzell has been a model winery for many small fine wineries in California, and its pioneering use of many modern winemaking techniques combined with Old World methods —principally the aging of wines in French oak—has been widely adopted by many larger wineries as well.

Hanzell was closed for almost two years after Zellerbach's death, until 1965, when Douglas Day, a former vice-president of Lucky Stores, purchased the property and declared his intention to continue Zellerbach's high standards. Nothing was changed, and the first Pinot Noir was produced, as had been Zellerbach's intention.

Mr. Day died in the summer of 1970; his widow, Mary Schaw Day, who continued the tradition without a break, herself died in the fall of 1973. The winery was purchased in 1975 by Barbara and Jacques de Brye.

THE WINES:

Hanzell produces only two wines, a Chardonnay and a Pinot Noir, both entirely from grapes grown on the property. Production is consequently very small, under a thousand cases of each. Its Chardonnay has long been regarded as one of the finest in California. Although aging California Chardonnay in French oak was pioneered here, it is not overdone, and the Chardonnay, which is consistently a superb, complex wine, exhibits great fruit and finesse. Of recent vintages, the

'73 was a good example: complex, harmonious, and well-balanced, with subtle hints of spiciness.

Pinot Noir is rarely as successful in California as Chardonnay, and Hanzell's Pinot Noir follows this pattern. While not as exalted as its Chardonnay, it is nonetheless often very fine indeed; the '66 I particularly remember as a complex wine with a haunting fragrance rather similar to crushed almonds. The '71 had an intriguing but closed nose and full, warm, intense flavors accented by oak, although it struck me as a trace acidic and short on fruit when I sampled it in mid-1976.

ZD Wines

ZD is a tiny winery near Vineburg in Sonoma, founded in 1969 by two engineers, Norman de Leuze and Gino Zepponi. At the moment, they have no producing vineyards of their own, but get their grapes from nearby sources, notably Rene di Rosa's Winery Lake Vineyards in the Carneros district of Napa Valley.

THE WINES:

While ZD has made Gewürztraminer, Chardonnay, Flora, and White Riesling, it is their Pinot Noir that has attracted the most attention. As several other wineries have discovered, the Carneros section in the Napa, rated a cool Region I in climate, is excellent for growing Pinot noir—at least when the year is favorable. The '70 and '71 Pinot Noirs I tried were both almost purple in color, with a quite arresting intensity of flavors. The '71, resampled in early 1977, had not aged gracefully; although its monotone, somewhat chocolatey flavor had a surprisingly long finish, it had developed a not altogether attractive rotting-vegetable pungency in the nose. However, the effort to make distinctive wines here is evident, and the label bears watching.

Kenwood Vineyards

Kenwood Vineyards was known as the Pagani Brothers Winery until 1970, when it was bought by the Martin Lee family and several other partners and named for the nearby town. The Paganis had been making sound table wine for sale in jugs since 1906, and were proud of their Zinfandel. The owners are continuing the Pagani label for jug wine and are using the Kenwood label for their new line of vintage-dated varietals. Their back labels are sometimes very detailed, even showing fermentation charts!

THE WINES:

The emphasis here is on reds, made primarily from grapes purchased from growers in the Sonoma-Mendocino region. The '74 Cabernet Sauvignon I tried in early 1977 was curiously mature-smelling, exhibiting tea-like hints and a touch of pungency in its aroma, but the flavors were quite attractive. Light and neither particularly complex nor tannic, it should be at its best in the late seventies. I was more impressed with the most recent vintage—'76—of the Chenin Blanc, bottled in January of 1977, with its soft, fruity aroma, hinting of oak, and dry but not overly austere flavor.

Chateau St. Jean

Chateau St. Jean (pronounced "Jeen") is one of the few California wineries that actually looks something like a château—although perhaps "villa" would be a better description of its Mediterranean style. More important, it has ambitions to match its imposing appearance and is already well on its way toward fulfilling them. Partners Robert and Edward Merzoian and W. Kenneth Sheffield—long-time Central Valley grape growers who wanted to create a fine wine "château"—purchased the former Goff estate and mansion near the village of Kenwood in the Sonoma Valley in 1973 and began planting some hundred acres of the property to top varietals. In 1975 construction began on a thirty-five-thousand-case-a-year winery; some four-fifths of its production will be white wines, the rest reds. The intention at Chateau St. Jean is to concentrate production on a half-dozen varietals and only produce a given wine when an outstanding one can be made. When its own vineyards come into bearing, the winery expects them to supply about half its grape needs; currently all the grapes are purchased from local growers. In fact, winemaker Richard Arrowood, who joined Chateau St. Jean in 1974, makes a specialty of obtaining grapes from outstanding vineyards and identifying the vineyard source on the label of each varietal he pro-

duces. This of course makes Chateau St. Jean more a
domaine operation on the Burgundian model than a Bordeaux
château estate.

THE WINES:

Arrowood's insistence on giving exact origins—county,
district, vineyard—on the wine label whenever possible
means that there are actually quite a number of Chateau St.
Jean wines. Distinctive lots of Chardonnay, for example, are
made, bottled, and labeled separately, allowing wine enthusiasts to make unusual and instructive comparisons of
wines from the same varietal and vintage but from different
vineyards. A case in point are the fine '75 Chateau St. Jean
Chardonnays from Alexander Valley that I tasted in the
spring of 1977. One was from the Robert Young Vineyards
on the east side of the valley and the other from the Belle
Terre Vineyards on the west side of the valley a quarter-mile
away. The former was rich, fat, oaky, with an impressive
balance and intensity of flavor; the latter lighter, more delicate, even elegant at that point, with attractive spicy nuances, hints of oak, and a long, lingering finish. Arrowood
thinks nothing of offering, say, seven such distinct Chardonnays in a given vintage.

Arrowood has also produced a rich, creamy '73 Blanc de
Blancs Napa Valley Sparkling Chardonnay (to be released
in the fall of 1977). His first Cabernet, a '74 Sonoma County
wine, was young and awkward (in early 1977) but has fine
balance and plenty of stuffing.

To date, however, his finest achievement has been with
"late-harvest" style Johannisberg Rieslings. The '75 Johannisberg Riesling from the March Vineyards in Mendocino showed
only a very delicate scent in early 1977 but had a delightful
flavor with dried-fruit nuances set off by excellent acidity
and a lightly sweet finish. The '76 vintage of the same
wine, tasted from the barrel, was more an auslese-style wine
at seven percent residual sugar, and had a rich, enticing,
apricoty aroma and flavor. I found the very dry '75 Johannisberg Riesling from the Robert Young Vineyards too acidic,
almost steely, and disappointingly dull and lifeless. But later
in the harvest season, botrytis infected the remaining crop
in this vineyard and the neighboring Belle Terre Vineyards,
from which Arrowood managed to create two stunning very
sweet Rieslings. The Belle Terre Vineyards "Individual bunch

selected late harvest" Riesling had an extraordinary honey-apricot-raisin nose and a thick, viscous honeyed flavor, with hints of emerging spice. A total acidity of 1.28 percent keeps its seventeen percent residual sugar from cloying the palate. The even more astounding Robert Young Vineyards "Individual bunch selected late harvest" Riesling, with a residual sugar level of over twenty-three percent (and total acidity of 1.35 percent), has a massive fruit-compote nose, a fabulously unctuous texture, and a fruity flavor so deep and honeyed it suggests butterscotch. Both should continue to develop in the bottle for many years.

Joseph Swan Vineyards

The Swan winery was started in 1969 in Forestville (near Santa Rosa), in the cellar under the Swan home. When Joe Swan, an airlines pilot, found the two-hundred-gallon limit on winemaking under a householder's permit too confining for his growing hobby, he bonded his winery. Swan has some small plantings of Zinfandel, and supplements his supply with grapes from local vineyards.

THE WINES:

Swan has already created a small stir with his "big-style" Zinfandels. A recent sample of his '72 Lot #1 Sonoma Zinfandel impressed me with its dark purple color, hard, tannic structure, and intense flavor, although it was not quite as rich or appealing as the '71. Still, it was a very fine wine, and indicates future Swan wines will be ones to watch for.

Simi Winery

Simi was built in 1876 by Giuseppe and Pietro Simi, who named the winery Montepulciano for their Italian homeland. Eventually the name proved too difficult for customers, and was finally changed to Simi. Located north of Healdsburg, the winery made mostly bulk wine before and after Prohibition, and finally began fading into a small local trade business when it was purchased in 1970 by Russell Green, a former president of Signal Oil. Green had planted grapes in nearby Alexander Valley back in 1959 when he had a summer home on the Russian River. At that time, the area was thought too hot for premium varieties, and had been mostly planted in

prunes. Later studies have shown it to be between Region II
and III, and it has now attracted a number of other growers.
In 1974 Green sold Simi to a subsidiary of Scottish & New-
castle Breweries Ltd., a British firm which in turn sold the
winery to Schieffelin & Co. of New York in 1976. Green
still retains his three hundred seventy-five acres of vineyards
in the Alexander Valley and sells his grapes to the revitalized
Simi. The winery aims for an eventual ninety-thousand-
cases-per-year production, consisting of nine vintage-dated
varietals, all but the Zinfandel from Alexander Valley. Mary
Ann Graf, one of the few women winemakers in California,
continues at Simi under the new owners, as does consulting
enologist André Tchelistcheff, one of California's most re-
spected fine winemakers.

THE WINES:

Under Russell Green, Simi produced some excellent wines,
including some non-vintage Cabernet Sauvignons and Zinfandels that had the advantage of being blended with Simi's
stock of older wines, some vintages of which rank with the
best California wines of the post-Prohibition era. (The 1935
Zinfandel and the '35 and '41 Cabernet—particularly the latter—were still magnificent drinking in early 1977.) Under its
present owners, Simi is concentrating on producing a shorter
list of fine varietals.

The Simi wines are all clean, well-made wines emphasizing style and polish over boldness of flavor, but so far many
fall only in the very good to fine category. The examples
I've had of Chenin Blanc and Johannisberg Riesling lacked
charm and distinction, and the Pinot Noir and Zinfandel
lacked character and appeal. However, among the Simi wines
I tasted in early 1977, the light, lovely '72 Cabernet Sauvignon had a very attractive flavor, and the '73 (not yet
bottled) promised excellent balance. The light, intensely
fruity '75 Gamay Beaujolais is quite pleasant drinking now.
In whites, Simi has been particularly successful with
Gewürztraminer and made a light, spicy delight from this
varietal in '74. Their '74 Chardonnay is a fine though not
outstanding wine, with an attractive, full, almost figgy-fruity
nose and a refined, slightly earthy flavor set off by moderate
oak aging. The '76, tasted out of the barrel, struck me as
richer, fatter, and heavier, and seemed to promise more
complexity. Simi's lone rosé is first-rate, one of California's

best—a rosé of Cabernet Sauvignon that typically offers, as it did in the '75, light olive-ish hints of Cabernet aroma in the nose and a fine, fresh, just off-dry flavor.

Cambiaso Winery and Vineyards

The Cambiaso family has been running their Healdsburg winery and its fifty-two acres of vineyards in typical Italian country-winery fashion since 1934. For years they made only a red, a white, and a rosé, but in the last few years have added Cabernet Sauvignon and a few other varietals to their list. Recently a Hong Kong investor bought the entire place, and substantial expansion is planned.

THE WINES:

The reds I have sampled are robust and full-bodied, as is usual from producers with an Italian country-winery heritage, and vary from ordinary to very good. Their non-vintaged "Vintners Reserve" Cabernet Sauvignon was typical of their table wines; it had a full, rich nose and a warm, round flavor with ripe, raisiny notes.

Dry Creek Vineyards

Located near Healdsburg, Dry Creek was bonded in 1972 and produced its first wines that year. Dry Creek's owner, David Stare, has some fifty acres of vineyard surrounding the small concrete-block winery; these will eventually supply about half the winery's needs, with additional grapes coming, as they do now, from the Dry Creek–Healdsburg area. Current production of a number of vintage-dated varietal wines is in the twelve-thousand-cases-a-year range; the goal is twenty thousand cases per year.

THE WINES:

From his first vintage, Stare has been remarkably successful with Chenin Blanc and Fumé Blanc. The '76 Chenin Blanc (the latest example) was a delight in early 1977: Its almost floral aroma was so expansive that it spilled over the glass, and its very light, delicate body, lively balance, touch of *pétillance*, and just off-dry finish added up to a tremendously charming wine. It is surely one of the finest, if not the

finest, fresh-fruity style Chenin Blancs in the state. The '75
Fumé Blanc Lot #2 had an undeveloped scent in early 1977,
but good flavor and acidity; it may need some months in the
bottle to develop. Stare ages his Chardonnays in oak, but his
deft, light touch with whites is evident in this variety as well.
The '74 was particularly lovely by early 1977, with vanillan
hints of oak in the scent and flavor, a fine balance, and a
complex finish.

So far, I find the reds less impressive than the whites. Most
have been intense and well-balanced, but—at least in their
youth—lacked some varietal character and the ripe, soft,
roundness that makes the whites so charming and appealing.
Among recent red releases, however, I did enjoy the spicy
'75 Zinfandel, which had good acidity and tannin and an
almost peppery finish; a few years should make it a fine
bottle. Stare's Cabernet Sauvignons are austere and well-built,
but a bit short on varietal flavor. The '74 had a rather closed
character in early 1977; the '76, tasted from the barrel, appeared to have much the same medium-weight structure and
character as the '74.

Souverain Cellars

This large, relatively new winery near Geyserville has un-
dergone a rapid series of changes in the past few years, including new owners and new labels. It was originally con-
ceived as a companion winery to the now defunct Souverain
of Rutherford winery in the Napa Valley, and produced its
first wines in 1972 under the "Villa Fontaine" label, which
was dropped in favor of "Chateau Souverain," which has
now been dropped in favor of "Souverain of Alexander Valley." Now that it is the only Souverain around, it will probably become known as just plain Souverain. Its new owners,
a partnership of grape growers called North Coast Cellars,
purchased the enterprise in 1976 from the Pillsbury Corporation. It will doubtless continue to purchase its grape needs
from local growers as it did when owned by Pillsbury.

THE WINES:

I have found the North Coast wines bottled under Souverain's previous labels in the good to very fine range, and it
appears safe to assume that the winery's new owners will continue to build on its previous successes. I enjoyed several of

the whites in the past, but of current releases, the '73 Souverain of Alexander Valley North Coast Cabernet Sauvignon was particularly attractive.

L. Foppiano Wine Company

John Foppiano left Genoa in 1874 to look for gold in California. Whether he found any isn't known, but in 1896 he bought a winery where the present one stands near Healdsburg. The winery has remained in family hands ever since. During Prohibition the family shipped fruit, and after Repeal enlarged their operation to its present two hundred acres of vineyards, and million-gallon storage capacity. In the 1960's Foppiano switched from bulk wine to varietals.

THE WINES:

Judging by several recent Foppiano releases, the wines here are beginning to make a slow transition from sturdy to stylish. An estate bottled '71 Petite Sirah had a full, rich, powerful nose, full-bodied flavor, and a moderately tannic texture with a very attractive underlying Italian-style ripeness when I tasted it in early 1977. An estate bottled '75 Sonoma Fumé (dry Sauvignon Blanc) had a pleasant fresh, crisp, scent but a rather dull flavor because of its lack of acidity.

J. Pedroncelli Winery

Founded in 1927, Pedroncelli began making the shift from bulk wine when John Jr. and James Pedroncelli, sons of the founder, took over the winery and began bottling premium varietals in the mid-fifties. Their hundred and ten acres of vineyards and winery building is north of Geyserville, and recent plantings have emphasized varieties like Cabernet Sauvignon.

THE WINES:

The Pedroncelli wines have become increasingly sophisticated in recent years and now have left most of their country origins behind. The whites range from good to excellent, most emphasizing a tart, sappy fruitiness that is particularly attractive in the '76 Chenin Blanc. The '75 Gewürztraminer I sampled featured a lovely honey-clove scent and a mild spicy fruitiness. The reds are a shade less distinctive than the whites, well-made but not particularly distinguished. I found the '73 Pinot Noir round, full-bodied, and satisfying, and the Cabernet Sauvignon of the same vintage well-built, with sufficient tannin and balance to develop into a fine-drinking, characterful, though not outstanding wine. It was, however, already pleasant and approachable when I sampled it in early 1977.

Sonoma Vineyards

Sonoma Vineyards rapidly expanded to its present substantial size from a tiny store-front operation, begun in 1959 as Tiburon Vintners by Rodney D. Strong, a former dancer and choreographer. Tiburon, located in the waterfront town of the same name north of San Francisco, had no vineyards, so in 1961 Strong established Windsor Vineyards near Windsor in Sonoma County. Wine was sold under both labels, and a substantial business in mail-order wine was created, featuring personalized labels. By 1970 a huge new modern winery had been built at Windsor, and national distribution of a line of sixteen varietal and generic wines led to adoption of the Sonoma Vineyards label. In 1973, the parent company decided to rename itself Sonoma Vineyards in keeping with the wine.

At one time, the enterprise planned to plant five thousand acres, which would have given it one of the largest vineyard holdings in California outside the San Joaquin Valley, but too rapid an expansion caused financial difficulties. In 1976, Sonoma Vineyards entered into a long-term agreement with Renfield Importers, which now controls the winery, although Strong remains as winemaker. Another new step: The winery has dropped its generic and jug wines and will concentrate on a dozen vintage-dated varietals. Currently, it makes a quarter of a million cases of wine per year.

THE WINES:

Recently, I tried the winery's top-of-the-line estate bottlings of Zinfandel, Johannisberg Riesling, Chardonnay, and Pinot Noir. Of these, I found the '73 Zinfandel most interesting: It had a rich, almost tarry nose with hints of oak and cherries, and an intense, fruity flavor. Rather high in alcohol (13.9 percent), this concentrated wine should lose some of its present harshness by 1980. The '75 Johannisberg Riesling, on the other hand, was light (eleven percent alcohol), rather delicate in style, and had an appley-fruity flavor. Its balance suggests it ought to be consumed young. The '74 Chardonnay I tried was, alas, badly oxidized; it appeared to be a fairly substantial specimen on the order of previous Sonoma Vineyards Chardonnays. The '73 Pinot Noir was a disappointment: thin in body, grapey-flavored, with a rather hard finish.

Among the non-estate-bottled wines, I found the '74 Ruby Cabernet coarse but characterful, the '73 Petite Sirah big, brawny, and appealing, and the '73 Cabernet Sauvignon very good, medium-bodied, young, and olive-ish.

Korbel Champagne Cellars

Korbel (actually F. Korbel & Bros.) is situated on the banks of the Russian River near Guerneville in redwood country. In the 1860's, three Czech brothers named Korbel came to the U.S. and worked at a variety of careers, at one time even running a cigar box factory, and ended up with a sawmill on the Russian River. They eventually planted the cleared land to vineyards in the 1880's, and by 1896 made the first Korbel Brut champagne. Since 1954 the winery has been owned by the Heck Brothers, who expanded its vineyards to seven hundred acres and added its most famous product, Korbel Natural.

While the Korbel champagnes are all made by the *méthode champenoise*, the Hecks have introduced a number of technological improvements in the processing to cut down on the excessive number of hand operations the process requires, without sacrificing quality. Machines now perform the operations of riddling and disgorging automatically, and enable Korbel to produce several million bottles of sparkling wine each year. Korbel added a line of table wines, both varietal and generic, and dessert wines as well as brandy in the midsixties.

THE WINES:

Korbel takes its line of a dozen table wines and jug wines seriously, and although the wines vary considerably in quality, some recent bottlings have shown improvement. The '75 Chablis had an aggressively greeny taste with a bitter finish, doubtless because of a heavy proportion of press wine, but the '74 Zinfandel was delightful, with a sprightly fruity nose and flavor. Korbel also makes a popular brandy, but its sparkling wines continue to be its best products. The Korbel Brut is thought by many to be the standard of quality for California champagnes of this type. I have always found it reliable, if not memorable, and there are a number of producers now who make sparkling wines of equal or better quality. The Korbel Natural, whose base wine is almost half Chardonnay, and which receives extra aging on the yeast, was for years the finest American champagne. Now it is only one of the best, which is to say that it is still a fine product—bone-dry, characterful, with a touch of yeast in the nose, and lingering vinosity—it makes an excellent aperitif. Korbel also makes an Extra Dry, a Sec, Rouge (a sparkling burgundy), and a Rosé (a pink champagne).

Italian Swiss Colony

One of the most commonly seen labels in the U.S., Italian Swiss Colony started as a philanthropic scheme to help Italian and Swiss immigrants to America. It began in 1881 as the brainchild of Andrea Sbarbaro, a San Francisco grocer turned banker, who purchased a fifteen-hundred-acre tract in Sonoma with the idea of creating a colony of vineyard owners. The utopian aspects proved unworkable, and Sbarbaro turned the operation into a private enterprise that soon prospered enough to enable him to build a mansion filled with gadgets to play practical jokes on his friends. After Sbarbaro's death and following Prohibition, the winery revived and passed through several hands, acquiring other labels and becoming, eventually, part of the giant Allied Grape Growers, a cooperative of some sixteen hundred grape-growers, whose marketing arm is United Vintners. They are now owned by Heublein, Inc. (which also owns Inglenook and Beaulieu Vineyards in Napa, among other labels).

THE WINES:

The winery at Asti, with its eight-million-gallon storage capacity, makes a number of United Vintners wines, including some of the non-estate-bottled Inglenook wines, but only a few Italian Swiss Colony wines. The most interesting of these is the Italian Swiss Colony California Chianti

"Tipo," a simple, tangy, acidic Italian-style red that comes in a round, wrapped, traditional chianti bottle. The rest are made in other wineries in the state operated by United Vintners, principally in the San Joaquin Valley; for comments on the rest of the line of wines, see the entry for United Vintners in Chapter 9.

Geyser Peak Winery

Geyser Peak is a prime example of the fact that a massive injection of capital is all it takes to startle a sleepy country winery quickly into new life, premium production, and national distribution. This former bulk winery was purchased by the Joseph Schlitz Brewing Company of Milwaukee in 1972; prior to that time the winery was best known for producing Four Monks wine vinegar. The enterprise added another country winery, Nervo, best known for its stocks of old Zinfandel, and now boasts a large new winery complex and six hundred acres of Sonoma vineyards. Geyser Peak hopes to be producing a million cases of wine (or nữto) per year by the early eighties.

THE WINES:

Geyser Peak's initial offerings seem to indicate an interest in both ends of the wine spectrum, from jugs to fine wines. Its first wines came on the market in 1974 under the Summit and Voltaire labels, the first used on generics and the second on non-vintage varietals. Now, after thinking it over, Geyser Peak has decided to phase out the Voltaire label, stick with the Summit tag for generics and jugs, and produce vintage-dated varietals under the Geyser Peak label. The Summit wines so far are competitive with other jug offerings from the big California producers. Several of them are available in handy one-gallon (and larger) dispenser cartons with collapsible inner plastic liners that keep opened wine fresher longer.

The nine varietals in the Geyser Peak line are made primarily from Sonoma and Mendocino grapes. Of recent releases, I found the '74 Pinot Noir a lively, grapey, attractive wine whose lightness suggests it ought to be consumed before 1978. The '74 Chardonnay was a characterful, though not particularly rich example, with a pronounced nose and noticeable oak flavor, but the '73 Zinfandel lacked fruit, depth, and varietal character, and was rather acidic. I preferred the light Cabernet Sauvignon of the same vintage with its olive-ish, somewhat stemmy-stalky aroma and flavor. I also sampled an intriguing '74 Limited Bottling Cabernet Sauvignon made from Central Coast grapes that showed good dark color, a strong herbaceous-stemmy nose, and a good depth of fruit. An undeveloped, awkward wine in early 1977, it should be quite nice by 1980.

Parducci Wine Cellars

Parducci is another small family operation that made the transition from bulk and local trade production to vintage-dated varietal wines. Parducci has made the transition better than a good many country wineries have, and has already produced some very fine wines.

Parducci is the pioneer post-Prohibition winery in Mendocino County. The founder, Adolph Parducci, actually began making wine in Cloverdale in 1916, but moved his winery to its present location north of Ukiah in Mendocino County in 1931. Two of his sons, John and George, now run the winery, and since the mid-sixties have planted new varieties, extended their vineyard holdings—they now have three hundred and fifty acres—and added modern equipment as they have shifted their emphasis to premium wines. As part of an expansion program, the winery gained new owners in 1971, but remains family-run.

THE WINES:

Parducci's current production level of about one hundred thousand cases a year consists primarily of vintage-dated varietals. One of the winery's most popular wines is its French Colombard (a wine Parducci pioneered as a varietal in 1947), doubtless the best example of this varietal in the state. Colombard is a rather undistinguished variety that usually makes a very neutral wine, but Parducci's—perhaps because the grapes come from the winery's low-yield vineyards—is always remarkably light, crisp, and fragrant. I sampled the '76 before bottling and was delighted with its fresh, appetizing fragrance and lively balance of soft fruitiness and crisp acidity. The '76 Chenin Blanc I tried had a similar fresh, fruity appeal.

John Parducci is not fond of the flavor wood aging gives

to wines, believing that oak masks the fruit more often than it adds to it. Thus, none of the Parducci whites see wood save Chardonnay—and then not always. The very attractive '75 Chardonnay—not aged in wood—showed a fine, full, almost fig-like varietal nose and a full, fruity core of varietal flavor when I tasted it in early 1977; a marvelously rich, fully developed '71 Chardonnay (also not aged in wood) tasted at the same time was as convincing an example as one could want that superb Chardonnays can be made without oak aging.

As one might expect, Parducci reds are aged primarily in large redwood cooperage to soften them, and even the ones that spend some time in small oak barrels do not have a noticeable oak note. In fact, Parducci has gone so far as to make a '73 Mendocino Cabernet Sauvignon that was not aged in wood at all, a tight-knit, very closed wine when I sampled in early 1977, which, while well-made, showed little in the way of young Cabernet scent and flavor. This suggests that quite a bit of the classic Cabernet character may derive from traditional wood aging. Less exotic and more attractive was the '72 Cabernet Sauvignon released under the "Cellar Master's Selection" label that Parducci uses for particularly outstanding lots of wine. Nineteen seventy-two was a good vintage in Mendocino, and this wine already had a lovely herbaceous Cabernet nose, a soft, lovely texture and flavor, and a long, nutty-sweet finish in early 1977. With just a little tannin to lose, this wine ought to be excellent drinking by 1980.

Parducci also makes several other reds, including a fruity Gamay Beaujolais, a Pinot Noir, a Zinfandel, and a Petite Sirah. The '72 Mendocino "Cellar Master's Selection" Pinot Noir was light and silky with a delicate fruity scent, but was perhaps a shade too acidic. The '72 North Coast Zinfandel had a curiously mature nose but thin body, which made its acidity and alcohol stand out. The "special selection" Mendocino Petite Sirah of the same vintage, however, had plenty of stuffing—in fact, it will take several years for its tannic bite to soften and its appealing, just-evident spice to emerge.

Fetzer Vineyards

Although Fetzer Vineyards was bonded in 1968, its ninety acres of vineyards were planted some eight years earlier in a Mendocino area north of Ukiah considered marginal for grapes like Cabernet Sauvignon. But Bernard Fetzer had strong beliefs in the potential of the area, and after several years of selling the grapes to home winemakers, built and bonded the modern winery, which he now runs with his family. Fetzer has one hundred and twenty acres in vines, but expects to continue to buy half the grapes he needs. Current production is around fifty thousand cases a year; about eighty-five percent of that is red wine.

THE WINES:

Fetzer likes his Cabernet Sauvignons to show plenty of color, tannin, and stuffing, and as a consequence many of them can be awkward and unharmonious when young, although their concentration and structure promise future rewards after enough bottle age. The '73 Mendocino Cabernet Sauvignon (estate bottled) had a full, deep, undeveloped scent with a faint earthy note and an angular taste structure when I tried it in early 1977. It should develop handsomely by the early eighties. The estate bottled '74 is similar, with an aroma that hints of olives, earth, fresh oak, and spice, and a solid matching flavor. The '76, sampled from a barrel, was still yeasty when I tried it, but appeared well-built.

The Zinfandels from this winery have varied in style much more than the Cabernets, and some have been thin and sharp. A recent bottle of the light non-vintage Lake County Zinfandel showed little but vinous warmth in the nose and was a trace green in the finish. The '74 "Ricetti" Mendocino Zinfandel, however, was full-bodied, tannic-textured, and mouth-filling, with a spicy-ripe aroma; it was a first-rate example of a rich Zinfandel that should develop magnificently over the next several years. Fetzer has also produced some fine Pinot Noirs—by early 1977 the '70 had developed a rich nose hinting of peppermints and almonds and a superb velvety flavor texture; it was easily one of the best California Pinot Noirs of recent years. It overshadowed the fine '74 Mendocino Pinot Noir I tried at the same time, which had a ripe-fruit flavor and full, oaky aroma.

Fetzer makes a considerable amount of everyday table wine—a Premium red blend and a Premium white blend. For the red, of which he makes most, he draws primarily on the large local plantings of Carignane. The warm, characterful, non-vintage Premium Red also goes to market labeled as "claret" and "burgundy."

At present, Fetzer is planning to add a·dry-style Johannisberg Riesling to his list.

Cresta Blanca Winery

Cresta Blanca is one of the best-known names in California's wine history, but it is now a label used by the giant Guild company for its Mendocino and other north coast wines. As Guild intends to run Cresta Blanca as a separate division, I will discuss its wines here.

Begun by Charles Wetmore in the Livermore Valley in 1882, Cresta Blanca in the years after Repeal became most famous for its Premier Sémillon produced in the mid-sixties, made from grapes hand-inoculated with botrytis mold to create a sweet white wine on the order of a French Sauternes. After slipping into inactive days, and finally closing in the late 1960's, Cresta Blanca was purchased in 1971 by Guild and has its principal winery in Ukiah, in Mendocino County.

THE WINES:

At present, the Cresta Blanca name appears on about eighteen non-vintage varietals and generics. The generics are unremarkable but well-made, and while the varietals, many of which carry Mendocino appellations, are not exciting wines, the ones I have tried have all been good to fine in quality.

As with all non-vintage wines, there is no way to tell one lot from another. While at first I was not favorably impressed with the Cabernet Sauvignon, recent bottles have been very good drinking indeed. The Gamay Beaujolais and Grignolino I've tried varied from good to very good. One of the better wines I have had from Cresta Blanca is their Petite Sirah, which exhibited an attractive oaky-mint nose, a great knot of flavor, and sufficient tannin to repay a few more years of aging. The Zinfandel showed an almost port-like raisiny ripeness in its nose and it had a slightly stewed-fruit character to its taste as well. I find the whites less exciting; the French Colombard, however, is most refreshing. The revived Cresta Blanca has also put a great deal of effort into its sherries; the most attractive, to my palate, is the very good "Dry Watch"—an excellent aperitif. As the Guild concern has enormous resources, and apparently intends the Cresta Blanca name to stand for its best wines, the label bears watching.

Other Wineries

As in other areas of California, there are new wineries of all sizes beginning operations in Sonoma and Mendocino; as might be expected, small ones are more common than large ones.

Included in the growing list of new Sonoma wineries are Alexander Valley Vineyards, Hop Kiln Winery, Gundlach-Bundschu Wine Company, and Lambert Bridge. Older tiny operations include Davis Bynum Winery and Trentadue Winery, as well as country wine producers like Valley of the Moon Winery.

The wines of two additional Sonoma wineries will probably be seen out of state sooner than wines of the above wineries. Hacienda Wine Cellars in Sonoma was founded in 1973 by Frank Bartholomew, the former owner of Buena Vista Winery, until he sold it in 1968. Hacienda will concentrate on fine wine. The 1886 Lemoine Winery in Glen Ellen was renamed Grand Cru by partners Allen Ferrera and Robert Magnani when they bought it in 1970. At first they planned to concentrate on wines made from grapes in their thirty-acre vineyard, primarily Zinfandel, but are now in the process of expanding their small production.

Mendocino has two new small wineries, both near Philo in the Anderson Valley, quite near the Pacific. Husch Vineyards has some twenty acres of vineyards so far, and Edmeades Vineyards, first planted in 1964, has some twenty-five acres. Both aim to make fine wine.

Chapter 8

Livermore to Monterey

The wineries north of San Francisco Bay in Sonoma and Napa include some of the most prestigious names in California. But Sonoma and Napa do not have a monopoly on fine wine, and they have nothing to match the sheer variety of sizes and extraordinarily different approaches to winemaking that one finds among the wineries south of the Bay that stretch across six counties from the Livermore Valley to the Monterey Peninsula.

The climate and grape-growing conditions in these south-of-the-Bay districts vary considerably. In the Livermore Valley in Alameda County, the soil is composed of an alluvial deposit, washed down eons ago from the Eastern Hills. Winemakers in this long-cultivated area point with pride to their stony soil, which is often more than half rock and hundreds of feet deep. This gravelly basin is Region III in climate. The Santa Cruz Mountains that run parallel to the ocean on the coast south of San Francisco have a number of small vineyards whose climate is Region I; although close to the ocean, the fir-forested steep slopes of the mountains keep out fog and allow the grapes the unhindered benefit of cool, slow ripening. The long Santa Clara Valley inland from the Santa Cruz Mountains is basically Region II, as is the long Salinas Valley that extends farther south into Monterey County.

These districts have their share of long history as well as fine wine. In Santa Clara, two of the largest premium wineries in California today, Paul Masson and Almadén, date their origins to the 1850's, as does Mirassou; the Livermore Valley has been cultivated almost as long, and the Santa Cruz Mountains have a number of vineyards and wineries of nineteenth-century origin. The Salinas Valley, however, is practically an instant wine district.

Almadén, Paul Masson, Mirassou, and other wineries in the Santa Clara Valley, as well as Wente Bros. in the Livermore Valley, have been forced to look for vineyard land elsewhere in recent years because of the increasing threat of urbanization. In the past few decades the creeping growth of housing tracts, shopping centers and just plain pavement has transformed some formerly sleepy agricultural valleys into smog-filled suburbs. The result in the Santa Clara Valley was that land taxes soared, water tables dropped, and pollution burned vines. With little space left, vineyard owners had to look elsewhere, and while some wineries, like Weibel, have gone north to places like Mendocino, most have gone south to Monterey County.

Monterey's Salinas Valley, a long, funneling corridor ten to twenty miles wide and a hundred and eighty miles long, opens onto Monterey Bay on the north and is bordered by the Santa Lucia Mountains on the west and the Gavilan Mountains on the east. Were it not for the cooling ocean breezes, this region would bake the vines during the summer, and were it not for its vast submerged rivers that permit easy irrigation, the scant rainfall would not support vines. Until 1960 the Salinas Valley could only boast of some thirty or forty acres of vines. It now has nearly forty thousand acres, and may have fifty thousand by 1980. The first plantings here were begun by Mirassou, and Paul Masson and Almadén quickly followed when it became apparent that the skimpy rainfall and stiff afternoon winds did not pose insurmountable difficulties in an area which the University of California had long ago analyzed as potentially fine vineyard land.

As startling as this jump in vineyard land is, perhaps even more surprising is that *non-grafted* vines are so widely planted here. Many wine lovers claim pre-phylloxera wines—wines made in the days before grafting of the vines was necessary— were better than any since. Of course, the number of such wines with life left in them after a century are few and fading, and the glorious vintages since are solace great enough for all but those whose romanticism about wine tends toward the melancholic. But is is hoped that "direct-producing" *vinifera*—*vinifera* grown on its own roots— might well yield better fruit than grafted vines. Almadén, Paul Masson, Mirassou and others are relying on soil sterilants and careful quarantine to keep the danger of phylloxera insignificant to their huge plantings. It is important to note, however, that no one is planting *vinifera* on its own roots except in areas where grapevines have never been previously planted. To plant ungrafted vines in long-cultivated areas like the Napa Valley would be very risky, as phylloxera may still be present in the soil.

The technology that is employed in both setting out and harvesting these bold new plantings is equally impressive. As much of the soil in the Salinas Valley has a dense "hardpan" layer some two to four feet below the surface, this has to be broken up to let the vines' roots penetrate deeper. In order to do this, a huge five-foot steel shank as thick as a post is sunk in the earth and dragged behind four giant crawler tractors. This plowing technique, called "ripping," has actually transformed the fertility, drainage, and soil composition of huge tracts of land. This is followed by extensive deep gas treatments in the soil to kill any possible pests, planting, and the laying of mile after mile of irrigation pipes. Most of these vineyards are laid out in such a way as to permit mechanical harvesting as well, in which giant machines rumble down rows of vines which have been pruned and trained to hang their bunches on long wires that run down the row; current models shake or knock the berries or bunches off. Some wineries, principally Mirassou, have topped this labor-saving innovation by having the grapes crushed, and then capped right in the field with a neutral gas to prevent spoilage, thus insuring maximum freshness and delicacy in the wines.

This sort of approach to grape-growing takes enormous amounts of capital, and most of these operations are funded by large corporations aiming for a substantial share of the growing wine market. In many cases, were it not for the use of these modern techniques on a grand scale, it would not be possible to offer good wine and sometimes fine wine at reasonable prices.

The first wines that were produced in the early seventies from Monterey grapes showed a surprising fruitiness and intensity of character. Several varieties, in fact, showed such strong varietal characteristics that they seemed imbalanced. Some of the first Cabernet Sauvignons, for example, had distinct vegetative aromas and a few showed the unsubtle scent and flavor of fresh-cut grass. It is important to note, however, that this so-called "Monterey character" only appeared in wines from Bordeaux grape varieties—Cabernet Sauvignon, Merlot, Sauvignon Blanc, and Sémillon. This note is probably a plus in Sauvignon Blanc (North Coast versions are not always that distinctive); Monterey-grown Sauvignon Blancs can have an attractive, unmistakably individual bell-pepper scent.

No one likes a "grassy" Cabernet, however, and theories abounded as to the origin of this disconcerting flavor note. Some ascribed it to the infancy of the vines; others to the soil; but research to this date seems to point clearly to the fact that Bordeaux varieties harvested before the sugar levels in the grapes reach 21° Brix (or, less technically, before they are completely ripe) are liable to show this overly strong varietal character, whereas the same varieties harvested at higher sugar levels will not. In fact, this "grassy-pepper" character is said to show up in Cabernet grown in a very cool season anywhere—including Napa and Bordeaux. Some Monterey winemakers harvested their initial crops too early in the season because they had not yet discovered that the district was far cooler than anyone had imagined, so cool that some varieties don't ripen until December! What can legitimately be called "the Monterey character"—very intensely flavored wines with high levels of acidity—is really the result of Monterey's extremely long, cool growing season.

That is only the beginning of Monterey's unique growing conditions. The area is also extremely dry, very windy, and has some of the lightest soil in California—all of which mean very low yields, often a plus in terms of wine quality. It also seems to have the most frequent occurrences of botrytis in the state, certainly a viticultural bonus for many white varieties. For all these reasons, the long-term outlook for the quality of Monterey wines is extremely promising.

The great interest in small individual enterprises is just as much in evidence south of San Francisco Bay as it is north of the Bay, so that polarization of size seems inevitable. Small wineries are not hostile to large wineries, only wary of them, like mice among elephants; they regard themselves in a different market, and are confident that wine lovers, when they want an especially fine or unusual wine, will seek them out. If the premium wineries south of the Bay can be considered bold, the small fine winemakers here are downright adventurous. They are ready by turns to be more scientific, or more traditional, or more daring, or more innovative, it seems, than in other areas of the state—anything to make finer and finer wine.

The Santa Cruz Mountains in particular are home to a handful of small wineries with a roughly similar approach to wine, and in some respects it is quite distinct from the Napa-Sonoma approach to fine wine. I say "roughly similar" because these wineries are fiercely individual, and perhaps in keeping with this maverick outlook, occupy lonely mountain sites. They share only the outlook that wines should be made in the most natural way possible. They are not by any means traditionalists, but are among the most experimental and daring of California winemakers, and their products are among California's most distinctive and impressive wines.

These individual wineries, whose approach to wine is best represented, I think, by Ridge and Chalone, see wine differently from the wineries in the Napa and Sonoma Valleys. In the Napa, the wineries strive for elegance and balance, even if the wines sometimes must be light and thin. The small mountaintop wineries south of the Bay strive for power and intensity of flavor, even if the wines sometimes must be coarse and heavy. At their best, the wines of the Napa are rich, stylish, and hauntingly beautiful; at their best, the wines of these small mountain wineries are arresting, austere, and overwhelmingly profound. Their greatest wines abound in what the French call *"goût de terroir"*—earthiness—that seems to capture in the dimensions of the wine the wild, raw settings of their vineyards.

Some wineries in the area, like Ridge, have only recently come in for their share of recognition; others, like Martin Ray, have stopped making wine after years of pioneering this style. All alike, however, have come in for their share of controversy and heated debate. Like their wines, these small wineries of the Santa Cruz and other mountain areas seem to elicit strong responses.

Suggested Samplings

Anyone wishing to sample some of the current high points of the region's wine production will certainly find some of them among the following types and producers. These are offered as a starting point, not a definitive list of the best, and readers are encouraged to go on and explore for themselves. Bear in mind that some of these wines are produced in small quantities and consequently may not be easy to find; many of them are readily available, however, at least in major U.S. cities.

RED:
> *Cabernet Sauvignon*
> Concannon Vineyard Limited Bottling
> Ridge Vineyards

Gamay Beaujolais
   The Monterey Vineyard

Petite Sirah
   Concannon Vineyard

Zinfandel
   Mirassou Vineyards
   Ridge Vineyards

WHITE:

(Pinot) Chardonnay
   Chalone Vineyard
   David Bruce
   Wente Bros.

Muscat Blanc
   Concannon Vineyard

Pinot Blanc
   Chalone Vineyard

Gewürztraminer
   Mirassou Vineyards
   Almadén

Sauvignon Blanc
   Concannon Vineyard
   Wente Bros.

White (Johannisberg) Riesling
   The Monterey Vineyard
   San Martin
   Wente Bros.

Emerald Riesling
   Paul Masson (Emerald Dry)

Sémillon
   Wente Bros. (Dry Sémillon)

OTHER:

Sparkling Wine
   Mirassou Vineyards Au Natural
   Paul Masson Brut

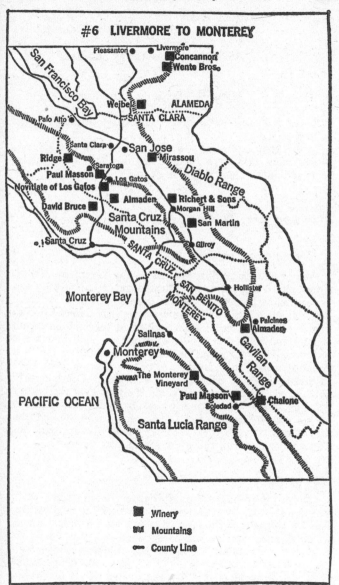

#6   LIVERMORE TO MONTEREY

San Francisco Bay

Pleasanton   Livermore
              Concannon
              Wente Bros.

Palo Alto

Weibel   ALAMEDA
              SANTA CLARA

Santa Clara   San Jose
              Mirassou

Ridge

Saratoga   Diablo Range

Paul Masson   Los Gatos
Novitiate of Los Gatos

David Bruce   Almaden   Richert & Sons
                         Morgan Hill

Santa Cruz   San Martin
Mountains

Santa Cruz   SANTA   Gilroy

              CRUZ

              SAN BENITO

Monterey Bay MONTEREY   Hollister

                         Palcines
                         Almaden
Salinas

Monterey   Gavilan

              The Monterey Range
              Vineyard

              Paul Masson   Chalone
              Soledad

PACIFIC OCEAN
              Santa Lucia Range

■ Winery
▨ Mountains
•─ County Line

Dessert Wine
Novitiate of Los Gatos Black Muscat
Paul Masson Rare Souzão Port
Richert and Sons Tawny and Ruby Ports

Rosé
Mirassou Vineyards Petite Rosé

These and other wines of the region are discussed in the
following pages.

In this chapter I will begin with the wineries in the Livermore Valley, then work south, down the Santa Cruz Mountains and Santa Clara Valley to Monterey County.

Principal Wineries

Concannon Vineyard

Among the pioneering wineries in the Livermore Valley,
Concannon Vineyard now produces some fifty thousand cases
a year, virtually all of it from grapes grown in its three
hundred stony acres of Livermore vineyards. James Concannon, the founder, came from Ireland in the mid-nineteenth
century and worked at a number of careers until he made a
fortune selling rubber stamps, and on the advice of the then
Archbishop of San Francisco, settled in Livermore in 1883
to make wines for religious use. This stood Concannon in
good stead, for during Prohibition his sons kept the winery
going by making sacramental wines. Ownership passed to one
of his sons, "Captain Joe" Concannon, who headed the
winery until his death in 1965. His sons, Joe Jr., and Jim
Concannon, now run the operation and its vineyards.

THE WINES:

Concannon produces more than a dozen wines, both
whites and reds. Over the years it developed a solid reputation for soft, clean whites—particularly its Sauvignon Blanc,
which in some vintages was exceptional—but these were not
noted for outstanding freshness and liveliness. Now, with
the installation of a battery of jacketed temperature-
controlled fermentors in 1974, the quality of all the whites

has improved markedly. While recently sampling their latest releases, I found even the non-vintage Chablis (mostly Chenin Blanc) had surprising freshness and fragrance. The '75 Johannisberg Riesling was lovely, featuring a touch of wintergreen in the scent and a light, tart-fruity flavor, but the '75 vintage of Sauvignon Blanc was superb: the aroma almost floral-fragrant and the delicate flinty flavor whistle-clean and crackling crisp on the palate. The winery's two new white varietals are also excellent. The '76 Muscat Blanc has only eleven percent alcohol, a positively exuberant Muscat perfume that spills out of the glass, and a lightly sweet, marvelously lingering grapey flavor—all of which add up to delicious drinking. The other new white is a more sober grape, the Rkatsitelli. So far, there's only one acre of this Russian variety in California, and the Concannons have it. The '76 I tried had a most intriguing spicy-perfumey aroma and, in contrast to what my nose led me to expect, a surprisingly stony, lightly spicy flavor with a faintly peppery finish.

Concannon also has some noteworthy reds. The '73 Zinfandel struck me as thin but pleasant, while the '73 Petite Sirah (which Concannon pioneered as a varietal wine in California) was excellent; round, robust, not too tannic, with a pleasant full texture to the body, intense flavor, and a "warmish" spicy-fruit scent to the nose, it was typical of past vintages. The '74 I sampled out of the barrel in early 1977 was much more impressive: So dark and purply it stained the glass, it was a tremendously rich wine, the aroma and flavor simply packed with fruit. This marvelous mouthful of a wine will be released sometime in 1978 as a "Limited Bottling."

The Concannon Cabernet Sauvignon is issued only in "Limited Bottlings." This wine, with its own unique "Livermore" character, is one of my favorites; while not terribly complex, it can be enormously satisfying. Of recent examples, the '70 is particularly fine, with a big, curranty, almost meaty nose and a generous core of flavor. The '74 that I sampled out of the barrel, which won't be released until 1978 or 1979, was impressively dark and extremely concentrated, and is likely to be even bigger and finer than the '70.

Wente Bros.

Wente Bros. (the name is always abbreviated on the la-

bels) was founded by the brothers' father, Carl Wente, a
German immigrant who made wine while working for
Charles Krug, one of Napa Valley's winemaking pioneers, in
1880. In 1883 Wente founded his own winery in the Livermore Valley, across the road from James Concannon's
vineyard. Wente's sons, Herman and Ernest, presided over
the winemaking and the vineyards respectively during the
years after Repeal, while the operation grew from a fifty-acre
vineyard to its present holdings of nearly fourteen hundred
acres, and the winery from a bulk-wine to a premium producer with a great reputation for white wines. Ernest's son,
Karl, oversaw Wente's expansion into vineyards in Monterey
and its continued experimentation with new wines until his
death in early 1977. He is succeeded by his sons Eric and
Philip. The winery now produces nearly four hundred thousand cases a year, some ninety percent of which is white
wine.

Wente has long been known for white wines; this is in part
due to the fact that the first wine pioneers in Livermore,
many of them Frenchmen, were attracted to the possibilities
inherent in its stony soil, and one of them, Louis Mel, obtained cuttings of Sauvignon blanc and Sémillon from
Château d'Yquem. Wente's El Mocho vineyards, acquired
from Mel, still have vines from Château d'Yquem cuttings.
That, plus the fact that such grapes seemed to do well in the
area, gave Livermore Valley wineries a reputation for white
wines.

THE WINES:

Wente was probably the first American winery to gain critical attention for its Chardonnay, and although now there are
far more wineries producing top-quality Chardonnay,
Wente's, in better years, is still very fine indeed. In years like
'75 it has a ripe appley quality which is most attractive.
In spite of the fact that both the Wente Chardonnay and
Pinot Blanc may spend a short time in oak, Wente Bros.
has not jumped on the bandwagon for oak flavor in the
whites, and continues to believe strongly in letting the fruit
show. The Wente Sauvignon Blanc can be very fine; I recently tried the '75 from Livermore, and found it had a
fresh, spicy aroma and spicy-leafy flavor nuances. In some
years it has a very intriguing spice-earth aroma rather like
clean damp earth. The characterful Pinot Blanc is one of

my favorites. The '73 had a deep gold color, a heavy herbaceous aroma, and a mouth-filling weedy-clean acid-crisp taste. The Wente Dry Semillon has some character and a round, full texture to its body, but like the popular Grey Riesling is a rather soft, simple, merely pleasantly fragrant wine. The same is true of the "Blanc de Blancs," a blend of Ugni blanc and Chenin blanc grapes, mostly the latter.

To me the Wentes' most interesting wine is their "Riesling Spätlese," a late-picked Johannisberg Riesling that is produced from time to time from their three-hundred-acre Arroyo Seco vineyard in Monterey, some fifteen miles from Carmel. Fog conditions occasionally permit the growth of Botrytis cinerea mold, the "noble rot" responsible for some of the great sweet wines of the world; botrytis occurs fairly frequently in Monterey, and the Wentes have made the most of it, producing in '69, '72, and '73 luscious honeyed sweet Johannisberg Rieslings with full flowery aromas and enough tart acidity to balance the sweetness. The '74, the latest example, had a deep, "botrytis"-floral nose and a superb, long, luscious-sweet lingering flavor. It should develop for several years if stored in a good cellar, which is just as well, since Wente made no late harvest Johannisberg Rieslings in '75 or '76.

The Wentes also produce ordinary to very good red wines, including a spicy, berry-like Livermore Zinfandel.

Weibel Champagne Vineyards

At the southern end of Alameda County, southwest from Livermore, is Mission San Jose, first planted by Franciscan Fathers in 1797, and now the home of the Weibel winery. The most important early figure in the area, however, was not a padre but Leland Stanford, railroad magnate, U.S. Senator, California governor, and wine-grower of great ambitions. Phylloxera put an end to his vineyard, first planted in 1869.

Rudolf Weibel and his son Frederick had come from Switzerland to San Francisco and made sparkling wines under other labels. In 1945 the Weibels purchased the old Stanford property. Since then the town of Fremont has expanded to threaten the vineyards there, and Fred Weibel, now head of the firm, purchased land in Mendocino and is completing a new winery there. Their Mendocino vineyards will supplement the production of their home vineyards, which goes into their extensive line of wines, some three dozen in all.

THE WINES:

Weibel specialized in sparkling wines until 1950, and still produces champagnes for other wineries. The process used for all the sparkling wines is the transfer method. The winery now also makes a good many varietal and generic table wines and while they are typical of many long lines of wines put out by large wineries in that they vary considerably in quality, many recent examples have been rather poor. A non-vintage Chardonnay I tried recently had peculiar off-odors and a very dull flavor. In the past I have enjoyed the Pinot Noir, however, and was pleased to find that a recent bottle of the non-vintage release had good aroma, fine, ripe flavor, and good acidity.

Ridge Vineyards

Ridge began in 1959 when four electronics engineers purchased an old vineyard and winery on the southeast side of Montebello Ridge near Black Mountain overlooking the Santa Clara Valley. One of the partners, David Bennion, began making wine from grapes from the old vineyard that had been planted first in the 1880's and then later replanted in the forties. Encouraged by the results, the winery was bonded in 1962, and by 1968 Bennion was working full-time at the winery. In 1970, another winemaker, Paul Draper, joined the growing staff, Bennion became president and vineyard manager, and the winery was on its way to an eventual goal of twenty thousand cases a year.

Ridge has produced a number of wines from its own fifty acres of vineyards, some of which are at twenty-five hundred feet elevation—the highest in the state. However, it buys most of its grapes from growers. In fact, Ridge has purchased its Zinfandel from areas as far apart and different in climate as Mendocino and Amador.

It devotes three-quarters of its production to Zinfandel and the rest mostly to Cabernet Sauvignon, although it does produce a miniscule quantity of Chardonnay. Eventually it plans to devote most of its production to Cabernet. Like many small wineries, it experiments constantly and makes wines from a number of different red varieties whenever it finds grapes from which it feels an interesting wine can be made. In almost all instances that means grapes from low-yield, highly stressed, unirrigated mountain vineyards.

Ridge is one of the principal exponents, if not the leading exponent, of a particular style of winemaking in California. It places great emphasis on natural winemaking and rarely fines or filters its wines; the wines are clarified mostly by patient racking, and the reds as a result show considerable extract and tannin. As Ridge's aim from its beginning has been to produce wines with as much fullbodied grape character as possible, it has been willing to forego early finesse and subtlety to achieve dramatic, mouth-filling power and dimension in its products. Most of the reds take years to develop and are sold young with the hope that customers will lay them down until they mature. Bennion feels that the wine-buying public is simply going to have to get used to the idea that not every bottled wine is ready to drink, just as many have got used to the presence of sediment in fine wines. This approach to winemaking makes Ridge a wine lover's winery; not every wine from it is an unqualified success, but every bottle is an adventure.

Ridge wants its customers to share in the experience of unique individual wines, and part of its effort in this respect is to be as informative as possible on their labels. These are exceptionally detailed, showing exact alcoholic content, whether or not the varietals are blended, the bottling date, and information on what sort of oak it was aged in, and the like. Most Ridge labels simply state "California" for geographical origin, rather than a county name, because the vineyard location is usually given. A great effort is made to accentuate the differences between vintages and vineyard locations, which makes it possible for one to compare a half-dozen Ridge Zinfandels of a given vintage from locations all over California.

THE WINES:

Ridge's style of winemaking has its risks. In the effort to produce assertive, arresting, and even awesome wines, Ridge has made some that were simply harsh and unpleasant. Its approach seems much more suited to red wines than whites, and in fact only about five percent of Ridge's production are whites—some two hundred cases of Chardonnay made from the small plantings of this varietal on Montebello Ridge. Big, strong, unfruity, sometimes weighty to the point of being ponderous, these are impressive wines, often very complex, but can lack charm and harmony.

Ridge's reds have understandably received the most attention. Through the '70 vintage, the Montebello Cabernets were typically inky in color, complex in aroma, and intensely fruity, though the fruit was masked by great, puckering, mouth-coating tannin: All of these have been wines to be appreciated in the late 1980's. Brimming with potential, they give one the hope that what is overwhelming and a little breathtaking about them in their youth will be their glory and grandeur in their prime, when the grim tannin eases its grip. Some people have mistakenly thought that the Cabernets made since then have been purposely made in a less awesome style, but '71, '72, and '73 were simply lighter vintages, and at Ridge, the grapes dictate the style of the wine to be made from them. One happy result is that the elegance and balance of the Montebello Cabernets from those vintages aren't hidden, waiting to be discovered by future generations. This does not mean they lack character and stuffing. The rich, ripe '71 with its lingering layers of flavor has already shown well against—even beaten—first-growth Bordeaux in blind tastings. The elegant '72, one of the best of that weak vintage, is leaner but more intense than the '71; its rich, well-knit texture will probably not open up before the early eighties. The '73 is rich and stylish, and while really requiring at least a decade's development before it can be adequately appreciated, already shows a great deal of suppleness and hints at future charm. Since 1974, Ridge has been making an additional Cabernet Sauvignon from grapes from a mountain vineyard in the Napa Valley, York Creek; it has not yet been released. The '75 York Creek has fifteen percent Merlot added in, but was nonetheless inky with tannin when I tried it out of the barrel in early 1977, and was more backward, austere, and undeveloped in flavor than the already currant-nosed, rich, balanced '75 Montebello sampled at the same time.

Ridge is rapidly becoming best known for its Zinfandels, however; it was one of the first wineries to take Zinfandel seriously as a "big" wine, and has made some of the finest, if not the finest Zinfandels in California: big, bold, whacking wines, chewy with tannin, and simply alive with flavor. While some of the early Zinfandels had hot, harsh qualities, recent releases have been more polished—which is not to say tame.

Of the many individual vineyard Zinfandels Ridge has produced in recent vintages, I have been particularly impressed with the '74 Lytton Springs, a deep, rich wine with superb texture and spiciness. It is, of course, still developing. The concentrated '76, tasted out of the barrel, may surpass the '74.

From time to time, Ridge produces a botrytized Zinfandel with considerable residual sugar, a unique and extraordinary natural red dessert wine; in the years it is produced, it is labeled "Zinfandel Essence."

Paul Masson Vineyards

As is mentioned in the entry on Almadén, the early history of Paul Masson is entwined with that of Almadén. Charles LeFranc inherited the Santa Clara Vineyards his father-in-law, Etienne Thee, had planted in 1852. Later he started a winemaking concern with *his* son-in-law, Paul Masson, a native of Burgundy, who later (in 1892) bought LeFranc's son's share of the business and formed the Paul Masson Champagne Company. Four years later he began building his winery in the Santa Cruz Mountains above Saratoga.

In the days before Prohibition Paul Masson was one of the industry's most important and influential winemakers, as well as being the sort of man who inspires legends. He managed to get permission to make "medicinal champagne" during Prohibition and after Repeal made wine for three years before finally retiring; he finally sold out to Martin Ray, a Saratoga stockbroker who long had the ambition of owning Masson's mountain vineyards. A year after a disastrous fire in 1941, Ray sold the Masson enterprise and moved to another mountaintop nearby to start again.

Since 1942, Paul Masson has been owned by Seagram & Sons, and since that time has grown into one of California's largest premium wineries (now four million cases per year); its growth can only be matched by Almadén's. Under the direction of men like Otto Meyer, Masson has become not only one of the best-known labels in the U.S., but is now exported to some fifty foreign countries as well, and has pioneered such successful wines as its "Emerald Dry" (Emerald Riesling). Masson has over six thousand acres in vines, mostly in the Pinnacles vineyard near Soledad and in Santa Clara Valley, and has four wineries—the old Paul Masson Winery at Saratoga, the Saratoga Champagne Cellars, one at

Pinnacles in Monterey, and one in the Central Valley near Madera.

THE WINES:

Masson produces an extensive list of wines—some forty-eight products—which are neither especially complex nor exciting, but are usually soft, light, attractive, and reliable; many of the "Riesling" types can be quite ordinary. Masson's "Emerald Dry" (Emerald Riesling) can be really delicious, however, with its lovely muscat-floral nose, a touch of *pétillance* to its light-green-gold body, and its refreshing, tart, simple flavor. A fine value among the generic whites is the non-vintage Dry Sauterne (a Sauvignon Blanc/Sémillon blend) which, in the samples I've tried, offers an intense spicy-leafy aroma and flavor.

A number of the reds are quite good and attractive, notably the proprietary blend, "Baroque," which, in the bottles I've tried, featured a full vinous scent and a soft, full, rich flavor. The other proprietary blend, "Rubion," is pleasant, but not as full and flavorful as the "Baroque."

Masson also does a good job with its champagnes (especially the crisp Brut), and has a very fine port (the "Rare Souzão") which is much superior to the vast majority of wines of this type in its price range.

Like several other giant producers, Paul Masson is not ignoring the growing market for fine wine. The existence of this market and the quality of grapes from their Monterey plantings have inspired Masson to take the plunge into vintage-dated varietals. The first four will be released in 1977; additional varietals will follow in succeeding years. Most will carry a Monterey appellation. The initial offerings, which I tasted in early 1977, are cautious in style, but impeccably clean and well-made. The relatively light '73 Cabernet Sauvignon (most of which is from Monterey grapes) showed good olivey Cabernet character and youthful intensity. The three whites all carry an "Estate Bottled" Monterey appellation. The '76 Gewürztraminer had a fresh, spicy nose and good varietal flavor, but its greeny finish tended to accent its dryness, and this detracted somewhat from its appeal. The '75 Pinot Chardonnay lacked varietal intensity, but showed good lingering fruit. The '75 Johannisberg Riesling, however, had a fine, floral aroma with hints of botrytis and a fresh, lively, tart fruitiness.

Novitiate of Los Gatos

The Novitiate of Los Gatos is one of two church-owned and operated wineries in California, the other being The Christian Brothers. The Sacred Heart Novitiate was founded in 1888 and has operated a sacramental wine business from that time. The Novitiate has about six hundred acres of vines and in the past few years has begun to take its small production of commercial wines—for many years a sideline—seriously. Expansion is planned, and wines such as their Pinot Blanc, Cabernet Sauvignon, and deservedly famous Black Muscat will be seen more often.

THE WINES:

The Novitiate's best wine, the Black Muscat, is a sweet intense dessert wine with a fascinating complex muscat scent with fruit nuances that remind one of things like marmalade, dried apricots, or maybe ethereal prunes.

The non-vintage Cabernet Sauvignon I've tasted has had a solid olive nose, good olive flavor and character, and was not bad though a bit light in body.

David Bruce

Experimentation is the watchword among the smaller wineries in the area, and is certainly in evidence at David Bruce. Dr. Bruce, a San Jose physician, began the winery and vineyards that bear his name in 1961, when he purchased land in the Santa Cruz Mountains not far from Los Gatos. In 1964 he bonded his small winery, but by 1968 had built a larger winery to take in the production of his thirty-seven acres of top varietals, which are planted at an elevation of two thousand feet. In the tradition of the area, Bruce follows his own dictates on winemaking, and his hangar-like winery building houses equipment he designed himself. Bruce makes wine for the wine enthusiast, and the adventurous one at that. He shuns filtering and fining and continues to offer many of his wines in cask bottlings, so that the individuality of each separate lot can be emphasized.

THE WINES:

Bruce makes Pinot Noir and Zinfandel (ocasionally pro-

ducing white versions of these reds, too) as well as Cabernet
Sauvignon and Chardonnay, the last of which has attracted
considerable attention and controversy among wine enthusiasts. His Chardonnay, sampled on several occasions, is
always something of an unusual white wine experience, not
just because it usually requires decanting. The '74 Chardonnay Lot #2, sampled in spring 1977, was gold with a hint
of green and had an impressively pungent Chardonnay aroma
with strong earth and oak overtones. The oak flavor was
penetratingly strong, but considering the incredibly heavy
extract did not seem out of balance. The body was thick and
weighty on the tongue, and the overall impression, although
stunning enough, was of a wine to be saluted as a far pole
of one style of California Chardonnay rather than simply
to be sipped for enjoyment. Yet according to the label, Lot
#2 is the lighter of the two '74 Chardonnays offered!

The '71 Late Harvest Essence Zinfandel smelled like a raw
young port with fleeting vegetative aroma notes, and had a
powerful (17.5 percent alcohol), rather raw flavor. It should
certainly last. A '72 Zinfandel, however, was much more
approachable in scent and had a fine flavor and good balance.

Such wines have their fans, others dislike them; but they
are anything but blah. Dr. Bruce's ability as a winemaker is
impressive, and it is evident he is not interested in tame
wines or timid wine drinkers.

Mount Eden Vineyards

This tiny Santa Cruz mountaintop enterprise has some two
dozen partners, a resident manager, Bill Miller, and a winemaker, Merry Edwards, and makes only one thousand cases
of wine a year. The winery, which draws on twenty-two acres
of vineyards originally planted in the forties by the controversial California fine-wine pioneer Martin Ray, plans to
plant an additional twenty to thirty acres of vineyard on
Mount Eden, and recently started a second line of wines under the MEV label made from grapes purchased from other
growers.

Martin Ray was a successful stockbroker who purchased
Paul Masson's winery and vineyards in the Santa Cruz mountains near Saratoga in 1936, when that pioneer winemaker
retired. After a disastrous fire in 1941, Ray sold the name
and business to Seagram's, moved to Mount Eden, and estab-

lished a winery and vineyards under his own name some two thousand feet above the Santa Clara Valley.

Ray was one of the pioneers of vintage-dated varietals and could be considered the father of the big, austere style of winemaking that many of the small wineries south of the Bay have adopted. Some of his wines were quite superb and complex; some were merely dramatic failures. Highly controversial because he thought little of other winemakers and said so, Ray scorned the California wine industry in general, and considered his own wines vastly superior to all other wines in California as well as to all but the great wines of pre-war Europe. His aloofness and ego became legendary. Finally, he became involved in protracted litigation over the five vineyards he helped establish on Mount Eden with other partners. All but three acres of Chardonnay are now owned by Mount Eden Vineyards. Ray died in 1976.

THE WINES:

So far I have only tasted three Mount Eden wines, all sampled in early 1977. The '74 Chardonnay has a complex but rather unattractive nose with curious hints of mustiness mixed with oak and impressive flavor dimensions marred by an unpleasant grassy, apple-skin finish. Whether additional time in the bottle will bring these disconcerting elements into harmony, I can't say. I preferred the crisp, characterful '75 MEV Chardonnay. The '73 Mount Eden Pinot Noir had a varietal, pepperminty, vaguely pruney aroma, but a rather acetic quality to its complex flavor, causing me to question its staying power. It appears that Mount Eden intends to make highly individual, unusual wines, pursuing a style similar to the late Mr. Ray's.

Almadén Vineyards

The history of Almadén is curiously tied to the history of Paul Masson. Both date from 1852, when Etienne Thee, a Bordeaux farmer, planted his vineyard near Los Gatos in the Santa Clara Valley. His son-in-law, Charles LeFranc, inherited the vineyards, and later *his* son-in-law, Paul Masson, a native of Burgundy, went into winemaking with him. In 1892 Masson bought out Charles LeFranc's son's share of the business, and formed the Paul Masson Champagne Company. But the Santa Clara vineyards, named Almadén for a local

quicksilver mine, remained in the LeFranc family, then went
dormant during Prohibition, were briefly revived after it under other hands, and finally in 1941 were bought by Louis
Benoist. Under his direction the vineyards and winery grew—
Benoist had an extensive list of wines and even introduced
Grenache Rosé to the American public—and Almadén eventually became the largest premium producer in the U.S. Since
National Distillers purchased it in 1967, its production has
continued to expand; in 1976 Almadén sold some six and a
half million cases of wine.

Its vineyard holdings alone are enormous: almost seven
thousand acres in four counties are now planted to twenty-
nine grape varieties. One of its vineyards near Paicines in
San Benito is thirty-eight hundred acres! Over two million
vines (all direct producers) are planted there, all of which
are irrigated by seven hundred and ninety miles of sprinkler
system, which can also be used for frost protection. In addition, Almadén has some nine thousand acres of vineyard
under long-term contract.

THE WINES:

Almadén's current line of products is now over sixty items
long, the major portion of which are merely clean, sound
wines. The jug wines offer no more vinous interest than do
its competitors' products, and a number of the generic and
varietal wines I've had lacked freshness, life, and character.
Doubtless this tired quality is a result of extra-cautious processing and excessive cellar treatment to ensure a reliable
product.

More interesting are the vintage-dated varietals Almadén
has introduced recently in an attempt to enter the fine wine
market. Many are labeled "special selection," some are estate
bottled, and quite a few carry specific appellations of origin
(principally Monterey and San Benito). I sampled some of
these new efforts in early 1977 and found most of them a
definite step up in quality from the wines in the regular line.
The '74 Pinot Chardonnay Special Selection had a fruity,
varietal aroma and a light fruity flavor with a nice finish. The
'75 Johannisberg Riesling Special Selection had a lovely color
and a fresh floral aroma with a hint of botrytis complexity.
Its body was light and the soft, fruity flavor just off-dry;
although nice, it could have used higher, more refreshing
acidity. The Gewürztraminer has been Almadén's best white

for some time; the '75 is an excellent specimen, with a spicy-sweet but not cloying fragrance and a clean, soft, refreshing, lightly spicy flavor.

Among the reds, I found the '74 Gamay Beaujolais Special Selection light, fruity, and well-made, but the '73 Cabernet Sauvignon Special Selection was even more attractive, with a young olive-ish aroma and a soft, mellow, balanced flavor. The most interesting of all was the '74 Petite Sirah, a big dark wine with a fine, almost blackberry-fruity flavor. Approachable now, it will no doubt develop into a satisfying, rich, round wine by 1980.

Almadén's latest sparkling wine—and to my taste, the best —is the very pretty bronze-colored "Eye of the Partridge," a blend of about one quarter Pinot Blanc, one quarter Pinot Noir, and half Chardonnay. The '74 had a clean, fruity scent and a delightfully fruity lightly sweet flavor with some richness.

Mirassou Vineyards

Mirassou is one of the oldest names in California wine-making, but one of the youngest labels. For many years, the Mirassous only made wines in bulk for sale to other wineries; not until the fifth generation and the late sixties did they begin to market wines under their own name. Their vineyards, facilities, and expertise have enabled them to quickly join the ranks of medium-sized premium wineries making standard to fine wines.

Pierre Pellier brought cuttings with him from France which he set out in what is now downtown San Jose in 1858. Then in 1881 Pierre Mirassou, another French immigrant, married one of Pellier's daughters, and ran a winery in the Evergreen district. His son, Peter, continued winemaking in the area and sold grapes during Prohibition. Peter's sons, Edmund and Norbert, built up the wine business, and in fact, still own it. The fifth generation is both numerous and active in the business, and has formed a separate marketing arm to buy the grapes from the vineyards and make wine to sell under the Mirassou label. Mirassou has over a thousand acres of vineyards in both Santa Clara and, since the early sixties, in Monterey, near Soledad. Due to the urban squeeze in the valley, Monterey is where Mirassou, like other wineries in the area, see the future. For now, however, the winery remains near San Jose, but the labels clearly indicate whether the grapes have come from Monterey or Santa Clara or both. Production of wines under the Mirassou label is now about 175,000 cases a year.

THE WINES:

Mirassou produces a line of wines, over two dozen if you include special "Harvest" selections (essentially special selection wines), but unlike the large lines of wines of many wineries, most are at least interesting even when they are not successes. Because many of the wines are made from Monterey grapes, which make wines of intense, even penetrating flavor, and because the Mirassous like the fresh, forthright character of the grape in wines, their wines are strong-flavored and fruity, with a good deal of varietal character. They are almost always above average compared with the good or indifferent vintage-dated varietals of many large premium wineries.

The whites include a dry, fairly characterful Chablis and a very fruity Chenin Blanc. The '76 vintage of this latter wine from Monterey grapes had a rather pungent (whiff of sulphur?) aroma but a delightful, peachy-sweet, soft flavor when I tried it in early 1977. The '75 Chardonnay, also of Monterey origin, was kept in oak, but not too long, and showed a fine, fruity-varietal aroma and a somewhat earthy, austere flavor. The '76 Johannisberg Riesling from Monterey was rather delicate in scent, and could have used a higher and more refreshing level of acidity to balance its grapey-sweetness. I was more impressed by the '76 Monterey Gewürztraminer, sampled from a holding tank. With a full, spicy-floral aroma and a delightfully balanced, sweetish, spicy flavor, it will be most attractive if it can keep its lively style after bottling. Most of the '75 Gewürztraminer went into Mirassou's newest white, Fleuri Blanc, a very appealing sweet (eight percent residual sugar) wine that will carry a vintage date from '76 on. Made from sixty-five percent Gewürztraminer and thirty-five percent Pinot Blanc and Johannisberg Riesling, it exhibited a big, full, heady, spicy aroma and a rich, round, unified, lingering fruity flavor with a touch of leafiness and spice in the finish.

To many, the intensely varietal character of wines made from Monterey grapes is far more attractive in whites than in reds. It is certainly true that for a time some of the Mirassou reds—notably the Cabernet Sauvignon—were troubled with aroma and flavor nuances that suggested various kinds of vegetables (asparagus, celery, etc.) and sometimes just plain grass. Whatever the cause of Mirassou's initial difficulties with certain reds, the problem is now under control, and all the vegetative hints that remain in the Cabernet are now simply a distinctive herbaceousness.

After the light, disappointing vintages of '71 and '72, the '73 Cabernet Sauvignon (Monterey) is back to form, and showed a strong herbs-and-olives nose and flavor and an attractive, lingering, cinnamon-spice finish when I tasted it in early 1977. Mirassou also makes a fruity Gamay Beaujolais and, every few years ('71, for example), an attractive Pinot Noir. The best of their reds, however, is the Zinfandel, which comes from both Santa Clara and Monterey. The '69 Late Harvest from Santa Clara I remember for its rich and concentrated nutty-spicy character and almost port-like pungent nose. The '74 Santa Clara bottling has a strong raspberryish aroma and plenty of mouth-prickling briary flavor and acidity. The Monterey Zinfandels seem to have more pepper and spice, even leafiness, than the ones from Santa Clara; a barrel sample of the '76 Monterey showed plenty of intensity of flavor and a full, warm, berry-like aroma.

Mirassou also makes a very fine, somewhat austere "Au Natural" champagne, and an intriguing rosé from Petite Sirah, called "Petite Rosé."

San Martin Vineyards

San Martin dates fram 1892 and was operated by the Filice family of grape growers from 1932 until 1973, when it was purchased by the Southdown Corporation, a Houston-based conglomerate. San Martin owns sixteen hundred and fifty acres of vineyards in Monterey. Southdown, which plans to expand San Martin's production considerably, has already invested heavily in new winery equipment.

THE WINES:

Ed Friedrich, San Martin's German-born and -trained winemaker, is in the process of upgrading San Martin's extensive line of wines, which includes fruit and berry wines and vermouths as well as the usual varietals and generics. Under the Filices, San Martin's wines could charitably be considered picnic fare. Many of these wines of indifferent

quality still crowd the current list, but are rapidly being replaced. To alert consumers to the change, the new labels
carry tags such as "limited vintage" and many have Monterey
and/or Santa Clara appellations.

The recent red releases include a big-flavored, almond-
cherry-scented '74 Amador County Zinfandel; a '74 Monterey
County Cabernet Sauvignon that showed a peppery-spicy
character, fine balance, and a trace of leafiness in the finish;
and a '73 Santa Clara Petite Sirah that featured a big,
stemmy-stalky aroma and heavy tannin. All three could use
some bottle age.

Good as these new reds were, I was more impressed by
the whites, particularly San Martin's new "Soft" Chenin
Blanc and "Soft" Johannisberg Riesling, both purposely made
low in alcohol (ten percent) to enhance their delicacy. The
'76 Soft Chenin Blanc is quite fragrant, faintly peachy, and
deliciously light and fruity-sweet; its charm is enhanced by a
touch of *pétillance*. The golden-hued '76 Soft Johannisberg
Riesling is appealingly delicate, but also round and flavorful,
with an apricoty tang. San Martin's other whites, while well-
made, are not as exciting, at least so far. The '75 Monterey-
Santa Clara Pinot Chardonnay is moderately characterful;
the '76 Monterey Emerald Riesling tart and quaffable; and
the '75 Santa Clara Muscat di Cannelli light and pleasantly
perfumed.

Chalone Vineyard

Chalone is located in one of the most unpromising areas of
California, but the severity of its grape-growing conditions
is undoubtedly partly responsible for the impressive intensity
of its wines. At some two thousand feet above the Salinas
Valley on the Chalone bench of the Gavilan Mountains is a
thirty acre vineyard first planted in the late nineteenth century by a Frenchman in search of chalky, unfriendly-looking
limestone soil similar to that of Burgundy. It was not until
1916, however, that the present vineyard was laid out by
William Silvear to Chenin blanc, Pinot blanc, Chardonnay,
and Pinot noir. The grapes grown on the property gained a
reputation for quality during Prohibition despite several
changes of ownership. Finally in 1966 Richard H. Graff,
after several stints at other wineries and study at Davis, purchased the property with several other partners, and began
making wines from the grapes. Now Graff has been joined by

more partners, as well as his brothers, John Graff and Peter Watson-Graff, who act as winemaker and vineyard manager, respectively.

Current plans call for eventual expansion of the now tiny annual production to about ten thousand cases a year. Ninety-five acres of new vineyards have been planted, and in 1974 a new small winery building was constructed. Until the new vineyard plantings come into full bearing, Chalone wines will continue to be hard to come by, as the original thirty-acre planting yields only about two tons an acre. Rainfall in the area is so limited that until a well was recently dug water had to be trucked from Soledad and fed to the vines through a special hose system.

THE WINES:

Chalone's main whites—Chenin Blanc, Pinot Blanc, and Chardonnay—have all been remarkably complex and flavorful. To some palates the Chalone style might seem overly oaky and ponderous; admittedly, "delicious" and "charming" are not terms that come to mind when tasting these austere, weighty wines. But at least one of the whites, the Chardonnay, has often been magnificent, unquestionably ranking among California's greatest achievements with that grape. Doubtless the intense richness of these whites is due in part to the concentrated fruit from the old, low-yielding vines in the original Chalone planting, but it is also surely a result of the painstaking winemaking, which includes fermentation (as well as aging) in Limousin oak barrels, a troublesome method used by only a few California wineries.

The most unusual white offered is the Chenin Blanc, which tastes like no other California effort with this wine: The '74, for example, featured an expansive nose with traces of oak and smoke and pears, a complex, lingering flavor with sharp notes of oak, and a crackling dry finish. Impressive as it can be, this style of Chenin Blanc is something of a stunt, and although several hundred cases of it will continue to be made each year from the grapes from the original Chenin blanc plantings, no additional Chenin blanc vines have been planted.

The Chalone style really comes into its own with the Pinot Blanc and the Chardonnay. Of recent Pinot Blancs I sampled in early 1977, the '73 was typical: golden-hued, heavy and thick, with an earthy, smoky-oak nose that hinted at the weedy character of the grape, it had a deep, austere flavor edged with crisp acidity and an earthy tang to its lingering finish. The '74 struck me as a shade lighter and fruitier; the '75, though undeveloped, was big and rich, on the order of the now-mature '73. The Chalone Pinot Blancs stand comparison with the best Chardonnays, and in fact are not always easy to distinguish from them, particularly from big-style oaky Chardonnays like Chalone's own. The deep-gold '71 Chardonnay is surprisingly mature at six years of age—in fact, probably at its peak—and is big, fat, and tangy-rich with oak. Its heavy vinosity weighs on the palate and its monotone flavor lingers. The '74 was a mélange of impressions—lush but austerely oaky, earthy but fruity, powerful but elegant; in short, magnificent.

To augment current production, Chalone also produces "vin blanc" and "vin rouge" from the young vines in its new plantings and makes a French Colombard from purchased grapes; all have been marketed under both the Chalone name and the winery's second label, Gavilan Vineyards. I found the '75 Vin Blanc (from three-year-old Chardonnay vines) soft in scent and delicate in flavor; it had been given added character by oak aging. The '76 French Colombard, the most successful Chalone offering of this varietal to date, tasted crisp and fruity with hints of oak when I tasted it out of the barrel in early 1977. This wine is by no means in the same league with other Chalone whites; it is not fine or complex, simply very good drinking.

The Chalone Pinot Noir—made in distressingly small quantities—comes from the original plantings, and, to judge by a sample of the '71, is one of the rare California Pinot Noirs that reminds one of the peppermint-rosebud aroma and silky richness of fine Burgundy.

The Monterey Vineyard

Monterey county is something of a an instant wine district. In 1970, there were less than eighteen hundred and fifty acres of vineyards planted; by 1975 there were well over thirty thousand! Along with the rapid expansion of vineyards came some very ambitious winery enterprises, including The Monterey Vineyard. Some ninety-six hundred acres of vineyards in the Salinas Valley were to supply an equally impressive winery operation. The massive building—looking something like a Spanish-modern airplane hangar—was built near the town of Gonzales in 1974 and was designed to have an eventual storage capacity of ten million gallons. It was also lavishly equipped to handle tiny to vast lots of wines separately, since the original intention was to offer single vineyard wines as well as generous amounts of varietals under The Monterey Vineyard label. A complicated enterprise consisting of interlocking and overlapping grape-growing partnerships, it was underfinanced and found itself unable to launch into the millions-of-cases-per-year production originally planned.

The Monterey Vineyard has now been scaled down considerably, and since January, 1977, has been owned and controlled by the winemaker brought in to oversee the original operation, Richard Peterson. (Peterson succeeded André Tchelistcheff as winemaker at Beaulieu.) Presently, the winery owns no vineyards and contracts to purchase grapes from local growers. Current production is definitely small-winery scale: twenty thousand cases a year. Peterson plans slow growth to about one hundred thousand cases annually. Certainly no small-sized producer in the state occupies such an impressive-looking and impressively equipped winery, and since The Monterey Vineyard has far more production and storage capacity than its needs for its own label, Peterson crushes grapes and produces wines under contract for other California wineries.

THE WINES:

The Monterey Vineyard presently offers a dozen varietals and one blend, all vintage-dated, from Monterey grapes grown in the cool Region I zone of the upper Salinas Valley. Its first wines, all exceptionally clean and well-made, came from the '74 harvest, and showed the sometimes surprising intensity that has come to be associated with Monterey-grown wines. The whites released so far show an attractive forthright varietal character, in certain cases at the expense of delicacy and subtlety. In the winery's white wine blend, Del Mar Ranch, however, this bright, fresh quality contributes to its refreshing, dry, crisp character—at least in the '74. A '75 Chenin Blanc had a strong, fruity-varietal aroma and good acidity but lacked softness and appeal. A '74 Chardonnay (labeled "late-bottled" to indicate oak aging) showed a very European-style light fruitiness and assertive acidity rather than the full, fat quality typical of most California Chardonnays.

The '75 Grüner Sylvaner (Sylvaner) had a light, leafy-vinous aroma and a lively, fresh, attractive flavor. I preferred the '75 Gewürztraminer, which had a very lovely heady-spicy scent and a lively, tart, dry (less than one percent residual sugar) spicy flavor. One of the most promising whites produced here—to judge by the '74—is the Johannisberg Riesling, a golden, rich-scented, round wine with a pronounced citrusy grapiness to its flavor, hints of botrytis complexity, and good mouth-filling vinosity.

The '75 Rosé of Cabernet Sauvignon was sharp, light and refreshing, with something like a strawberry-herby aroma. I found the '74 and '75 Gamay Beaujolais sharply assertive and very tart and fruity and light-bodied. The '74 Zinfandel from the El Camino Ranch had a very lively berryish nose and taste, but was overshadowed by the richer dark-ruby "December Harvest Special Reserve" of this same wine, which showed a riper, richer scent, almost raspberryish, with a curiously leathery-earthy note, and a very intense, deep, and lingering berry-like flavor with an intriguing peppery finish. Its normal-level alcohol makes it less port-like and more approachable now than many late-harvest Zinfandels, and its racy acidity augurs fine future development.

The Monterey Vineyard already produces very interesting and distinctive wines, and certainly has the potential to become one of California's important fine-wine labels.

Other Wineries

There are a number of wineries in the area between Livermore and Monterey whose labels will be more frequently seen in the future. These range from small fine wineries to large operations now gearing up for volume production to tiny country outlets now being readied for expansion. Of all California's wine districts, the Santa Clara Valley seems to boast the largest number of country wineries. West of Gilroy in south Santa Clara are found a group of wineries, some dating back to pre-Prohibition times, that for years have conducted a bulk-wine business and a brisk highway trade in their very informal roadside tasting rooms. As is typical with country wineries, their best wines are their robust reds. Live Oaks, Bertero, Rappazzini Bros., Pedrizetti, and Bonesio have recently been joined by Fortino Bros. and Thomas Kruse.

The most interesting small winery in the Morgan Hill area is Richert & Sons, founded by enologist Walter R. Richert in 1953. Like most of the wineries with roadside tasting rooms, Richert has no vineyards, but unlike most of them, it specializes in dessert wines. His "Full Dry Sherry" is a pleasant, nutty, medium-sweet and above-average wine, while the Richert Tawny Port is quite attractive, with a prunish-woody nose and smooth, unfruity flavor.

The Santa Cruz Mountains were home to some fifty wineries as recently as the 1930's, but the number dwindled to a handful until the resurgence of interest in wine in the 1960's. Now nearly two dozen wineries dot the mountainsides. All are very small—most produce well under a thousand cases a year—and very individual in outlook. Many, however, lean toward the "natural style" of winemaking. Some produce very fine wine; others only curiosity pieces; a few have not yet passed out of the amateur stage and their products show it. Some of the older and better-known names not already discussed in the text include Martin Ray (the label is being continued by his son, Peter Martin Ray), Woodside Vineyards (in San Mateo County), and Nicasio Vineyards.

In San Jose is the Turgeon and Lohr Winery, founded in 1974. It has two hundred and eighty acres of vineyards in Monterey and offers a full line of varietal wines under the J. Lohr label. Current production is about twenty thousand cases a year; eventual expansion to one hundred thousand cases annually is planned. Of the initial wines that I tasted in early 1977, I found the whites, many of which show the characteristic intensity of Monterey-grown grapes, particularly promising.

Monterey has not been the only new wine district developed south of the Bay in the seventies. The Central Coast—at least that is what many of the wineries call the wine country of San Luis Obispo and Santa Barbara counties—lies directly south of Monterey county. As many wine lovers realize by now, "south" does not necessarily meant "hot" in California's ocean-cooled mountain-and-valley coastal geography. All three fine-wine climatic zones—Regions I, II, and III—are found in the Central Coast and there are already eight wineries in the area. Two of these—Pesenti Winery and Rotta Winery—have been making country-style jug wines for years. I have sampled wines from two others: Hoffman Mountain Ranch and The Firestone Vineyard. The Hoffman family founded Hoffman Mountain Ranch in the Santa Lucia Moun-

tains west of Paso Robles in 1972 and built the winery in
1975. The family hopes the chalky limestone soil of their
seventy acres of new plantings will yield an outstanding Pinot
Noir, so far produced only in miniscule quantities. I tried
a fresh, light, fruity '75 Chenin Blanc and a pale, mildly
spicy '75 Late Harvest Franken Riesling (Sylvaner); they
were both attractive. The Firestone Vineyard near Los Olivos
north of Santa Barbara was founded in 1974 by A. Brooks
Firestone, grandson of the tire magnate Harvey Firestone.
It has about three hundred acres of vineyards and will be one
of the biggest premium producers in the Central Coast. I
tried an attractive, lively, very flowery '75 Johannisberg
Riesling and a charming, characterful dry '75 Rosé of Pinot
Noir (made with thirty-four percent Chardonnay); both were
very clean and well-made.

Chapter 9
Lodi to Cucamonga

The San Joaquin Valley stretches almost three hundred miles from Lodi to Bakersfield. Often called the Inland or Central Valley region, it is east of the Livermore to Monterey district and runs north to south between the coastal range and the Sierra Nevada mountains. Including the much smaller but climatically similar Cucamonga district east of Los Angeles, it is a vast grape-growing area that ranges between Region IV and V in degree-days. Far too hot a climate for fine wine grapes, the area is most noted for its volume production of ordinary quality table wine, its ordinary to fine dessert wines, and its brandy.

In these districts the application of technology to winemaking reaches its zenith in the largest wineries, where unpredictable elements such as wooden cooperage and corks have been replaced by glass and steel tanks and aluminum screwtops for bottles, and the computer has been put to use in the blending of wines. Impressive as the production-line methods of the giant wine-factories of the area are, what is most impressive to many is how good much of their wine is. Many have claimed that what is most unique about California is not that it produces some fine wines to rival the world's best, but that its least ambitious table fare is so superior to the *vin ordinaire* of most wine-producing countries. What enables these giant wineries to produce enormous quantities of good, sound wine at reasonable prices are the conditions found here.

The Lodi (pronounced "low-die") area in the north of the San Joaquin Valley includes the fifty-square-mile grape-growing district surrounding the city of Lodi. Grapevines grow huge in its sandy-loam soil and Region IV climate, and its principal grape is a table grape, the Flame Tokay. Lodi has almost twenty thousand acres of these vines, and fourteen thousand acres of wine grapes, mostly Zinfandel and Carignane. At least some of the Zinfandel grapes grown here can be made into very fine wine. But in recent years wineries looking for Zinfandel to make rich, concentrated reds have largely turned to the vineyards of nearby Amador county.

The main San Joaquin Valley, from Escalon and Modesto to Fresno and Bakersfield, produces two-thirds of California's entire production of wine, and most of that is made by just two firms, E & J Gallo and United Vintners (the principal wine subsidiary of Heublein, Inc.). There are almost seven hundred square miles of vineyards stretched along the thirty- to fifty-mile-wide valley, and its rich soil, irrigation systems, and the sun and heat of a climate that ranges between Region IV and V allows yields of up to twenty tons of grapes per acre. While the Mission grape of the padres is still widely grown here, the most famous grape of the area is Thompson Seedless, the "three-way" grape which can be used as a fresh table grape, turned into raisins, or made into extremely neutral wine—what some flippantly refer to as "Fresno Chardonnay" or "Château Thompson." This portion of the San Joaquin Valley, not surprisingly, produces virtually all the raisin crop of the U.S., a vast amount of fresh table grapes, and almost all the port, muscatel, and brandy of California, as well as half the state's production of table and sparkling wines. In fact, a number of the largest premium wineries whose table wine production takes place in other districts have branch wineries here or contract with wineries in the area to produce their sherries, ports, and brandies.

The Cucamonga district east of Los Angeles, while not part of the Inland Valley, is similar climatically—it is Region IV—and produces mostly ordinary table wine and some good Zinfandels. Unfortunately what vineyards it has left may not be able to withstand encroaching urbanization. Besides, viticultural interest in Southern California is now focused on the considerably cooler Rancho California district to the south, between Cucamonga and San Diego.

The bountiful grape-growing conditions in the Region IV and V districts permit production on a grand scale; the term "agribusiness" is said to have been coined here. The staggering size of the vineyard tracts, in some cases requiring the use of private planes to inspect them, and the city-like sprawl of the winery complexes is eye-opening to those whose image of a winery is an ivy-covered stone cellar nestled in a field of vines. Most of the important wineries here, with their huge storage tanks glinting in the sun, look about as romantic as oil refineries.

The largest firms put out wine under dozens of labels, buy grapes or own vineyards up and down the valley as well as all over the state, and truck grapes and wine back and forth between as many as a half-dozen wineries. Such firms are more business empires than wine estates, and their histories have more to do with corporate takeovers and other business machinations than they have to do with wine. If the size and spread of the industry here makes it difficult to identify who makes wine under what label, the ease with which grapes and wine are transported makes it nearly impossible to identify the viticultural source of the grapes that go into a given wine.

Ninety percent of the wine consumed in the U.S. sells for under two and a half dollars a bottle, and this enormous market is supplied mostly by the wine factories of the Inland Valley. While fine wine cannot be mass-produced, ordinary to good wine can, and these giant concerns have improved their production techinques to the point where a number of their best jug wines compete favorably in quality with the less outstanding premium wines, and in terms of dollar value, often offer more.

It is, however, extremely difficult to characterize ordinary-to-good wines. It has to be recognized that non-vintage generic wines may be made from any sort of grapes whatsoever, and many times what determines what grapes make up a particular lot of wine may depend on the availability of certain varieties and the prices that are asked by the growers. One bottle from a particular batch of a given winery's Mountain Red may be attractive, and the next bottle, from a different batch put out by that winery, may be dull or coarse. In wines whose outstanding feature is that they offer inexpensive inoffensive drinking, one cannot expect to find much character. In aiming their wines at a large and largely non-wine-drinking public, most of these wineries have tried to make a virtue of blandness. While one jug wine may taste better than another at a given time, there is little consistent difference in character and quality between one large winery's burgundy or chablis or another's. In other words, there is not enough to say about them that one couldn't also say about dozens of other wines as well. This is not to say that products in the jug wine category are beneath a wine lover's notice; far from it; they provide the great majority of table wine in this country, without which most of us would go thirsty most days.

While it is rare to find a truly offensive jug wine from one of these large producers, they can often be faulted for traces of bitterness (which comes from squeezing the last drop out of the grapes), too much residual sugar (left in to appeal to sweeter palates, and because it masks defects), a kind of tired, thin blahness to the flavor, synthetic aromas, and sometimes a rough coarse finish. For the most part, however, they are pleasant enough, and considering their extremely reasonable price range, one should not expect them to be worthy of contemplation as well.

Jug wines may not excite a wine lover's imagination, but their virtues are apparent to anyone who has to think twice about the price of a bottle of wine. It's more difficult to see the vinous virtues of some of the region's other popular products, particularly "pop" wines. About fifteen percent of all wine consumed in the now wine-thirsty United States falls into the category of "special natural wines." Whether or not such creations will become America's contribution to the world's *vin ordinaire*, people are buying up the fruity, fizzy concoctions at an impressive rate: nearly sixty million gallons in 1975.

Although dubious about what these new wines might taste like, I was surprised to find that a few of them are quite as pleasant, innocent, uncomplicated, and enjoyable as cotton candy. Many of the mad admixtures on the market, however, require a missing nose and a lead-lined gullet to choke down.

Flavored wines, of course, are nothing new; vermouth is probably the most common example. But pop wines—low alcohol, fruit-flavored wines made specifically for the soda-and-fruit-punch palate—have been around only for the past fifteen years. Until the improvement of filtration techniques, it wasn't possible to make a stable flavored table (low-alcohol) wine—that is, one with a long shelf-life. However, since the late sixties, pop wines have become an important part of many large wineries' output, especially that of E & J Gallo.

The wineries from Lodi to Cucamonga are not ignoring the fine wine market, however. New hopes have been raised by the development of grape varieties specifically suited to hotter regions. Primary among these are Emerald Riesling and Ruby Cabernet, both developed by the University of California at Davis, and both have already produced good wines with considerable character, while yielding up to ten tons per acre. A new red grape "Variety 12" (now renamed "Carnelian") is a cross between Cabernet Sauvignon, Grenache, and Carignane, yields eleven tons per acre in warm districts, and yet produces a wine with good acid balance. It is this sort of viticultural advance that holds out the promise the growers in the Inland Valley, long devoted to Mission, Flame Tokay, Thompson Seedless, and other undistinguished varieties, will now be able to grow better grapes in their climate without sacrificing yield. The result will be an increase in the production of better inexpensive table wine, something which will always be in great demand.

Suggested Samplings

This list of suggested samplings is necessarily short; virtually all this vast region's production is sold under the broad appellation "California" and its finest products—dessert wines and brandies—are often sold under the labels of wineries whose principal winery is located elsewhere. Again, some of these are produced in small quantities and may not be easy to find; others are among the most readily available wines in the U.S.

RED:

Ruby Cabernet
Conti-Royale (East-Side Winery)
M. LaMont (Bear Mountain Winery)
E & J Gallo

Zinfandel
Ambassador (A. Perelli-Minetti and Sons)
Angelo Papagni
Italian Swiss Colony
E & J Gallo

Red Blends
E & J Gallo Hearty Burgundy
Guild Tavola Red

WHITE:

French Colombard
Italian Swiss Colony (United Vintners)
M. LaMont
E & J Gallo

Muscat Alexandria
Angelo Papagni

White Blends
E & J Gallo Chablis Blanc
Winemaster's Guild Sauterne

OTHER:
Dessert Wine
Ficklin Tinta Port

Brandy
Guild 12-year-old

These and other wines of the region are discussed in the following pages. I will discuss the wineries located near Lodi first, and then work south to Cucamonga.

Principal Wineries

Guild Wineries and Distilleries

Guild is the third largest winemaking firm in the U.S. Its history is a complicated one, since it grew out of a number of cooperatives and corporate mergers. It emerged in the early sixties under its present name and after joining forces with a number of well-known Fresno labels, assumed nearly its present size. In 1970, Guild acquired the Roma and Cresta Blanca labels. It now operates eight wineries from Mendocino to Fresno, and its total storage capacity exceeds fifty million gallons. The range of its wines is enormous, around seventy, counting all brands, from its best-selling robust red table wine "Vino da Tavola Red" (Tavola Red for short) to its quite good north coast wines bottled under the famous old Cresta Blanca label. Cresta Blanca is now operated as a separate concern by Guild, which should help its rejuvenated label gain a reputation of its own (see Chapter 7). Among premium wines, Guild also has the Winemaster's Guild series, some of which are made from Mendocino and other north coast county grapes. Guild imports wines under this label as well. Some other labels in the Guild family, acquired mostly by merger over the years, are Cribari, Ceremony, and just plain Guild.

THE WINES:

Guild's Tavola Red, with its familiar red-checked-tablecloth label, is said to be made mostly from Lodi Zinfandel and Carignane and is currently being made in a lighter, less robust style. The result is a not-quite-dry, soft, pleasant-drinking wine. The Winemaster's Guild Mountain Red Wine is also pleasant and, to judge from the bottle I tried, appears to be made mostly from Ruby Cabernet. The Roma line can be quite good, notably the burgundy and sauterne. The Cribari line of wines is noticeably on the sweet side, or as this style of wine is called, "mellow." In contrast, the Winemaster's Guild sauterne is a dry, refreshing white blend. In short, Guild appears to be attempting, and largely succeeding, to make ordinary to good quality table wine for every palate. Some of the most distinctive products of this giant firm are its brandies, particularly the smooth Guild 12-year-old.

A. Perelli-Minetti and Sons (California Wine Association)

This Lodi firm dates from 1895 and at its height during pre-Prohibition days controlled most of the state's output. During Prohibition its members reorganized into Fruit Industries and then in 1950 changed back to the original name. At that time it had eleven member wineries, which accounts for its still seen Eleven Cellars label. But by 1971, only one member winery was left, A. Perelli-Minetti and Sons of Delano in the southern San Joaquin Valley. (Mr. Perelli-Minetti, by the way, first made wine in California in 1902, and was still active in the business at age 92.)

Nonetheless, the California Wine Association is still of considerable size, having twenty million gallons in storage capacity and marketing a complete line of wine under a number of brands. Due to the California Wine Association's colorful history, it actually owns some two hundred labels, though it uses only a few these days. Fino Eleven Cellars, L & J, Vino Fino, Guasti, Ambassador, and Calwa appear on table wine, sparkling wine, and vermouth labels, and the Aristocrat and A. R. Morrow appear on brandy labels.

THE WINES:

Eleven Cellars is the top of the line brand of the California Wine Association, and in some cases its varietal and generic wines are made from Napa Valley grapes—in which case it is stated on the label. I find these typical ordinary to good table wines, with the Cabernet Sauvignon and the Zinfandel showing some varietal character and flavor. A recent sample of the non-vintage Ambassador Zinfandel had a rich, warm, almost port-like nose, a distinct dried-fruit flavor, and a slightly sweet finish. Not an unattractive wine, but very different in style from the light, fruity character of most North Coast Zinfandels.

East Side Winery

Of the large cooperatives in the Lodi area, East-Side is the only one to bottle a good deal of its wine; the others mostly sell in bulk to other wineries. Founded in 1934, it is composed of over a hundred grower-stockholders, who supply the six-million-gallon winery with grapes from their own vineyards. While it has developed a reputation for its brandy and dessert wines (it also sells its brandy to other wineries, who often sell it at a higher price under their own labels), since 1962 it has been actively developing a program of growing and bottling premium wines, especially newly developed grapes like Ruby Cabernet, Emerald Riesling, and Gold (this last was derived from Muscat and intended as a table grape, but makes a light, sweetish white wine). Recently East-Side has installed a good deal of the latest modern equipment as part of their commitment to producing better wines.

THE WINES:

East-Side's line of wines appears under the labels Gold Bell, Mission Host, Conti-Royale, and Royal Host. The Conti-Royale Ruby Cabernet is quite a good wine—it shows substantial character and the strong olivey-weedy flavor of this variety. Nonetheless, East-Side remains best known for its well-made Royal Host dessert wines and Conti-Royale brandy.

Franzia Brothers Winery

Founded in 1906 and operated by the Franzia family at

Ripon near Escalon until its recent purchase by Coca-Cola Bottling of New York, Franzia has been known in the past for its line of reasonably priced table, dessert, and sparkling wines, vermouth, and brandy, all under one form or another of the Franzia label. With its twenty-eight-million-gallon storage capacity and four thousand acres of vineyards, Franzia will probably become a much more frequently seen label. Coca-Cola of New York, incidentally, now owns Mogen David (see Chapter 11), the large Chicago and New York producer, as well as Tribuno Vermouth in New Jersey, which makes it one of the nation's largest wine producers.

THE WINES:

Franzia markets a complete line of inexpensive wines, mostly generics, and a varietal Zinfandel; I have never found any of the Franzia wines memorable, but under its new ownership this may change and its label may come to stand for more than jug wine.

E & J Gallo

The E & J Gallo Company is an empire of wine rather than a winery. One out of every three bottles of wine Americans drink is made by Gallo—over one hundred million gallons of wine a year. Ernest and Julio Gallo started their enterprise with rented tanks in a rented warehouse in Modesto in 1933; untrained in winemaking, they checked out a couple of two-page winemaking pamphlets from the local library and managed to make sound wine. Two years later they built their own winery on the outskirts of Modesto. It is now long since swallowed in the world's largest winery complex, including its own glass factory for bottle-making. This, together with their new wineries in Fresno and Livingston, has a total storage capacity of a hundred and sixty-five million gallons. There are said to be over a hundred thousand acres of vineyards in California that grow grapes for Gallo. The two brothers still own every nut, bolt, and bottle cap of the enterprise, and have proved to everyone's satisfaction that what sells wine is quality at a reasonable price. To that end, they have extraordinary research facilities devoted to insuring the uniformity and quality of every one of their vast line of products. Their use of technology is already at the computer stage, at least in blending. Their marketing ability is second to none.

While the Gallos' main business is based on good, sound, everyday table wine, they have pioneered a number of taste trends in wine and wine beverages. When their Boone's Farm wines became popular among young adults in the late sixties, Gallo began marketing fruit-flavored wines aggressively and captured ninety percent of the pop wine market. Gallo rarely takes a back seat on any major trend, and introduced a line of varietal wines in the fall of 1974.

THE WINES:

None of the Gallo products are fine wines; at their best, they are quite good. The success and reputation of their wines are built on reliability, drinkability, and price. Perhaps the two best-known Gallo jug wines are Hearty Burgundy (which sells two million cases a year) and Chablis Blanc. These regularly take top honors in blind tastings of wines in their category. I am personally not a Hearty Burgundy fan, as I prefer a lighter, drier red, but the slight residual sweetness found in the Chablis Blanc is quite attractive and, remarkably enough for a wine of its price, it actually has a pleasant floral nose.

Gallo also makes pleasant sparkling wine labeled proudly "Eugene Charmat bulk process," a refreshing trend, and a range of typical, ordinary quality table wines—Pink Chablis, Sauterne, Rhinegarten, etcetera—which vary in sweetness and fruitiness. Like all the Gallo products, these are very clean in flavor, although their residual sweetness can be rather wearing.

The less distinguished Gallo products—Paisano, André, Carlo Rossi, Red Mountain, and the flavored and pop wines— are for the most part marketed under other labels rather than the Gallo name (though all, so far, show Modesto as the address). Of the flavored wines, Thunderbird and Twister are unpleasant, potent-tasting high-alcohol wines which apparently have their fans. The pop wines—the Boone's Farm series, Tyrolia, Madria-Madria Sangria, Pagan Pink Ripple, etcetera—are all clean, fruity and as innocuous as soda pop, apple juice, or fruit punch. As might be expected, however, the new non-vintage varietals are very well made and exceptionally clean, but also very neutral, making them reliable and consistent but rather characterless. Still, they are pleasant drinking, particularly the French Colombard and Ruby Cabernet.

United Vintners

United Vintners, the main wine-producing division of Heublein, is the second largest wine producer in the United States; unlike Gallo, however, it has a complicated corporate structure and produces a great number of wines with an enormous range of quality. The history of the firm is more interesting from a business than a wine viewpoint—its story seems one of little fish being swallowed by bigger fish. In brief, its origins after Repeal begin with Louis Petri, who built a California wine empire (including, at one point, a wine tanker ship) to rival the Gallos in the late 1950's. He sold the Petri wineries—which included by 1953 Italian Swiss Colony—to the Allied Grape Growers Cooperative. United Vintners became the marketing arm of Allied, and among its acquisitions, added Inglenook in 1964. In 1968, Heublein, the international marketer of vodka, imported wines, and other potables, bought United Vintners, and picked up Beaulieu a year later. Thus the basic arrangement is that Heublein is the parent company, while United Vintners is its biggest wine subsidiary, to which Allied supplies most of the grapes.

Allied Grape Growers is composed of over sixteen hundred member growers—there are even some in Washington State—and United Vintners has eight wineries in California with a total storage capacity of one hundred million gallons. Their biggest winery, however, is located near Madera in the mid-San Joaquin Valley, which holds some forty million gallons and, following the lead of the Gallo brothers, cuts bottling costs by runnings its own glass factory there as well. Most of the United Vintners wines, except for the "estate line" of Inglenook and Beaulieu wines (these Napa Valley operations are run more or less separately), are made in Madera from grapes from all over the state, and carry a whole string of labels: Inglenook Navalle, Italian Swiss Colony, Lejon, Petri, Santa Fe, Jacques Bonet, Bali Hai, Annie Green Springs, T. J. Swann, and others. (United Vintners also owns the Gambarelli and Davitto label used in the East.) Most of these labels give "San Francisco" or "Italian Swiss Colony, California" as the address, but are really bottled at the main winery at Madera.

THE WINES:

Inglenook and Beaulieu estate-bottlings are discussed under their own headings in Chapter 5, and the history of Italian Swiss Colony was given in Chapter 7.

The Italian Swiss Colony line includes burgundies, chablis (even a very grapey sweet "Ruby Chablis"), a pleasant Rhineskeller Moselle, an attractive French Colombard, a very light Cabernet Sauvignon (whose quaffability doubtless depends on heavy blending), and various rosés, all well-made and of competitive quality with other giant producers like Gallo. In some bottlings, the Italian Swiss Colony Zinfandel is quite good and shows some varietal character, really remarkable for such an inexpensive wine. The Inglenook Navalle line is no better (and no worse) than the competitive jugs from other giant producers, despite the Inglenook name.

Bali Hai, a redolently fruit-flavored wine, first introduced in 1964, has sold up to two million cases a year. Its sticky-sweet exuberance and green after-bite is anything but subtle. The lemon punch of Swiss-up and Silver Satin continue to find a market, but until Annie Green Springs, United Vintners had no real challenge to Gallo's Boone's Farm wines. After eighteen months of research into customer taste preferences in the early 1970's, United Vintners came up with several Annie Green Springs flavors, including "Peach Creek" and "Country Cherry"; however, I find Annie Green Springs "Berry Frost" the best of the pop wines. It smells like a jar of homemade preserves and grows on you, like a good raspberry sherbet. Annie Green Springs has sold millions of cases so far. The T. J. Swann wines are eminently forgettable.

Ficklin Vineyards

Ficklin is one of California's smallest wineries and its label is one of that state's most prestigious. Founded in 1946 by Walter Ficklin, its reputation is due to the fact that since the late forties, Ficklin has devoted itself almost exclusively to a single product—port. Its first-quality port has had little competition in California. Ficklin is also virtually the only small top-quality winery in the entire San Joaquin Valley.

Ficklin's greatest accomplishment has been to show that fine wine can be produced in Region V areas in California, if grapes suitable for such a hot climate are grown and an appropriate wine is made from them. Following the advice of the University of California at Davis, the Ficklins have planted classic Portuguese varieties—Tinta Madeira, Souzão, and three others—on their fifty acres of vineyards near Madera. Their vinification techniques approximate Old World methods where suitable, and the result is a ruby-style port with considerable finesse and aging potential.

Although Ficklin's choice to specialize in dessert wine has long been appreciated by wine lovers, curiously enough, it is probably Ficklin's success growing table wine grapes that is showing the valley the direction for the future. Originally the family grew additional grapes to make table wine for its own use, and planted an experimental plot of Emerald Riesling and Ruby Cabernet, the two Davis-developed grapes for hot climates. The quality of the wines that resulted impressed upon many growers the fact that it is possible to make good premium table wine from San Joaquin grapes. The Ficklins, however, only sell very small amounts of these table wines at the winery, preferring to stick to their main business: fine port.

THE WINES:

The Ficklins market one wine, their Tinta port. It is a full ruby port, non-vintage, a blend made from the solera of all their vintages since 1948. The wine spends four years in wood and a year in bottle before being released, and although quite enjoyable then, gains considerably in the bottle. If properly cellared it would undoubtedly last for decades. The examples I have tasted have all been excellent, dark, rich-looking heavy wines with an unctuous body that coats the glass in thick waves and drips. A rich, full, complex, fruit-compote nose with a hint of crushed nuts and a long, velvet sweet taste to match are its hallmarks. It is a very fine wine and a superb one with age; while it lacks the finesse and complexity of the very best of Portugal, its achievement is best appreciated by comparing it with other attempts in California to produce a fine port wine.

The winery does produce from time to time a vintage port, usually using the opportunity to experiment with such things as making the wine entirely from one grape variety. These are available only at the winery, and then rarely, as are the small amounts of Ruby Cabernet and Emerald Riesling produced.

Papagni Vineyards

Angelo Papagni firmly believes fine table wines can be made from grapes grown in the Central Valley. After having grown grapes in the region for some twenty-five years, he built a winery in Madera in 1973 to make wine from the roughly two thousand acres of vineyards he owns in Madera and Fresno counties. Papagni released his first wines in 1975 under the Angelo Papagni label.

THE WINES:

Papagni currently offers seventeen wines, including sparkling and dessert types, and a fruity, quaffable proprietary white blend, "Fu Jin," intended to accompany oriental food. It is his vintage-dated varietals, however, that are the most interesting. Papagni offers a number of reds: Zinfandel, Barbera, a very fruity off-dry Grenache (not a rosé, but very light), and varietals made from very humble valley grapes, Alicante Bouschet and Carignane. Neither is thought to be a fine wine grape, and the Alicante is often scorned as worthless. The '73 Alicante Bouschet I tried in mid-1976 was a dark, substantial-looking wine with a full, vinous aroma and a heavy, tannic body, but its lack of flavor made it seem curiously hollow. Although not what I would call a fine wine, it is a good one, and shows what a skilled vintner can get out of very unpromising material.

To me, Papagni's most exciting wines are his fine Muscats, which rank with the very best produced in the state. There are actually several different but closely related Muscat grapes grown in California, all of which share the sweetly floral, grapey perfume fresh Muscat grapes have. Papagni makes the Muscat Alexandria variety—frequently used to make sundried raisins—into a delightful white wine. His light, pale '73 Muscat Alexandria was extraordinarily fragrant and fruity, full of spicy-perfumey Muscat character and just off-dry. His non-vintage Moscato d'Angelo is even lighter and sweeter, its intense Muscat grapiness enhanced by considerable *pétillance* (at least in the sample I tried).

M. LaMont (Bear Mountain Winery)

This large thirty-two-million-gallon winery grew out of the Di Giorgio vineyards in south San Joaquin Valley in 1966, when it became part of a huge cooperative and was renamed Bear Mountain Winery for the large mountain of the same name on the eastern side of the valley near Bakersfield. Bear Mountain was the first winery in the area to bottle its own wines, although like most wineries in the area, it sells a considerable amount of wine in bulk to other producers. Its goal now is to produce good wine at a reasonable price, and it offers a line of varietals and generics to prove its point. Almost all its grapes come from its member-growers, and in this area, yields of six to ten tons of grapes per acre are common. The surprising thing is the number of better varietals that are now being grown here with some success, considering this is primarily Region V.

THE WINES:

Most of the Bear Mountain wines reach the market under the M. LaMont label (there is a small town, Lamont, near the winery), and others carry labels like Mountain Gold and Mountain Peak. The M. LaMont generics, like the chablis and the burgundy, also indicate the principal grapes used in the blend (a welcome trend). Their varietals range from Emerald Riesling, Sémillon, and Chenin Blanc in the whites to Barbera, Zinfandel, and Ruby Cabernet in the reds. The Ruby Cabernets I have tasted to date are good, consistent wines. All showed some oak character and had a pleasant dusty-vinous aroma, along with a full, dry, flavorful, and tannic character. The burgundy is similar and also good. It has a good deal of Ruby Cabernet in it; it could be a touch drier. The Zinfandel is light-bodied and lacks character, but provides good drinking. The Barbera is tart and dry.

Among the whites, the Chenin Blanc is good, light drinking; the French Colombard is drier and more characterful than most from this area, and the Sémillon is simple and crisp. Its new Chardonnay is good but lacks varietal character.

Brookside Vineyard

Secondo Guasti, an Italian immigrant from the Piedmont, founded the first winery in the Cucamonga desert east of Los Angeles in 1900, when he organized the Italian Vineyard Company and settled the town of Guasti with the families he brought over from Italy to work the land. By 1917 he had four thousand acres of vineyards and had built an impressive mansion. During Prohibition sacramental wines were made and the winery passed into a cooperative. The Brookside label actually dates from the 1880's, but it was not until the 1950's and 1960's when the Biane family bought the old Guasti winery and expanded their operation to thirty direct-to-the-customer outlets (including two in Arizona) that it has become well-known.

They sell eighty wines under Brookside, Assumption Abbey, and other labels. Brookside now has new plantings in the area even further south, known as Rancho California. This hilly region boasts a cool microclimate rated Region III. Brookside's new wines from this area, coupled with its recent purchase by Beatrice Foods of Chicago, should go far to spread its label and upgrade its quality.

THE WINES:

Only the Assumption Abbey label is marketed outside the wineries, of which the Zinfandel, long thought to be one of the better Cucamonga varietals, is a good example. It has a full "warm" pungent nose and a heavy, ripe flavor, almost port-like; a good, robust wine. Future Assumption Abbey varietals will come from Rancho California as well as Cucamonga.

Calloway Vineyard and Winery

Ely Callaway retired from the presidency of Burlington Industries, Inc., to grow grapes in the Rancho California district. The first vines were planted near Temecula in 1968. Promising experimental batches of wine made from these grapes in the early seventies inspired Callaway to build a winery in 1974. Grapes for the Callaway wines come from his 135-acre vineyard and neighboring vineyards.

THE WINES:

The first wines, mostly all from the '74 vintage, showed that it was possible to make very good to fine wine south of Los Angeles. Of the half-dozen vintage-dated varietals, the White Riesling is so far the most interesting of the lot even if it lacks varietal character. The '75 was pale, just off-dry, very clean and fresh and had excellent vinosity. The scent is not particularly expansive or flowery but the flavor is intriguing: complex, austere, and a touch woody, with high acidity, light fruitiness, and a very long-lingering finish with hints of tea and cloves.

The most interesting of the reds is the ponderous Petite Sirah. The '74 was so inky-dark it coated the glass, and so concentrated, aggressively tannic a mouthful that it offered little pleasure. The '76—tasted from a barrel sample—was similar, but rougher, and in early 1977 featured an aroma as intense as cough syrup. Both lack real underlying flavor and balance despite enormous substance; if flavor and balance are there, they are certainly safely disguised for a decade.

Other Wineries

Although there are a number of small country wineries scattered throughout the area, these are more isolated than most, and virtually unknown even to Californians. Some of the largest wineries in the area bottle no wine of their own, but make only wine in bulk for other wineries.

Some of the smaller wineries, like Barengo, north of Lodi, have been purchased by larger corporations and will doubtless expand their production. Among the new wineries in the Lodi area is the Filice Winery. The Filice family formerly owned San Martin Vineyards in Santa Clara, but recently acquired the defunct Montcalm-Acampo enterprise, which failed to transform itself from a bulk-wine operation to a premium winery in the early 1970's. The Filices may revive the Montcalm Vintners and Acampo Village labels, or they may just market wine under their own name.

Although founded in 1936 as a cooperative, California Growers Winery at Cutler, south of Fresno, has only recently entered the premium wine field. Until 1972, it was mostly a bulk-wine producer, but its present twelve-million-gallon storage capacity indicates its wines will be seen more frequently in the future. Its president, Robert Setrakian, owns his own vineyards nearby as well, and wines will appear under both his name and the Growers label.

Chapter 10
New York

New York is the second most important wine-producing state in the U.S. Although it produces only one-tenth the wine that California does, and trails California considerably in grape acreage—California has over six hundred thousand acres in vines, while New York has only forty thousand—it is the home of some of the nation's largest and some of its most unusual wineries.

The Eastern United States is unique among viticultural areas of the world in that it produces wine from three distinct types of grapes: native American types (mainly *labrusca*), *vinifera,* and hybrids of those two. Of its total grape acreage, over ninety-five percent is planted to *labrusca* types, of which the Concord is the principal variety. *Labrusca* types have long been the basis of New York's wine industry, and only recently have any large plantings of hybrid grapes been undertaken. *Vinifera* acreage is minute—probably under a thousand acres.

There are several major grape-growing districts in the state: the Hudson River Valley, the Finger Lakes area, and the Chatauqua and Niagara districts in the western parts of the state near Lake Erie. In each case, the proximity to large bodies of water permits grapes to be grown in what would otherwise be very cold latitudes, and even so, the grape-growing season is quite short, around a hundred and fifty days.

The weather, unlike that of Europe, however, is generally consistent, and a good crop is possible every year. The Finger Lakes district is the most important winemaking area in New York—producing thirty million gallons of the state's thirty-eight million gallons annual production—while the Chatauqua district supplies most of the grapes for the state's large production of fresh table grapes and grapes for juice and jellies.

Grapes for winemaking have been cultivated in the state since the 1600's, when they were planted on Manhattan Is-

#7 PRINCIPAL WINE GROWING AREAS OF NEW YORK

Lake Ontario

Finger Lakes
GENEVA

Niagara Falls

Chatauqua

Lake Erie

NAPLES

WESTFIELD

HAMMONDSPORT

Hudson River Valley

Hudson River

HIGHLAND
MARLBORO

■ Wine Growing Area

NEW YORK

land, but the wine industry in New York was smaller than that of other Eastern states until the latter part of the nineteenth century. The Reverend William Bostwick is generally credited as the first person to grow grapes in the Finger Lakes. He planted Catawba in his rectory garden at Hammondsport on Lake Keuka in 1829; by 1860, the Pleasant Valley Wine Company (U.S. Bonded winery no. 1) had begun operations; today, the area boasts about a dozen important wineries of various sizes, from the Taylor Wine Company (the largest U.S. winery outside California and the largest U.S. producer of sparkling wines) to the seventy-eight-acre Vinifera Wine Cellars estate of Dr. Konstantin Frank, the first man to grow *vinifera* grapes successfully in the Eastern United States.

In spite of the fact that the vast majority of wines made in New York State are made from grape species and varieties which are unknown to most of the world's viticultural areas and often taste strange to palates unaccustomed to the wines made from them, the wineries in New York State have quadrupled their business in the past two decades. This success no doubt accounts for the limited interest taken by most of these wineries in growing *vinifera*, even though this can now be done in at least some of the warmer parts of the state, and the *vinifera* that has been planted so far has yielded some wines as outstanding as any produced in this country. This reluctance to grow *vinifera* is a rather curious historical phenomenon, since the beginnings of viticulture in the East were largely devoted to attempts to grow these European grape varieties.

The reason why so much effort was expended on the effort to grow *vinifera* in the East was that the wine native grapes yielded was unpleasant. Today the principal *labrusca* varieties used in the East are probably due to accidental crosses of native grapes cultivated by early viticulturalists and *vinifera* (see Chapter 3). Most of these varieties—Concord, Ives, Elvira, Delaware, Moore's Diamond, etcetera—yield wines which vary in quality from good to strange, so strange, in fact, that a great many people find them distinctly unattractive. The musky, perfumed scent and flavor of wines made from these varieties has come to be called (for some mysterious reason) "foxy."

Efforts to grow *vinifera* in the East continued for some time, even after the discovery that the phylloxera pest present in Eastern U.S. soil prevented *vinifera* from growing on its own roots. Attempts were made to grow it on native root stock, just has had been done in California.

But experimental plantings yielded only inconclusive results, and the general view of Eastern winemakers up to the 1950's was that *vinifera* could not be consistently grown in the Eastern U.S. The principal reason for this failure seemed to be excessive cold: fifteen degrees below zero is common in the Finger Lakes region of New York, while temperatures of five below zero are most unusual in the northernmost viticultural regions of Germany. Such temperatures can kill or severely damage *vinifera*, while the hardier native species are much less subject to "winterkill."

Thus, an entire industry in the U.S. has developed out of making wines from native grapes. While efforts were made to tame the taste of *labrusca* and make the wines taste more like *vinifera* wines, the fruity appeal of many of them has led many of the larger wineries to make a marketing virtue out of what some would call a taste defect—the "foxiness."

Winemakers in the Eastern U.S. often claim that wine lovers find the taste of *labrusca*-based wines strange only because it is unfamiliar to them. It is something one has to get used to, they say, like caviar or olives. However, the taste of most *labrusca* wines is extremely simple and strong and frankly has little to offer the sophisticated palate. Almost without exception they lack subtlety and complexity, and unless their rather intense flavors are made more palatable by dilution, blending, and other ameliorating procedures adopted during the winemaking process, the end product overpowers rather than complements food and is often found tart and cloying by people who are acquainted with the more subtle sensations better *vinifera* wines offer the nose and mouth. Yet it seems clear that for the foreseeable future there will be a continued market for *labrusca* wines; of the best-selling *labrusca* types in the East, some appeal to a pop wine palate and the rest can be described as "transitional" wines, wines that appeal to palates that like semi-sweet whites and reds.

The enormous popularity of *labrusca-based* wines is no more puzzling a phenomenon than the enormous popularity of simple fruit-flavored pop wines: they both appeal to similar palates and satisfy the demand for a simple, uncomplicated, anytime beverage with a direct, fruity zing to its taste. It makes no more sense to frown at the widespread consumption of these wines than it does to look down one's nose at cider, fruit punch, mixed drinks, or soda pop. Taste preferences are taste preferences; what does these wines a disservice, however, is to claim qualities for them that they do not have. They are, by and large, quite ordinary and undistinguished in quality apart from their unusual flavors, just as the vast majority of *vinifera* wines produced in the U.S. and elsewhere are quite ordinary in quality. This does not mean that they cannot be enjoyable; but it does mean that it is asking too much of a *labrusca* wine that it be worth the sort of intense contemplation to which the greatest *vinifera* wines can be subjected.

All of this, however, is not to say there are no *labrusca* wines worth tasting in New York State. On the contrary, some of the white wines made from native grapes like Delaware and Moore's Diamond can be quite good, and offer unique taste experiences for the wine lover. (In general, native white varieties yield better wines than the native reds, probably because they need much less amelioration with sugar and water in their production to yield balanced wines.)

New York State sparkling wines and sherries are of high quality, and can be attractive even to a *vinifera*-accustomed palate. The process of making sparkling wine helps to disguise the *labrusca* qualities of the base wine, and the baking and aerating or weathering process sherries are subjected to removes almost all the *labrusca* character from the final product.

When looking at the winemaking processes used in Eastern U.S. areas, it is important to note that what would be a process detrimental to quality in the making of *vinifera* wines would not necessarily·be detrimental to quality in making *labrusca* wines. Federal laws, it is often pointed out, allow the addition of sugar and water to musts in the East in order that the very low sugar/high acid *labrusca* grapes can be made into a balanced wine. While the addition of water to any *vinifera* wine would simply be watering down the product, adding water to some *labrusca* wines undoubtedly produces a blander, but more palatable product. Federal laws also permit up to twenty-five percent out-of-state-wine to be added to a wine labeled with a specific state name. Thus, New York State wine need only contain seventy-five percent New York State wine and, of course, that proportion can have water and sugar added to increase its volume thirty-five percent. It is no secret that the largest wineries in New York ship in bulk wine from California to blend with their own wine, and some even own their own acreage in California for this purpose. A comparison of the gallonage produced by New York State wineries each year with the state's acreage and yield indicates that a great deal of what appears in the bottle is out-of-state wine and water. On the other hand, without this careful amelioration of the must and blending with *vinifera* wine, their products would undoubtedly be far less pleasant to drink.

New York, like California, produces a vast amount of wines with more individuality in the labeling than in the bottle. But, recognizing that an increasingly larger share of the wine market prefers dry rather than semi-sweet table wines, and wines with *vinifera* characteristics, the large New York wineries have been producing more and more wines from French hybrid varieties. Just as the *vinfera* crosses Ruby Cabernet, Emerald Riesling, and other varieties developed for a warm climate are enabling California wine-growers in the Central Valley to upgrade the quality of their table wines, so too the cold-resistant French hybrids are enabling New York wineries to upgrade the quality of their wines. Thus, some thirty percent of the new plantings in New York State are in French-American hybrids, which these wineries hope, since these are crosses between native varieties and *vinifera,* combine the winter-hardiness of the former with the taste qualities of the latter. So far, the hardiness of the hybrids is more apparent than their suitability as superior fine wine grapes. There is no question, however, that many of them produce much better wine than native varieties.

The interest in French hybrids in this country can be traced to Phil Wagner, the man responsible for introducing French hybrids to the United States. An editorial writer for the *Baltimore Evening Sun,* Wagner became interested in home winemaking in the thirties, and at first made wine from *vinifera* grapes shipped East. Repeal ended these grape shipments and Wagner tried making wine from *labrusca* grapes, but disliked the taste. After reading about hybrid grapes developed in France, he ordered some vines, discovered they made a palatable wine, and soon his home winemaking operation developed into a nursery and winery complex. He and his wife, Jocelyn, bonded the Boordy winery in Riderwood, Maryland, in 1945, and their wines became the local *vin du pays.* The quality possible with the best of these hybrids interested others, and in the fifties and sixties these efforts attracted New York winemen, among them the late Greyton Taylor of the Taylor Wine Company and Charles Fournier of Gold Seal.

If the current research into hybrids is an effort to grow grapes that will make fine wine—or at least better-tasting wine—in the East, it may seem puzzling to a wine lover that little effort is being made to try growing *vinifera* first. Not only has *vinifera* produced superb wines in a number of lands, some varieties have already yielded some of the best wines of their type in the U.S. in the Finger Lakes region. It must be remembered, too, that the finest *vinifera*—the "noble" varieties—have been cultivated and selected over thousands of years specifically for their superior taste when made into wines. It takes a great deal of optimism to suppose that a grape variety developed by crossing *vinifera* with *labrusca* or some humble variety is going to taste as good as the *vinifera* one started with.

Why, in other words, should an Eastern wine-grower trying to make good to fine wine handicap himself by growing less than the best varieties?

The answer given by the large New York wineries is that *vinifera* cannot be grown commercially on any large scale in New York State because of the severe winter climate. This claim seems to be supported by research, but what makes it somewhat controversial is that *vinifera* has been grown successfully in the Finger Lakes region since 1957. The story of this achievement is basically the story of one man, Dr. Konstantin Frank (his winery will be discussed later).

Dr. Frank, a Russian-born German with extensive experience in growing *vinifera* in the Ukraine, came to the U.S. in 1951 and first tried unsuccessfully to convince the state experimental station at Geneva, New York, that it was possible to grow *vinifera* commercially in New York. In 1953 Charles Fournier, the winemaster of Gold Seal wineries, gave Frank a chance to try some experimental plantings, and Frank soon demonstrated his claim that the solution to growing *vinifera* in the East depends on the careful selection of cold-resistant root stock and the proper selection of *vinifera* clones to graft on them. Frank used Canadian root stock, which allowed grapes grown on it to blossom later and ripen earlier and the vine itself to have a longer dormant season, thus avoiding the damage an early frost would normally cause *vinifera* vines. That, combined with proper selection of *vinifera* clones, allowed the experimental vines that Frank planted at Gold Seal to survive a twenty-five-degree-below-zero freeze in 1957, and still produce up to four tons an acre.

Dr. Frank eventually left Gold Seal to found his own winery above Lake Keuka, Vinifera Wine Cellars, and since then has had yields of up to seven to ten tons an acre from White Reisling and Chardonnay! When one consider that a yield of five tons an acre is considered excellent for Concord, these are impressive figures indeed.

It is true that *vinifera* must be carefully grafted on the appropriate root stock, but this is also true of many of the hybrid grapes, which do poorly on their own roots, and whose yields are no better than those of *vinifera*. From the viewpoint of making fine wines, growing *vinifera* has another advantage over native and hybrid types. Unlike native grapes or most hybrids, they have excellent sugar levels and much lower acidity and therefore need no addition of sugar or water to produce a palatable, balanced wine. Grapes that need sugar added to them rarely yield wines that have the body, flavor, and richness of wines made without amelioration from fully ripened grapes.

But the major New York wineries and the state's research specialists as well are not as enthusiastic about Dr. Frank's achievements as a wine lover is apt to be. In spite of the fact that no one disputes that a number of his wines are unquestionably superb, and that his grape-growing efforts have been crowned with success, the New York wine industry is not taking his accomplishments as a signal that the *vinifera* revolution has come to the East. For one thing they note that viticultural research has not yet confirmed that winter cold hardiness of *vinifera* vines is directly affected by the choice of root stock; vigorous root stock, they claim, may lead to overbearing, and consequently weaken the vine. Only the most careful selection of vineyard sites and expert vineyard management, they say, could ensure viable large-scale commercial production of *vinifera*. But the argument, at bottom, tends to revolve around commercial considerations.

What would make the the large-scale cultivation of *vinifera* difficult and expensive for many Eastern wineries is that few of their methods, from vineyard to bottle, could be adapted easily to the production of fine *vinifera* wines. Grapes in the Finger Lakes district, for example, are largely machine-picked by the calendar, which means that their sugar/acid ratios may not be at their best. Only the widespread use of amelioration permits this to be a useful method. It would be pointless to grow fine *vinifera* grapes which do have excellent sugar/acid balance, and then fail to pick them at the proper stage of ripening. Hybrids, on the other hand, hold out the prospect of allowing Eastern wineries to upgrade their entire line of wines significantly without having to change their methods or raise their prices dramatically in order to cover what they see as the great effort and expense of nursing *vinifera* through cold winters and the like. Thus, those Eastern wineries that have become interested in *vinifera* on a large scale have chosen to begin operations in California rather than commit themselves to the higher risks and expense of *vinifera* cultivation in the East.

It is true, too, that the cultivation of hybrids opens up the possibility of growing wine grapes in areas far too cold in winter for *vinifera*, and producing quite quaffable *vin du pays*. Hybrids also offer a unique, wholly different source of wine for the Eastern U.S. The desire not to try and compete with California is an understandable one.

Many of the hybrids already yield good wines, and in the future may yield fine wines as well. The increasing use of varietal labeling and vintage-dating for hybrid wines and even the better native wines, is a clear indication that the New York wine industry is confident that its use of better non-*vinifera* grapes enables it to offer something unique to the American wine-drinking public, even that segment with more sophisticated palates. There is little argument with this.

Because of the rigors of the climate and the demands of the vineyard, *vinifera* plantings in New York State may be small for some time. I suspect, however, there is a potentially good-sized market for very fine vintage-dated New York State *vinifera* wines, especially those varieties—like White Riesling—that yield uniquely delicate wines when grown in a cool climate. Nonetheless, all this seems in the future, and meanwhile New York finds itself arguing the merits of all these issues, with wineries often dividing over the prospective merits of each species or type of grape.

The following review of New York State wineries concentrates on those in the Finger Lakes district. These lakes are long, narrow, very deep glacial lakes that run north and south in the hilly area of the western half of the state south of Lake Ontario. The rounded hills, steep vineyards, deep blue lakes, and scattered farming communities make the area popular with tourists in the summer. Most of the major wineries and several of the important small ones are clustered around Lake Keuka and the little hamlet of Hammondsport at its southern tip, and it is there that the state's controversies over grape-growing are centered.

Suggested Samplings

Anyone wishing to sample some of the current high points of the region's wine production will certainly find some of them among the following types and producers. These are offered as a starting point, not a definitive list of the best, and readers are encouraged to go on and explore for themselves. Bear in mind that some of these wines are produced in small quantities and consequently may not be easy to find; many of these are readily available, however, at least in major U.S. cities. Note that native American and hybrid varieties as well as *vinifera* varieties are listed here.

RED:

> *Baco Noir*
> Great Western (Pleasant Valley Wine Co.)

> *Foch*
> Widmer's Wine Cellars

> *De Chaunac*
> Benmarl
> Widmer's Wine Cellars

> *Red Blends*
> Boordy Red
> Bully Hill Red

WHITE:

> *(Pinot) Chardonnay*
> Benmarl
> Dr. Konstantin Frank (Vinifera Wine Cellars)
> Gold Seal

> *White (Johannisberg) Riesling*
> Benmarl
> Dr. Konstantin Frank (Vinifera Wine Cellars)
> Gold Seal

> *Gewürztraminer*
> Dr. Konstantin Frank (Vinifera Wine Cellars)

> *Seyval Blanc*
> Benmarl
> Bully Hill

> *Delaware*
> Widmer's Wine Cellars

(Moore's) Diamond
    Bully Hill
    Great Western
    Widmer's Wine Cellars

White Blends
    Boordy White
    Bully Hill White
    Gold Seal Chablis Nature

OTHER:
    Sparkling Wine
        Gold Seal Charles Fournier Blanc de Blancs
        Great Western Naturel
        Taylor Brut

    Sherry
        Great Western Solera Sherry
        Widmer's Special Selection Sherry

These and other wines of the region are discussed in the following pages.

Principal Wineries

The Taylor Wine Company

The Finger Lakes produce three-fourths of New York State's wines, and most of the grape-growing areas line the shores of Seneca, Canandaigua, and most importantly, Keuka Lake. The sleepy little hamlet of Hammondsport at the foot of Keuka Lake, with its village green bordered by the post office, a drug store, and the local tavern, hardly looks like the center of a major wine industry, though grape posters are featured above the booths in local coffee shops. But the town is surrounded by some of the nation's largest wineries, and one of the biggest is Taylor's, with a storage capacity of twenty-two and a half million gallons, a sprawl of thirty-six buildings, and an annual production of over four and a half million cases of wine.

Taylor began very modestly in 1880, when Walter Taylor, a young cooper, settled with his bride on a seven-acre plot,

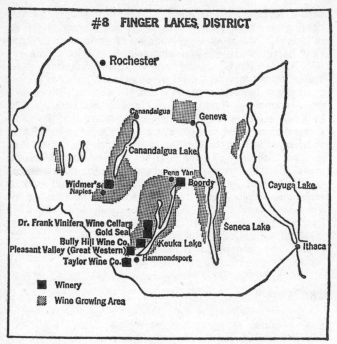

#8 FINGER LAKES, DISTRICT

later expanded to seventy, above Lake Keuka on Bully Hill just north of Hammondsport. Taylor planted his vineyards to native grapes, and did a prosperous business making barrels for some of the wineries already in operation in the area. Soon he was sending his own wine in barrels to New York City and by 1913 began buying grapes from other growers to supplement his yield. When Prohibition came in 1919, the Taylors and their five children decided to produce grape juice and moved into larger quarters just south of Hammondsport. After Repeal, the company grew considerably in size and in 1962 became a publicly held corporation (although it remained under family management until the late sixties), and purchased a controlling interest in the Pleasant Valley Wine Co., whose principal brand is Great Western. In 1977 Taylor merged with the Coca-Cola Company of Atlanta, Georgia.

Taylor operates its Pleasant Valley subsidiary as a separate enterprise, so I will discuss it separately. Taylor itself owns about thirteen hundred acres of vines, and also has contracts with some four hundred and fifty growers to supply the additional grapes it needs. It has extensive and increasing acreage in hybrids, and about three-quarters of its crop is mechanically harvested. Its modern winemaking facilities are impressive, from its banks of nearly one hundred hundred-thousand-gallon fermentors to its huge, automated transfer method champagne bottling lines. Interestingly enough, Taylor uses wood cooperage almost exclusively, and has building after building of redwood and oak tanks up to sixty-four-thousand-gallons' capacity which hold every Taylor wine at one time or another, as well as the blending wines which the winery ships in from California. Taylor does not ferment its reds on the skins, but "hot presses" the grapes instead, a process by which the must is heated before pressing to extract color, a technique which seems to have no deleterious effect on *labrusca grapes*. During fermentation, reds and whites are handled similarly. The entire winery operation, aided by over eight miles of stainless steel and Pyrex tubing, is geared to producing the consistent, reliable, and well-made *labrusca* products with which Taylor has been so successful.

THE WINES:

Taylor markets twenty-eight different wine products, almost all from native grapes or hybrids, including sangria and vermouth, none of them vintage-dated and all, except for the sparkling wine, screw-topped. They vary in quality from attractive, simple, ordinary wines to sweet *labrusca*-flavored types which are perhaps best judged as wine beverages rather than as wines. Taylor sherries, while lacking foxiness, lack character as well. The sparkling wines are more interesting and while the Brut champagne, made principally from Delaware, is slightly sweet, it is well-made, has a pleasant fruity scent, and a clean flavor. The Royal Quality Dry is sweeter than the Brut, and the other Taylor sparkling wines—the Cold Duck and Sparkling Burgundy—are quite noticeably *labrusca*-flavored and scented. So are, for that matter, the claret, the burgundy, the rosé, and the sauterne, none of which has much vinous interest or appeal. The rhine wine, however, is quite pleasant, although it lacks flavor and has a fast finish. It is made chiefly from the Aurora grape. Best quite cold, it shows how careful processing and blending can improve a *labrusca*-based wine. Taylor also markets an Emerald Riesling and a Ruby Cabernet. Both are blends made from out-of-state *vinifera* and home-grown Eastern native and hybrid grapes, and thus have a slightly Eastern flavor.

Taylor's most popular table wines are its proprietally named Lake Country White, Red, and Pink, made predominantly from Niagara, Baco Noir, and Catawba respectively. All are bland, soft, grapey, slightly sweet, palatable, and ordinary in quality.

Pleasant Valley Wine Company (Great Western)

Pleasant Valley was founded in 1860 by thirteen Hammondsport gentlemen and is consequently U.S. Bonded winery no. 1. It made the first New York State champagne in 1865, and by 1870, the wine had been dubbed "the great champagne of the West" by a Boston wine lover, which resulted in Pleasant Valley giving its champagnes the name "Great Western." For years the company prospered with its champagne, and for a while during Prohibition it had a monopoly on supplying sparkling wine to the clergy.

Located close to Taylor's main operation in Hammondsport, Pleasant Valley has its own vineyards on Lake Keuka as well as its own contracts with outside growers. Since 1962 it has been a subsidiary of Taylor, and in some ways operates as the parent company's prestige line. Under the late Greyton Taylor and his son Walter (son and grandson of the founder of Taylor's) Pleasant Valley's Great Western wines were expanded in the 1960's to include the state's first wines made entirely from French-American hybrids, and a number of varietals, a few of which were vintage-dated. Its production methods differ from Taylor's in a few respects: reds are fermented on the skins rather than hot-pressed, and their sherries are "weathered" in a solera system rather than baked, as at Taylor. It too uses large wood cooperage extensively.

Pleasant Valley expanded its operations along with that of its parent company and now has nearly five million gallons of storage capacity. It expects eventually to make a great deal more use of hybrids, and plans to emphasize its line of varietals.

THE WINES:

Pleasant Valley offers almost three dozen products, made from some thirty-five native and hybrid grape varieties, some

varietally labeled, the rest generic; all appear under the Great
Western label, and all are corked with something like a sherry
stopper, so that the cork can be removed without a corkscrew.

Pleasant Valley's transfer-process sparkling wines are
among its best products; its newly introduced Naturel champagne is its best sparkling wine, and one of the best in the
state. This light, straw-colored, fine-bubbled wine has an attractive yeasty aroma and a very dry flavor that points up its
crisp acidity. Very faint *labrusca* nuances in the nose and
finish do not detract from its pleasant, strong, clean character. The winery also produces good solera sherries, of which
the medium sweet is the best, full, round, and with some
flavor. Some of their table wines are among the better
labrusca products of the state while others are much less
attractive; the Diamond Chablis (Moore's Diamond) is a one
hundred percent varietal, according to the winery, and exhibits a pleasant, *labrusca*-scented nose, and gravelly-fruity
taste with a fast finish. The Dutchess Rhine Wine has an
attractive nose but is rather sweeter and more cloying. Most
of the other whites, like the Delaware Moselle, are quite
strongly *labrusca*-scented and flavored. The best reds currently
offered are the Baco Noir Burgundy and the Chelois: both
are rather soft, sweetish, lack depth of flavor, have green-
leafy nuances, and are quite ordinary, though well made. The
most exciting wine I have ever had from Pleasant Valley,
however, was a red, out-of-the-barrel sample of a 1975 De
Chaunac I tried in the spring of 1977. The winery is considering adding this promising varietal to its line of products, and
it's not hard to understand why. Dark ruby in color, it had
a full, vinous-fruity aroma and a very attractive, intense,
fruity-tart flavor that spread on the palate. The sample I tried
showed not the slightest hint of its Eastern origins and in fact
had the sublety of very good *vinifera* wine.

The Bully Hill Wine Company

Bully Hill was founded in 1970 by Walter S. Taylor, the
grandson of the founder of the Taylor Wine Co., on the site
of the original Taylor vineyard of the 1880's. Seven hundred
feet above Lake Keuka north of Hammondsport, Bully Hill
has two hundred acres of vineyards, some as high as seventeen hundred feet, almost all in hybrid vines. It produces
mostly vintage-dated varietal wines from its own grapes.

Walter Taylor, with the encouragement of his father, Greyton Taylor, purchased the original Taylor property in 1958 and by the mid-sixties had created a small Finger Lakes wine museum and an experimental winery, both housed in some of the original nineteenth-century farm buildings. The Bully Hill complex was even expanded to include a home winemaker's shop.

Bully Hill's founder and owner is a controversial figure in the New York wine industry. Formerly an executive vice-president of the Pleasant Valley division of the Taylor Wine Co., he was ousted from the firm in 1970 for being an outspoken critic of the statewide use of out-of-state wines and water to reduce acidity in New York State wines. Since then he has gone on to criticize and publicize through pamphlets and newsletters other practices he disapproves of, such as loose labeling and the use of poor native grapes like Concord.

Taylor has even adopted the phrase "wine without water" for his winery motto. The implication that these legal practices are deceptive and amount to stretching the product is strongly resented by the larger New York wineries, since, as was pointed out in the introduction to this chapter, without the addition of blending wines and water many New York State *labrusca* wines would not be as drinkable as they are.

Nonetheless Walter Taylor's efforts have focused attention on the lack of interest most New York wineries have in fine wine. Varietal labeling, vintage dating, and giving the source of grapes are little used in the state, and Taylor is probably right that unless New York State takes an interest in producing fine wines as well as everyday wines, it will remain behind California not only in quantity but also in quality of production. The production of any fine wine in a given viticultural area raises the reputation of all the wines produced in that area; the lack of any fine wine from a given district is often, justly or not, taken as evidence that no fine wine can be made there.

Perhaps because of his family's long involvement with the state's wine industry, Taylor takes a very personal interest in the future of the New York wine industry as a whole, and believes it his duty to try to raise what he considers the state's low standards of winemaking. Together with his German-trained vineyardist and winemaker, Hermann Wiemer, and a considerable fortune left him on his father's death in 1970, Taylor set out to show the industry what New York

State could accomplish with better grapes and better wine-making techniques. Curiously enough for an advocate of fine wine, Taylor appears uninterested in *vinifera* grapes, and stoutly maintains the superiority of the French hybrids, of which Bully Hill has about twenty varieties planted.

THE WINES:

Bully Hill produces about twenty thousand cases of wine a year; its line includes a number of varietals and a Bully Hill Red and White and Rosé, all vintage-dated. Many Bully Hill wines are unblended, and for the ones that are, the exact proportions of grapes used in the blend are given on the label. Taylor's enthusiastic claims for the hybrids—that they are capable of producing wines to rival the world's best—seem excessive, however. While the Bully Hill wines I have tasted have all been well-made and most could be describd as good, none exhibited the finesse and complexity of fine, much less great, *vinifera* wines. They are all a cut above the usual *labrusca* and hybrid wines produced in the state, however, and are made in a full-flavored style that is true to the grape variety—no small oak cooperage is used—and show what quality is possible in some native and hybrid types without the use of blending.

A '73 Bully Hill White I tried was palatable, but not as appealing as earlier examples. I found the '75 Seyval Blanc more subtle, with a high, light, perfumey nose and an apple cider green-tart finish.

To my palate, the most intriguing wines that Bully Hill produces are its reds, which are quite a bit better than the reds produced by the large New York wineries. The Bully Hill Red is a blend of seven French-American hybrids, and is a very individual wine with its own unique character. The '70 vintage tasted in early 1974 had a big, expansive, high, delicate, perfumey, and quite attractive nose, round and clean and curiously light, yet rich at the same time. Its taste is less impressive; light in body, low in tannin, soft and full but not deep or intense in flavor, it had good acidity and finished smoothly but quickly. The '74 of this blend, tried in early 1977, had a pleasant vinous nose and a spicy, intense flavor, but little depth. Good examples of *labrusca* and hybrid wines are said to gain with bottle age, and the Bully Hill reds seemed to uphold this view.

Many of the wines could not be identified as New York State wines, in spite of the grapes used. While the best are certainly not in the same league, as fine *vinifera* wines, they are quite the equal of the vast majority of *vinifera* wines one would class as ordinary to good.

Gold Seal Vineyards

Founded in 1865 as the Urbana Wine Company, Gold Seal occupies a large stone building with numerous wings and additions built into the hillside facing Lake Keuka a few miles north of Hammondsport. A mural inside the lobby depicts the days before the road was built when lake steamers brought grapes to the winery and took away barrels of wine.

Gold Seal's sparkling wine has been known as "Gold Seal" since the 1880's, but not until 1957 was the company named for its best-known product. Wine production at Gold Seal has always been in the hands of French winemasters, the last of which is the recently retired but still active Charles Fournier, who came from his position as winemaker at Veuve Clicquot in the Champagne district of France in 1934 to head Gold Seal's production after Repeal. (Like many of the large wineries in the area, Gold Seal made "medicinal" wines during Prohibition.) Fournier was one of the first to experiment with French hybrids in the Finger Lakes and, as was pointed out in the introduction to this chapter, was the man who in 1953 gave Dr. Konstantin Frank the chance to show that *vinifera* could be grown in the East. Gold Seal was thus the first winery to produce a commercial *vinifera* wine in the East, but has produced only occasional bottlings of Chardonnay and White Riesling from its several hundred acres of *vinifera* since, preferring instead to blend them into its other wines. Gold Seal uses a variety of winemaking methods, depending on the quality sought; it bakes its sherries, uses both hot pressing of red grapes and fermenting on the skins, and uses both wood and stainless steel for cooperage. The winery has eight hundred acres in native grapes and hybrids and *vinifera* on both sides of Lake Keuka and near Seneca Lake. Like other large New York State wineries, it buys the majority of its grapes from other growers. For its blending wines, however, Gold Seal has considerable acreage in California's Central Valley near Modesto, and has recently added fifteen hundred acres of vineyards in the cooler Salinas Valley in Monterey. Gold Seal eventually plans to produce and market a number of California wines (from *vinifera,* of course), and thus will join the small number of U.S. wine firms with wineries on both the East and West Coasts.

THE WINES:

Gold Seal, like many large California wineries, makes a conscious attempt to make wines of varying degrees of quality and sophistication. The top of its line are its vintage-dated Chardonnay and Johannisberg Riesling. These *vinifera* varietals are produced only in years with exceptionally bountiful vintages. In lean years the grapes contribute to the character of the Blanc de Blancs champagne and the Rhine wine, among others. In early 1977 I tried the pale '74 Pinot Chardonnay. It had a curiously perfumey aroma, as if some hybrid or native grape had been blended in. I found little detectable varietal character in this quite dry wine, which also featured a fast and somewhat bitter finish. I was less disappointed in the '75 Johannisberg Riesling sampled at the same time. An estate-bottled wine, it was rather faint in aroma, but had some body, a soft texture in the mouth, and good flavor. A pleasant enough wine, it too lacked real varietal character.

Apart from the *vinifera* wines, Gold Seal considers its Blanc de Blancs champagne and its Chablis Nature table wine to be its best. Both appear under the "Charles Fournier" signature, and both show the results of careful blending of hybrids, native grapes, and some *vinifera.* While the Blanc de Blancs is said to spend two years on the yeast, it does not exhibit any yeasty nuances in its nose; neither, however, does it have anything but slight *labrusca* traces in its pleasant aroma. The flavor is good, the *dosage* slightly sweet, and again the wine only shows slight *labrusca* traces in the finish. A good, palatable sparkling wine, it is widely thought to be New York State's best; it is not hard to see why this transfer method champagne is on a par with similarly made sparkling wines of California. I have been more impressed with the Chablis Nature, which has a very light, pale straw color, some *pétillance,* and a very pleasant apple-crisp flavor. A light, simple, and refreshing wine, it is best very cold, and has only a trace of *labrusca* flavors. The recently introduced "Charles Fournier Burgundy Natural Private Reserve" exhibited a vinous, faintly sweet aroma that hinted at a healthy percentage of California Ruby Cabernet. I found the flavor pleasant, but quite simple.

Gold Seal produces about a million cases of wine a year, and its strongest seller is its Catawba, which comes in white, red, and pink, and in either bottles or jugs. Gold Seal also produces the Henri Marchant wines, sherries, ports, various sparkling wines, Cold Duck, Concord, and even a wine called simply "Labrusca." These are all typical of the wines of the larger New York wineries.

Vinifera Wine Cellars (Dr. Konstantin Frank)

Vinifera Wine Cellars, founded in 1963, is the unique creation of a remarkable wine pioneer, Dr. Konstantin Frank. Born of German parents in the Ukraine in 1899, Frank studied agriculture at the Odessa Polytechnic Institute and after receiving his degree, taught viticulture and enology. Along the way, he also fought in the White Russian Army, organized collective farms in the Ukraine, and, during the German occupation and while the director of the state experimental station in Odessa, oversaw the planting of two thousand acres of vines. After the Second World War he emigrated to Austria, then Germany, and finally, in 1951, he came to the U.S. with his wife and three children and forty dollars. Frank spoke no English and lived in a Brooklyn slum while he picked up the language and saved enough money from dishwashing and other odd jobs to buy a one-way ticket to the nearest grape research facility, the New York State Agricultural experiment station at Geneva, New York, at the head of Seneca Lake.

After describing his qualifications and experience in grape growing, Frank was offered a job hoeing blueberries, and there he labored for two years. Although Frank had grown acres of *vinifera* in the Ukraine, where the temperature hit forty-below in the winter, everyone scoffed at his claim that it would be possible to grow *vinifera* in the Finger Lakes if enough attention were given to the selection of cold-resistant root stock. Puzzled that no one was growing *vinifera* in the state, he was told it had been tried unsuccessfully for over three hundred years.

Fortunately, Charles Fournier, then head of Gold Seal, listened to Frank's arguments and hired him as a consultant in 1953 to try to grow *vinifera*. Frank looked for root stocks which would permit later blossoming and earlier ripening of the grafted vines so that they would enter dormancy before the first killing winter temperatures. After searching as far as the St. Lawrence Seaway and Quebec for root stock, Frank successfully planted several experimental blocks of *vinifera* on Canadian root stock which withstood twenty-below-zero temperatures that severely damaged some *labrusca* vines. Triumphant, Frank established his own vineyard high above Keuka Lake after ten years of pioneering work at Gold Seal, during which time he personally grafted a quarter of a million vines and proved conclusively that it was possible to grow *vinifera* in the East.

Vinifera Wine Cellars is run by Dr. Frank and his family, and consists of a low rambling farmhouse and a small winery building partly sunk into a hillside overlooking Lake Keuka a few miles north of Hammondsport. There, seventy-eight acres of *vinifera* yield some extraordinary wines. Not content with simply producing some of the finest wines in the U.S., Dr. Frank continues with his efforts to convince dubious researchers, New York wine-growers, and other growers in the East that they should turn their entire attention to growing the finest varieties of *vinifera* rather than the hybrid varieties, which, he aruges, are no more winter-hardy than properly grafted *vinifera*, no more productive, and certainly do not yield anything like fine wine. Like many men who have a sense of mission, he does not suffer gladly those he considers fools, and cannot understand why anyone would be interested in hybrids when *vinifera* does so well in the East. He throws up his hands when he hears the claim that no one without his expertise could do as well with *vinifera*, and points out that he does nothing out of the ordinary. In order to prove his point, Frank has turned over much of his vineyard to experimental plantings which show the effects of grafting various clones of *vinifera* on various kinds of root stock. Frank has sixty-two kinds of root stock in his vineyards, and about sixty varieties of *vinifera*, not counting clones of very cold-resistant Eastern European and Russian varieties unknown in the U.S., with exotic names like Fetjaska, Sereksia Tschornay, Mzuny and others, and even a small plot of Concord and Delaware that Dr. Frank hopes to improve.

Dr. Frank points out that his *vinifera* grapes ripen every year in the reliable, although short, Finger Lakes growing season, something they do not do every year in the erratic seasonal variations in Europe. Thus, Frank never sugars his wines, something that must be done with most *labrusca* and most hybrids, even in good years. He is also proud of his remarkable yields—up to seven to ten tons per acre from Riesling and Chardonnay. Botrytis cinerea, the noble rot of Germany and Sauternes, Frank notes, occurs frequently in the Finger Lakes, and in fact he has a problem warding it off varieties other than his White Riesling.

As might be expected from a wine-grower who has an almost mythic conception of America's destiny to drink *vinifera,* Frank believes winemaking should be as natural as possible and is an advocate of minimal cellar treatment for the wine. He uses stainless steel fermentors, but uses minimal filtration and fining, preferring instead to rack the wine a number of times during settling. While he ages his wines in small oak cooperage, Frank does not believe the flavor of oak contributes to wine and uses only neutral fifty-gallon whiskey barrels. He also keeps his wines a surprising length of time before releasing them, even the whites, and often has nine-year-old White Rieslings for sale at his winery.

Dr. Frank takes his pioneering role very seriously and feels he has an almost patriarchal duty to speak out on what he sees as dubious practices in the wine industry. He is a stern critic of many of the legally permitted additives often used in U.S. wine as preservatives, charging that their long-term effects are unknown. If American consumers were not so frightened of a little sediment in their wines, he says, fewer wineries would feel impelled to overprocess their wines and use such additives.

In spite of the fact that most New York wineries haven't exactly rushed to make use of Dr. Frank's pioneering work with *vinifera,* he derives great satisfaction from the fact that small growers all over the East have come to him for cuttings and advice, and dozens of states now have small plots of *vinifera* successfully planted. Now that he is in his seventies, Dr. Frank is pleased to think all his work has not been in vain, and that what he thinks of as his contribution to his adopted country will not be lost or forgotten.

THE WINES:

Vinifera Wine Cellars produces ten wines for sale, but only a few are normally marketed outside the winery, as the number of acres planted to each variety is very small. Of the few thousand cases that reach the market each year (all labeled

under the Dr. Konstantin Frank signature), his most famous
and probably his most outstanding wine is his Johannisberg
Riesling Natur Spätlese (unsugared, late-picked), a wine
which in the best years is of astonishing quality. In fact,
the only Rieslings I have ever had from the U.S. which
approximate their style have been some of the new White
Rieslings from the Pacific Northwest. California, in spite of
the fact that it has produced some extraordinary Rieslings,
may have too warm a climate to produce Rieslings that consistently remind one of fine Moselles, as Dr. Frank's Riesling
does. Limpid in the glass, with a delicate floral-wintergreen
nose at its best, its flavor is remarkably mouth-filling, soft
and tart, with an exquisite balance of rich, ripe fruit and
almost a citrus-like acidity; its finish is long and lingering,
with a haunting nuance of wintergreen. It is not merely fine;
it is superb. This, of course, is the wine at its most memorable, and of the vintages I have had, the ones which most
approximated this character were '69, '68, and '65. The '67
in particular was not successful, though still refreshing, rather
too thin and tart, and marred by a whiff of sulphur. The '66
was similar, but not so thin. The Riesling is affected by
botrytis frequently, and is usually simply allowed to add its
nuance to the Natur Spätlese. As a means of gaining attention for his accomplishment, Dr. Frank produced a Trocken-
beerenauslese in the early sixties (long since sold out) and
has produced another one since (it is still slumbering in his
cellar). The older Riesling Spätleses have developed marvelously in the bottle, taking on an almost honeyed spicy
quality, though those adjectives best apply to Dr. Frank's
Gewürztraminer which, in a vintage like '65, makes a luscious
overripe, honeyed, unctuous wine, with a seductive clover-
floral-spice nose; the '69 on the other hand, while still attractive, was much lighter and had an unfortunate nose reminiscent of bananas.

His Chardonnay is also superb, and while it does not have
the oily, rich magnificence of some California Chardonnays,
it has its own marvelous distinction, lighter, more elegant,
with hints of chalk and a lingering leafy-green spiciness. A
complex wine with considerable finesse at its best, I was most
impressed with the '70 and '74 vintages. I was not taken with
his Muscat Ottonel, however, at least the one vintage I tried
('66), in spite of the fact that its beautiful apricot nose
reached way over the glass; I found its flavor sharp and thin.

Dr. Frank's reds are most intriguing, although not as excit-

ing as his whites, to judge by the '69 vintage. His Cabernet
Sauvignon, tasted in early 1974, was actually purple in the
glass, and had an extraordinary raspberry nose, overlaid with
a strong, pleasant, dusty-stalky smell. With a very light body
but a fine flavor, it is a well-built, tannic wine that needs five
more years at least to harmonize its elements. The Pinot Noir
had a similar dusty-stalky nose, this time with a vegetative
aroma; a long full flavor, light body, and fine mint-like finish
left an impression of a complex but not overwhelming wine.
Sampled against a '69 Gamay Beaujolais in early 1974, I preferred the Gamay, which had a marvelous dusty-stalky-
asparagus-mint nose and a tannic rich, full flavor, with a
nuance of olives and mint in the finish—a superb wine.

I should also mention that I have found considerable variation from bottle to bottle in some of Dr. Frank's wines. This
appears to be due principally to variations in storage conditions in retail outlets, a constant problem for any fine wine
made in a natural manner.

Boordy Vineyard

Boordy Vineyard is the name of the small Riderwood,
Maryland, winery begun in 1945 by Philip and Jocelyn Wagner that has become well-known for the wines made from the
French-American hybrids it helped introduce to this country.
(See the introduction to this chapter.) In 1968 the Wagners
joined their enterprise with that of Seneca Foods of Dundee,
New York, which is best known as a processor of applesauce
and fresh grape juice. Seneca has plants in several locations
in New York and in the Yakima Valley in Washington State.
The Boordy division of Seneca Foods is a unique operation in
that it operates in three states: at its home winery in Maryland; in Penn Yan, New York, at the head of Keuka Lake;
and at Prosser in the Yakima Valley of Washington. Each
winery will eventually devote its production to separate lines
of regional wines, and the two Eastern ones for the moment
are concentrating on the hybrids for which Boordy originally
became known.

THE WINES:

Currently the Penn Yan Boordy winery is the major
source of Boordy wines, since the Maryland winery is very
small. The wines (eight altogether) are usually vintage-dated

but not usually varietally labeled, as most of the wines are
blends of a number of grapes. The principal wines are a red,
a dry white, and a rosé, of which the red and white are
among the best of the wines made from French-American
hybrids. Of recent vintages, I've found the Boordy Red attractive, simple in flavor, with a soft, diffuse taste and a nice
finish; it is best cool, since *labrusca* hints emerge as it warms.
In short, it is a fruity, pleasant wine. The Boordy White has
a very slight *labrusca*-tinged nose, but a clean, quaffable
flavor.

One varietal wine produced by Boordy is their "Five-Two-
Seven-Six" (Seyve-Villard 5276) most commonly labeled
Seyval Blanc. It is an unblended wine. I found it rather pungent in nose, and heavy in flavor, and though it finishes well,
rather wearing.

The Wagners, to their credit, have never made any rash
claims about the quality of these hybrid wines, and, with refreshing candor, characterize them as *vin du pays*—simple
country wines.

Widmer's Wine Cellars

Over the hills at the foot of the next large lake, Lake
Canandaigua, some miles northwest of Hammondsport, is
Widmer's, the only winery in Naples Valley and by far the
largest business in the little town of Naples. Widmer's dates
its founding from 1888, when John Jacob Widmer, a Swiss
immigrant who came to America with his family six years
earlier, crushed his first vintage. There were already wineries
in the valley, but Widmer prospered, at first by selling wine
in barrels, then in bottles, and by 1910 could afford to send
one of his three sons, Will, to Germany to study winemaking
at the institute at Geisenheim. After struggling through Prohibition by making fresh grape juice and jellies, Widmer's began expanding its operations and pioneered a number of innovations in New York State, among them varietal labeling,
vintage dating, and the use of the solera-type system for
dessert wines. This last has become a trademark of Widmer's,
and consists in putting *labrusca* wines in barrels that are left
exposed on the roof of the winery through the year. This
"weathering" process takes a minimum of four years at
Widmer's and removes the *labrusca* quality of the wine. This
also results in a more interesting product than baked wines.
Widmer's has ten thousand barrels in tiers four-deep all over

its winery roofs, which presents a rather startling sight to visitors.

Widmer's grows a third of the grapes it needs for its production of a half-million cases a year and buys the rest from local growers. Its most popular product by far is its Lake Niagara White—a sweetish *labrusca*-flavored wine that Widmer's began marketing in the late thirties and which became wildly popular in the 1960's. It now sells in excess of two hundred thousand cases a year.

But Widmer's has long had its eye on the fine wine market. After Will Widmer's death in 1968, and the winery's purchase in 1970 by the R. T. French Company (best known for its mustard), which itself has been bought by Reckitt and Coleman, the London food firm, the winery took steps to add *vinifera* wines to its line. After reaching the conclusion that growing *vinifera* in the East on a large commercial scale would require considerable investment, Widmer's instead purchased five hundred acres in the Alexander Valley in California's Sonoma County. Widmer's has thus been able to begin purchasing *vinifera* grapes from California growers to make and market wine until its own new plantings come into bearing—something it could not do in the East. Until its new California winery is built, Widmer's is using another winery's cellars in St. Helena in the Napa Valley.

THE WINES:

Widmer's best dessert wines are its sherries. I found its dry cocktail sherry palatable and its medium dry Special Selection Sherry (usually aged eight to ten years) quite nutty and flavorful—in fact, it is quite the best New York State dessert wine I have tasted.

Widmer's most interesting Eastern products, however, are its vintage-dated varietal wines which are almost always unblended. The Naples Valley Delaware is probably the most attractive of the varietal whites to a *vinifera*-accustomed palate. I tried the '68 vintage in early 1974 and found its unfoxy, leafy-apple skin nose intriguing. The flavor was also interesting, almost apple cider-like, and flinty-dry. The Moore's Diamond of the same vintage was much more *labrusca*-scented, and featured a spicy-fruity, sweeter taste.

Of the Naples Valley reds, the '71 Foch exhibited a high, round, attractive nose somewhat reminiscent of strawberries and a rather tart flavor and finish. The most remarkable wine

I have ever tasted made from a French-American hybrid was an experimental lot of Widmer's 1970 De Chaunac. This red wine could easily have been mistaken for a fine, young, unusual Zinfandel. It had a dusty, berry-like nose, and a very *vinifera*-like, intense, spicy, and expansive flavor. Widmer's intends to market later vintages of this wine—probably the '73—in the near future, and its quality shows that the efforts to make truly fine wine from hybrids may not be an altogether vain enterprise.

Widmer's less distinguished Eastern wines are typical of most of the Finger Lakes wineries. It ought to be noted that Widmer's "Riesling," occasionally produced in Spätlese versions, has nothing to do with White Riesling; it is made from the Missouri Riesling, a *labrusca* variety.

Benmarl Wine Company

Although wine has been made from Hudson River Valley grapes for almost a century and a half, grape acreage has declined markedly since the 1800's. Once the region had scores of wineries and some thirteen thousand acres of vineyards. At present, there are only a handful of wineries and a mere several hundred acres of vineyards: In terms of quality, the most important of these is Benmarl Wine Company. After returning from Europe with his family, illustrator Mark Miller bought a former vineyard plot near the town of Marlboro overlooking the Hudson and named it Benmarl. First run as a cooperative in the late fifties, it was bonded in 1971 and Miller and his family now produce about six thousand cases of wine a year, virtually all from hybrid grapes grown in the seventy-two-acre vineyard.

Miller is a tireless promoter of small wineries; Benmarl is used in part as a kind of experiment station to try new varieties and to encourage local farmers to plant the vine before creeping suburbanization takes over the mid-Hudson. Currently the majority of Benmarl's production goes directly to members of its "Societé des Vignerons," who receive "vinerights" (a case or more of wine a year) in exchange for dues.

THE WINES:

Benmarl produces dozens of experimental lots and cuvées of its various hybrid varietals, but most of these go to its membership. A number of vintage-dated varietals are marketed, however, the best of which is the Seyval Blanc. The '74 was an outstanding example of the hybrid. I sampled various cuvées of the '76 Seyval Blanc out of the barrel in early 1977 and found several pleasantly tart and fruity, with attractive floral-perfumey aromas. The winery also has very small plantings of Chardonnay and White Riesling; production of both, as one might expect, is miniscule and proceeds on an experimental basis. Samples of the '76 Chardonnay struck me as light, sharply acidic and clean, and the '76 Riesling as light, steely-tart, and honeysuckle-scented.

The available reds are from hybrids, and are also rather light and sharp, which makes them somewhat less attractive than the whites. Still, they are all far superior to the average New York State red. To my taste the most promising of the '76 vintage was the De Chaunac, with its full grapey scent, good vinosity and flavor, and strong hints of oak aging.

Other Wineries

There are over three dozen wineries, varying considerably in size, in operation in New York State, though very few of the ones outside of the Finger Lakes area are well known. The Canandaigua Wine Company, which also owns Richard's Wine Cellars in Virginia, as well as several wineries in various parts of the state, is one of the largest wine producers in the country and one of the least known. Having purchased a few years back the Bisceglia Brothers winery, a California bulk-wine producer located in the San Joaquin Valley, Canandaigua will no doubt soon be adding a line of dry table wines. At present it markets traditional-style *labrusca* wines under the Virginia Dare label, among others. Its best-selling product is said to be Richard's Wild Irish Rose, which sold five million cases in 1976. Its *labrusca* character is fearsomely aggressive.

The Hudson Valley is home to a few wineries, none particularly large, and it is probably best known for the uncompromising *labrusca* products of medium-size wineries like Hudson Valley and the Brotherhood Winery. One small Hudson Valley winery, High Tor, recently closed its doors. It had been in operation since 1954 and had gained a good reputation for its hybrid-based wines. There are also, interestingly enough, several wineries in the Hudson Valley that supply grapes to several New York City wineries, which specialize in kosher wines. There are no longer any vines on Manhattan Island, but there are still several operating wineries in Manhattan's Lower East Side, like Schapiro's Wine Company, which quite accurately describes its *labrusca* products as wines with flavor "you can almost cut with a knife." One of the best-known kosher wineries in the country is the Monarch Wine Co. located in Brooklyn. (The other is the Chicago-based Mogen David Wine Corp., which has wineries in western New York as well.) Monarch obtains its grapes from Finger Lakes growers, and produces a long line of *labrusca*-based wines, under a variety of labels, the best known of which is Manischewitz. Most of Monarch's wines are based on Concord and are consequently quite *labrusca*-flavored; perhaps their best product is their sweet Manischewitz Cream White Concord.

There are small wineries attempting to make interesting wine in other parts of the state as well, including Johnson Vineyards and Niagara Falls Wine Cellar in the Chatauqua-Niagara district in the western part of the state; both produce French hybrid wines and the latter is growing *vinifera* in addition.

One very promising new venture is the Long Island Vineyards Winery in Cutchogue, New York, the only such winery-estate on Long Island. Its forty-four-acre vineyard is planted exclusively to top *vinifera* varietals, a bit of viticultural pioneering its owners, Alex and Louisa Hargrave, feel is feasible given the unusually moderate winters in their location. Their Pinot Noir has already been given excellent marks by experienced palates. They expect to release their first wines—all from the '75 vintage—in late 1977.

Chapter 11
Other States, New Directions

What is most remarkable about the wine industry in states other than California and New York is the great interest the wineries now take in hybrid and *vinifera* wines. The growing acreage of better vines in a number of states makes it clear that in a few years Americans will see many wines, perhaps a good proportion of them fine wines, carrying labels from states hitherto little associated with wine of any quality. Interestingly enough, however, some of the states which may become well known for wine production in the future were among the largest producers of wine in America's past. As mentioned previously, Ohio was the leading U.S. wine state in the 1850's, when it produced twice as much wine as California—over half a million gallons a year. Its wine industry, founded by Nicholas Longworth at Cincinnati, was destroyed by vine diseases, principally powdery mildew, in the 1860's, and the state's wine industry never recovered, except for a brief success by its Lake Erie wineries before Prohibition. Now, Ohio's wine industry (presently five thousand acres of vines) is expanding rapidly and experimenting with hybrid vines.

In other states old wineries have been revived, new ones started, and vineyards have been planted to *vinifera* in areas long thought to have impossible growing conditions for fine wine varieties. Michigan and Washington now have about twenty thousand acres each in vines (about half the acreage New York does), while Pennsylvania has roughly ten thousand acres, and a surprisingly long list of other states have lesser amounts. All these states are rapidly expanding their acreage, and in fact, the rapidly expanding vineyards of Washington may surpass New York's in total acreage in the next decade.

With a handful of exceptions, most of these states do not presently have wineries geared to the production of fine wines. Most produce sound, everyday *labrusca*-type wines for local markets, and sometimes neighboring states as well. This picture is changing rapidly, of course. Now that Dr. Konstantin Frank in New York has shown it is possible to grow the finest varieties of *vinifera* in the East and produce superb wine from them, wineries in the East, Midwest, and even the South are experimenting with small plots of White Riesling, Chardonnay, and Pinot noir, as well as with large plantings of French hybrids. Some new wine districts, especially in the Pacific Northwest, have shown astonishing potential as important fine wine areas, and in the next few decades American wine lovers are certain to hear of other areas, too.

The following brief notes cover some of the largest and best distributed wineries outside New York and California, the ones whose products are most likely to be of interest to wine lovers, and mention some of the small wineries which have begun operations recently with the intention of making fine wine.

The East Coast and Midwest

Vinifera is now grown in Connecticut, at least experimentally, and a new winery, White Mountain Vineyards, is producing wines from hybrid vines grown in New Hampshire. Pennsylvania, which until recently grew mostly Concords for grape juice, now has about a dozen small wineries growing hybrids and *vinifera*. The first of these was the ten-acre Conestoga Vineyards, founded by Melvin Gordon in 1963. In 1968 Pennsylvania—a control state—passed a law permitting small wineries in that state to market their own wines without having to sell them through the Liquor Control Board. Two new wineries promptly opened up in Erie County—Presque Isle Wine Cellars and Penn-Shore Vineyards—both of which produce a number of wines from French hybrids, and *vinifera* as well.

I have tasted the Penn-Shore wines, and while the *labrusca* wines are unremarkable, the Extra Dry champagne I sampled was on a par with the better sparkling wines of New York State. The best wine I tried from Penn-Shore was their nonvintage Seyval Blanc, one of the best wines from that variety I've had. It had a nose reminiscent of Sauvignon Blanc, and good fruit and balance. The winery's 1971 Chardonnay, however, was a disappointment; it was pleasantly scented and well-made, but was too green and unripe to be successful. A better vintage will doubtless produce a better wine.

Boordy Vineyard in Riderwood, Maryland, is well known locally for its small production of wines from the French hybrid vines that its proprietors, Philip and Jocelyn Wagner, helped pioneer in this country in the 1940's. Its red, white, and rosé wines from its Riderwood winery are similar in quality to the better-distributed wines from its Penn Yan, New York operation: all are clean, well-made, and pleasant.

Maryland is also the home of Montbray Wine Cellars, the creation of Dr. G. Hamilton Mobray, a research psychologist who now has an eighteen-acre vineyard planted to hybrids and *vinifera* northwest of Baltimore. Dr. Mobray markets tiny quantities of the first *vinifera* wines produced in the state since Lord Baltimore tried to grow the Old World vines in the 1660's.

New wineries and vineyards have begun in recent years in Missouri, Indiana, Illinois, and other Midwestern states. Some have begun producing wines from both hybrids and *vinifera*. Production of most is now quite small, but some of the wines are quite interesting; recently I tasted a *méthode champenoise* Illinois champagne ("Pere Marquette Brut"), principally from hybrid grapes by the Thompson Winery of Monee, Illinois, that was on a par with the best New York State sparkling wines. One of the best red blends from hybrid grapes I've had came from Mount Pleasant Vineyards in Augusta, Missouri, about thirty miles west of St. Louis. In the late nineteenth century the vineyard had a considerable reputation, but Prohibition put an end to its label. In 1966 the winery was revived and now produces wine from its twelve-acre planting of hybrids and *vinifera*. The 1972 Emigré Red I tried was a good wine with fine balance, and some complexity in the nose and flavor.

Ohio, too, is turning its attention to better wine grapes. Meier's Wine Cellars, while not the largest winery in the Midwest (that honor would probably go to the Mogen David Wine Corporation of Chicago, best known for their kosher *labrusca* wines), is one of the largest. Recently it has begun to market a red and a white table wine under the Chateau Jac Jan label, both made from French hybrid grapes, in addition to its well-known sherries and *labrusca*-flavored wines like Catawba. Meier's is also experimenting with *vinifera*.

Michigan remains the largest wine-producing state in the Midwest, however, and has a number of large and small wineries clustered in the southwest corner of the state near Lake Michigan. Among the largest are Warner Vineyards and the Bronte Champagne and Wines Co. Warner has recently begun plantings of *vinifera,* but for the moment is upgrading its line of wines with hybrids. While I was not particularly impressed with their new *méthode champenoise* Michigan Brut champagne, I found their Imperial Cream sherry attractive and well-made, and their Vineyard White a clean, light wine much like the best "Rhine" types of New York State.

Bronte expects to double its three hundred and seventy-five thousand gallons a year production over the next few years, and emphasizes hybrid wines. Their champagne is comparable to New York State champagne, cleanly made and palatable; their Baco Noir is a good product for this grape, though tart. (Bronte, by the way, is the originator of Cold Duck in this country.)

Among the smaller Michigan wineries, Tabor Hill Vineyards, founded in 1970, is already producing *vinifera* and hybrid wines from its forty-five-acre vineyard.

A recent sample of the non-vintage Tabor Hill Cuvée Rosé was assertive and unappealing, but the non-vintage Cuvée Blanc was light, sweetish, and quite pleasant. The '74 Johannisberg Riesling was rather light and tart and lacked varietal intensity, but otherwise well-made.

Experimental plantings of hybrids and *vinifera* have been made in Texas and Idaho, and Wiederkehr Wine Cellars in Altus, Arkansas, the largest winery in the Southwest, has begun plantings and limited bottlings of White Riesling and other *vinifera.* Wiederkehr has a good reputation for its sparkling wines.

Until recently, no large-scale plantings of *vinifera* have been undertaken in the East, but 1976 brought news that the Zonin Wine Company, a large Italian-based European wine producer, has purchased some eight hundred acres near Charlottesville, Virginia, and has begun planting top *vinifera* varietals. This turn of events is a belated vindication of Thomas Jefferson's (and other pioneering viticulturists') belief that fine wine grapes could be grown in Virginia.

Suggested Samplings

Anyone wishing to sample some of the current high points of the region's wine production will certainly find some of them among the following types and producers. These are offered as a starting point, not a definitive list of the best, and readers are encouraged to go on and explore for themselves. Bear in mind that some of these wines are produced in small quantities and consequently may not be easy to find; many of these are readily available, however, at least in some major U.S. cities.

RED:

Baco Noir
Bronte

Red Blends
Boordy Vineyard Red
Mount Pleasant Vineyards Emigré Red

WHITE:

Seyval Blanc
Penn-Shore Vineyards

Catawba
Meier's Island Sweet Catawba

White Blends
Boordy Vineyard White
Tabor Hill Vineyard Cuvée Blanc
Warner Vineyards White

OTHER:

Sparkling Wine
Pere Marquette Brut (Thompson Winery)
Penn-Shore Vineyards Extra Dry

Rosé
Boordy Rosé

Dessert Wines
Warner Vineyards Imperial Cream Sherry

The Pacific Northwest

While the experimental plantings in various Western states may prove to yield fine wine, in the past few years, Oregon and Washington have already shown themselves to be suitable for growing *vinifera*, and *vinifera* that can yield outstanding wines.

There are already a dozen wineries in Oregon, and although some of them make only fruit wines, a handful are engaged in the production of fine wines, all from *vinifera* varieties. Most, however, have extremely limited production. Even considering the relatively cool climate, and the fact that Oregon does not have vast flat acreage suitable for vineyards, it is obvious there are several thousand acres of hillsides which can yield top-quality wines, especially whites.

The first winery in recent years to grow and make *vinifera* wines is the Hillcrest Vineyard in the Umpqua Valley, founded in 1963 by Richard Sommer. His wines have improved steadily since his first vintages, and are very fine wines. The '72 White Riesling had a lovely, delicate scent, a light, delicate body, and refreshing, fruity acidity; a very attractive, though not complex wine. The quite dry non-vintage Gewürztraminer had an exceptionally spicy, fresh, and delicate nose, and a spicy-leafy flavor. Hillcrest also produces Cabernet Sauvignon, and the '71 vintage I tried had a light, varietal nose and good flavor; a bit light and thin, it rather reminded me of some of the fine Cabernet rosés California produces—though it was by no means as light as a rosé.

Hillcrest has been followed by a number of other small wineries, bonded very recently, who are intrigued with the potential that varieties like White Riesling have in Oregon's cool climate—in fact, of the other Oregon wines I have sampled, the White Riesling is much the best wine: light, fruity, and delicate.

The state of Washington has over a quarter of a million acres of flat land suitable for grape-growing, however, and in spite of occasional very cold winters, has ideal conditions for *vinifera*. In the past, a great deal of Concord has been grown here, but the extraordinary potential of *vinifera* in this climate has resulted in large new plantings of the Old World grape in Washington's major wine-growing district, the Yakima Valley. As there has never been any phylloxera in the area, *vinifera* vines are grown on their own roots—a considerable economic advantage.

Boordy Vineyard, since 1968 a division of Seneca Foods, has a new winery operation at Prosser, and while it is setting out the hybrid wines that Boordy founder Philip Wagner pioneered in Maryland in the 1940's, it is experimenting with *vinifera* as well. The first *vinifera* wines produced under its Washington label—a Cabernet Sauvignon and a Pinot Noir—were light and delicate, but showed the excellent potential that the area has to produce fine *vinifera* wines in a different style than California.

Washington's most prominent winery, Ste. Michelle Vintners, has already demonstrated that Washington has one of the nation's ideal climates for superb white wines. Formerly known as American Wine Growers, it is a merger of several Washington wineries that began after Repeal. After the great success of the *vinifera* varietals the firm introduced in 1970 under the Ste. Michelle label, it changed its name to match its best label. With its 1974 purchase by the United States Tobacco Co., Ste. Michelle gained the resources to become a well-known winery, and to judge by some of its recent wines, has stayed with its intention to produce outstanding wines.

All eight of Ste. Michelle's vintage-dated varietal wines are made from grapes grown in its seven hundred and fifty acres of vineyards in the Yakima Valley, some one hundred and ninety miles southeast of Seattle as is Ste. Michelle's new winery. (Not surprisingly, the winery has already made extensive use of mechanical harvesting and field-crushing.) The first of its wines to gain critical attention was its Johannisberg Riesling, and recent samples of the '73 and '75 showed the same lovely, almost pine-like aromas that distinguished earlier vintages. The flavor and balance struck me as more austere than earlier examples, but still fine and characterful. The '75 Sémillon had a pungent, somewhat earthy aroma and a rich, sharply tangy flavor that needs some time in the bottle to bring out its best. The gold-straw colored '75 Gewürztraminer, a new release, had a marvelous, heady, honey-and-spice scent and a surprisingly dry, crisp character despite its two percent residual sugar. The Grenache Rosé is consistently superb, and the '75 is no exception. Bright rose in color, it had an extremely intense, almost strawberryish aroma and a lovely, strawberryish, just off-dry flavor.

Most astonishing to me, however, were the samples I had in early 1977 of the Cabernet Sauvignons. The dark, rich-looking '74 had a fine, deep, classic Cabernet aroma laced with oaky notes and a closed, but round, well-knit, flavor, fine balance, and an olive-ish finish. The '75, tasted out of the barrel, was even bigger than the '74, heavy and powerful on the palate, with a full oaky-olive aroma and flavor that promised impressive future development. Both had plenty of tannin to lose, particularly the '75, but already stand comparison with the better California Cabernets of the same vintages, and make it clear that the Yakima Valley can produce fine reds as well as whites. Ste. Michelle has become an important label, and its success with Washington State wines will doubtless encourage others to join the handful of wineries in the region.

Suggested Samplings

Anyone wishing to sample some of the current high points of the region's wine production will certainly find some of them among the following types and producers. These are offered as a starting point, not a definitive list of the best, and readers are encouraged to go on and explore for themselves. Bear in mind that some of these wines are produced in small quantities and consequently may not be easy to find; many of these are readily available, however, at least in some major U.S. cities.

RED:

> *Cabernet Sauvignon*
> Hillcrest Vineyard
> Ste. Michelle

> *Pinot Noir*
> Ste. Michelle
> Boordy Vineyard

WHITE:

> *White (Johannisberg) Riesling*
> Hillcrest Vineyard
> Ste. Michelle

Sémillon
Ste. Michelle

Gewürztraminer
Hillcrest Vineyard
Ste. Michelle

OTHER:

Rosés
Ste. Michelle Grenache Rosé

*   *   *

H. Warner Allen once wrote, "After mildew, phylloxera, cocktails and Prohibition, wine-lovers have a right to expect from the New World some startling boon as compensation. Perhaps when time has swung its full circle and the boot-legger has become a historical curiosity, there will emerge from the West some great unknown wine, for there is no limit to the artistic possibilities of the fermented juice of the grape."

Now, some forty years after the Repeal of Prohibition, America has redeemed her early promise. The wine vine since its earliest cultivation has held a particular fascination for the peoples of many lands, and Americans have been no exception. Wine is a special kind of poetry—a poetry of place and time—that can be relived as long as there are bottles of it left to be tasted, for the harvest from no other plant can be made into a product that so well sums up the fruit and soil and season.

Americans have rediscovered this romance of wine, and if the glorious wines so far produced are any augur, the future of great wine in America is assured.

Glossary

The following list consists primarily of common wine-tasting and winemaking terms used in the United States. It does not include grape or wine varieties or label terms; consult the index for these. Omitted as well are self-evident terms of approbation such as "magnificent," "delightful," etcetera.
Note: Italicized words appear elsewhere in this list.

ACETIC: Wine which has gone *sour* or vinegary through excessive contact with air.

ACID: The acidic taste dimension in wine is primarily due to the presence of tartaric and malic acids, as well as citric, succinic, lactic, and *acetic* aid. The degree of acidity in a wine is described as *flat, sharp* or *tart,* or *green.*

AFTERTASTE: see *finish.*

AGED: *Mature,* fully developed wines are described as aged, and should possess *bouquet.* The age of a wine may be roughly determined by careful tasting. A wine's age, like that of a person, is described as *young, mature,* or *old.*

ALCOHOL: Alcohol is found in concentrations of from nine to fifteen percent by volume in table wines. Wines of low alcoholic content are described as tasting *light* or *weak;* wines high in alcohol are described as *heady* or *strong.*

APPLES: A fruit smell associated with the presence of malic acid and apparent in a number of white wines.

AROMA: That part of a wine's *nose* or *smell* that can be attributed to the grape variety used.

ASTRINGENT: A wine of high *tannin* content has a puckering effect on the mouth and is described as astringent, *tannic, rough,* or *harsh.* A wine of low tannin content is described as *smooth* or *soft.* Wines lose astringency with age.

AUSTERE: Austere wines are *fine* wines which exhibit *severity* of *character* and high *acidity* and/or *tannin.* They generally lack *charm,* usually because of a lack of *fruit.*

BAD: *Unsound* or *spoiled* wines are described as bad.

BAKED: The flavor that results from grapes grown in hot climates; a *warm, cooked,* or *roasted smell* and *flavor.*

BALANCED: Said of wine whose *flavor* dimensions are in harmony.

BIG: Big wines are *strong* and *full-bodied.*

BITE: Wines with high *acidity* are said to have bite.

BITTER: An excessively *astringent* wine.

BLACKCURRANTS: A fruit smell found in many reds, especially Cabernet Sauvignon.

BODY: The degree of non-sugar solids present in a wine affects one's perception of the wine's weight and texture in the mouth. High *alcohol* content adds to the impression of heavy body. Dry table wines are described as *light* or *thin, heavy, rich,* robust, or *full* in body.

BOTRYTIZED: Wines made from grapes affected by the beneficent mold Botrytis cinerea ("the noble rot") have a *distinctive,* perfumey scent.

BOUQUET: That part of a wine's *nose* or *smell* which can be attributed to aging in cask or bottle.

BREATHE: To let a freshly opened wine have contact with the air before consumption is to let it breathe. See *decant.*

BRIGHT: Said of a wine's color that is clear.

BRILLIANT: Said of a wine's color that is absolutely clear.

BROWNING: The color of well-aged red wines is often brick-red; the effect can be noticed at the wine's edge in a wine glass.

BURNT: A wine with a highly *cooked* flavor; sometimes used to describe the excessively woody *flavor* of some wines.

CHAPTALIZATION: Sugaring; the addition of sugar to the *must* to ensure complete fermentation.

CHARACTER: A wine of character has something to notice, whether it be virtues or defects.

CHARM: Attractiveness. Often said of *light, fruity* wines.

CLEAN: A wine free from defects is described as clean; also an impression of refreshing straightforwardness of *flavor.*

CLOUDY: A wine that is cloudy in appearance is always suspect and usually *bad.*

CLOYING: Often used to describe wines with a *sweet, heavy,* and tiresome *flavor.*

COARSE: A *sound* though crudely made wine, *poor* to *ordinary* in quality, often *rough* or *harsh* in *character.*

COMPLEX: *Fine* wines possessing a *subtle* mélange of several different scents and *flavors* are said to be complex; the opposite of *simple*.

COOKED: See *baked*.

COOPERAGE: Collective term for any and all containers wooden or otherwise, used for wine during its time in the cellar.

CORKY: The offensive *smell* of a wine spoiled by a moldy (not merely dried out) cork. Infrequently encountered.

DECANT: Decanting is the transferring of finished wine from its bottle to a carafe or decanter for serving, usually done to separate the clear wine from its sediment or *deposit*, if any, or to aerate the wine (see *breathe*).

DEEP: A wine is said to have a deep *nose* or deep *flavor* if the scent or taste has a number of layers or levels to it; usually used with *rich* but *subtle* wines.

DELICATE: A *light* wine is delicate as well if it also has some *subtlety* or *elegance*.

DEPOSIT: The sediment (mostly precipitated *tannins*) which is left as a powder or crust on the inside wall of undisturbed bottles of certain wines which have been aged.

DISTINCTIVE: Recognizable *character* in a wine. Certain varietal wines are said to be distinctive because they can be distinguished from one another. Not all distinctive wines are *distinguished*.

DISTINGUISHED: Exceptional, evident, and well-*balanced character* in a wine; a term of praise.

DRY: Dry wines lack perceptible *sweetness*.

DUMB: Undeveloped but potentially *fine* wines are said to be dumb.

EARTHY: Scents or *flavors* reminiscent of fresh earth; a virtue in some wines.

ELEGANT: Said of very *fine* wines that give one an impression of stylishness in the *balance* of their elements.

ENOLOGY: The science or study of wines and winemaking.

EXPANSIVE: A generous, spreading quality in *nose* or *flavor*.

FINE: Wine of *distinguished character*.

FINING: Clarification by the addition of certain substances to the wine. The fining agent settles to the bottom carrying with it fine suspended particles.

FINISH: The *aftertaste* that stays in the mouth after swallowing or spitting out the wine. It may be unpleasant or haunting and may disappear instantly or linger.

FLAT: A wine lacking *acidity* is said to be flat.

FLAVORS: The impressions left on the palate when the wine is worked over in the mouth.

FLINTY: A stony, gravelly, or mineral *nuance* in scent or taste.

FLOWERY: The *aroma* of some wines is distinctly floral or *expansive* and perfume-like in character.

FRAGRANT: A fragrant wine is one with an *expansive*, scented *nose*.

FRESH: The opposite of *tired*, used to describe *fruity, tart, young* wine.

FRUITY: Fruity wines have various ripe-fruit scents and/or *flavors*. A fruity wine is not always simply *grapey*.

FULL: Wines with substantial *body* are described as full.

GOOD: A better than *ordinary* wine, but not *fine*.

GRAPEY: A *fruity* wine with a fresh-grape smell.

GREAT: Along with *noble*, the highest praise that can be given to a wine.

GREEN: An excessively acidulous wine; unripe.

HARD: *Tannic* young red wines are said to be hard.

HARMONIOUS: A harmonious wine is a well-*balanced* wine.

HARSH: An excessively *astringent* and/or *acidic* wine.

HEADY: An attractively *strong* wine.

HEAVY: A *full-bodied* wine.

HONEYED: A *flavor* quality found in some very fine *sweet* wines.

HOT: Very *alcoholic* wines may have a hot or burning quality in the *finish;* certain dessert wines have a hot *character* as well.

INKY: A tinny, *metallic nuance* or taste.

INTENSE: A wine with highly concentrated qualities.

LEES: The heavy sediment which is thrown by *young* wine in *cooperage*.

LEGS: The drips apparent on the inner walls of the wine glass which reveal the viscosity of the wine.

LENGTH: The lasting quality of the *finish* of a wine.

LEAFY: A *green*, vegetative *nuance* in *flavor*.

LIGHT: Wines low in *alcohol* are described as light in *body*.

LITTLE: A wine with little *nose, flavor,* or *character* is described as little or small.

LIVELY: *Young,* fresh, well-made wines are lively in scent and *flavor*.

LUSCIOUS: A quality of the *body* and *flavor* of some very *fine* wines with a particularly rich attractive deliciousness.

MADERIZED: The *browning* effect caused by great age.

MATURE: A wine which has developed fully with age.

METALLIC: A tinny flavor; usually a defect.

MOLDY: An unpleasant *smell* and taste from rotten grapes.

MUST: The mass of unfermented, crushed grapes.

MUSTY: An unpleasant *smell* like that of a dank cellar.

NEUTRAL: An unexceptional, undistinctive wine is said to be neutral.

NOBLE: See *great*.

NOSE: The *smell* of a wine, including *bouquet* and *aroma*.

NUANCE: A *subtle flavor* or odor trace.

NUTTY: A nut-like odor and *flavor* found in better dessert wines.

OFF: A wine that is off is partially or completely *spoiled* or defective.

OLD: Old wine is past its peak of development.

ORDINARY: *Sound* and drinkable table wine, between *poor* and *good* in quality.

OXIDIZED: A condition caused in wine by excessive contact with air. It is a stage on the way to complete spoilage (see *acetic*) and is usually objectionable.

PEACHES: A fruity quality reminiscent of peaches and sometimes noticeable in Chenin Blanc.

PETILLANCE: Naturally occurring light sparkle.

POOR: A *sound* but barely drinkable wine. Below *ordinary* in quality.

POWERFUL: Used to indicate *strength* and *bigness*.

RACKING: The drawing off of wine from one vat to another during winemaking, usually for the purpose of separating it from its *lees* or sediment. The transferring of wine from one container to another in the cellar.

RASPBERRIES: A fruity *nuance* found in a number of red wines, especially Zinfandel.

RICH: Wines with substantial *body* are described as rich, round, *full*, robust.

RIPE: *Full, soft, mature* character.

ROASTED: See *baked*.

ROUGH: See *harsh* and *coarse*.

RUBY: Typical color of many red wines.

SAPPY: A *lively*, straightforward, *grapey character*.

SEVERE: See *austere*.

SHARP: *Biting acidity*.

SHORT: Said of a wine with a quick *finish*.

SICK: A diseased, *unsound* or disturbed wine.

SILKY: A description of the texture of the *body of* certain wines. See *velvety*.

SIMPLE: The opposite of *complex*.

SMELL: The odor of a wine; see *nose*.

SMOKE: An elusive quality found in some white wines.

SMOOTH: Descriptive of the *texture* of some wines; also said of a wine low in *tannin*.

SOFT: Descriptive of wines of low *acidity*.

SOUND: Soundness is the objective chemical state of a wine which is properly made and stored so that it is not *soured* or *spoiled*. It is not a judgment of quality as such, but is a necessary condition of all drinkable wines.

SOUR: See *acetic*.

SPICE: Quality found in many wines; particularly Gewürztraminer.

SPOILED: A wine rendered undrinkable by bacterial action. See *acetic*.

STALKY: A green-woody scent. See *leafy*. The terms "stalky" and "stemmy" are also used to describe the flavor of wines which have been fermented too long in the presence of stems.

STEELY: A certain kind of *severe* or *austere* quality. It does not mean *metallic*.

STRONG: Descriptive of *alcoholic* wines.

SUBTLE: Descriptive of wines with *complex* and elusive *nuances*.

SULPHURY: An obvious, nose-tickling, volcanic *smell* due to an overdose of sulphur.

SWEET: The opposite of *dry*. The sensation of sweetness in wines is caused by the presence of glucose and fructose sugars.

TANNIC: See *astringent*.

TANNIN: The astringent substance found in grape skins, seeds, and stems; it is an essential component of fine red wines.

TART: Wines with a refreshing *acidity* are often called tart.

TEXTURE: The "feel" of wine as it moves in the mouth. Some descriptive terms for various impressions of wine textures are: *silky*, satiny, grainy, chalky, fat, fleshy, viscous, *unctuous, velvety*. See *body*.

THIN: Watery or lacking in *body*.

TIRED: Descriptive of overprocessed wines which lack freshness. Opposite of *lively*.

ULLAGE: The airspace above the wine in an incompletely filled cask. The space develops by evaporation and is filled by "topping up," or the addition of more wine. Wine which has evaporated below the neck of the bottle is called an ullaged wine; in such a condition, it is usually spoiled.

UNBALANCED: The opposite of *balanced*.

UNCTUOUS: An almost oily texture to the *body* of the wine; found in *fine sweet* wines.

UNRESOLVED: Insufficiently developed for its elements to be in balanced harmony.

UNSOUND: The opposite of *sound*.

VANILLA: A scent most evident in brandies, it is imparted by certain varieties of oak used in casks. It is also apparent in many wines as well.

VELVETY: Descriptive of a rich, opulent *texture*.

VITICULTURE: Grape-growing. The science and technique of grape-growing.

VINIFICATION: Winemaking. All the stages of winemaking.

WARMTH: Flavor characteristic of wines made in hot climates. See *baked*.

WEAK: See *thin*.

WOODY: A quality of wines kept overlong in wooden cooperage, or too long in new oak casks (in which case the wine may be described as oaky).

YEASTY: A usually attractive scent in young wines; it is a pleasant overtone in sparkling wine.
YOUNG: *Fresh,* but undeveloped wine.

Further Reading

Many otherwise authoritative books on wine, especially those written by Europeans, are wholly inadequate in their treatment of American wine. There are exceptions of course—most notably the writings of Hugh Johnson and Harry Waugh. There are books by Americans on American wine which are quite dated and consequently unreliable, and some recent books, especially those which attempt to rate wines, have their drawbacks as well.

The following books, however, are highly recommended. It should be noted that the current rapid rate of growth in the U.S. wine industry means that information on certain specific wineries and their products may be already out of date. This brief list necessarily omits important works of an especially scholarly or technical nature, such as V. P. Carosso's *The California Wine Industry 1830–1895* and *Table Wines* by Amerine and Joslyn.

Wine: A Guide for Americans. M. A. Amerine and V. L. Singleton. University of California Press. Berkeley, 1965.
Dry, but eminently authoritative, reliable, and factual, this general guide to wine has special emphasis on California wine and winemaking. Its treatment of the chemistry of wine is excellent.

Guide to California Wines. John Melville, 5th edition revised by Jefferson Morgan. E. P. Dutton & Co., Inc. New York, 1976.
Despite its title, this book is really an informative survey of California's wineries rather than its wines, which are not specifically evaluated.

California Wine Country. Ed. Bob Thompson. Lane Books. Menlo Park, California, 1972.
This informative and indispensable guide for visiting California's wineries is written for the tourist, and features excellent road maps.

The Wines of America. Leon D. Adams. Houghton Mifflin Co. Boston, 1973.

A detailed, popular history of wine in the United States, it covers the American wine industry in depth. Since it is not a wine guide *per se,* few evaluations are made.

Harry Waugh's Wine Diary. Harry Waugh. Christie Wine Publications, 8 King Street, St. James's, London SW1, England. Published annually.

A large part of these books concerns the author's travels in the U.S. and his evaluations of American wines. An eminent wine taster, Mr. Waugh offers his tasting notes with a refreshing lack of pomposity.

The California Wine Book. Bob Thompson and Hugh Johnson. William Morrow and Company, New York, 1976.

An entertainingly written guide to California wines, one of the few that attempts to discuss regional and wine-making styles. Its strong opinions make it a book to read after having gained some familiarity with the subject.

California Wineries, Volume One: Napa Valley. Michael Topolos and Betty Dopson. Vintage Image, St. Helena, California, 1975.

The first of a series of handsomely illustrated volumes cataloguing the wineries in various districts. Informative and factual rather than evaluative.

Connoisseurs' Guide to California Wine. Ed. by Charles E. Olken and Earl G. Singer. P.O. Box 11120, San Francisco, California, 94101. Published six times a year by subscription ($15).

Easily the best of the various wine newsletters, it covers the wines of California and the Pacific Northwest. Each issue includes scores of objective wine evaluations, interviews with winemakers, regional analyses, and so on.

Index

Boldface numbers refer to main entries; italic numbers refer to illustrations.

284